FRA FOR

Scandinavian perspectives on
management consulting

Steinar Bjartveit og Göran Roos (Eds.)

Scandinavian perspectives on management consulting

CAPPELEN AKADEMISK FORLAG

© J.W. Cappelens Forlag as, Oslo 2005

Oversettelse: Kapitlene 4, 7, 8, 10 og 11 samt introduksjonene til del II–IV og forordet er oversatt av Adrian Peretz
Omslag: Stian Høiås
Omslagsbilde: «Hip, hip, hurra! Kunstnerfest på Skagen» av Peder Severin Krøyer, gjengitt med tillatelse fra Göteborgs konstmuseum. Fotograf: Lars Noord
Kapittel 6 er gjengitt fra boken *Making Sense of Management: A Critical Introduction* (1996), utgitt av SAGE, med tillatelse fra Mats Alvesson og Hugh Willmott.

Sats: Thor Holm Grafisk as
Trykking: Lobo Media AS

ISBN-10: 82-02-23423-9
ISBN-13: 978-82-02-23423-2

Det må ikke kopieres fra denne boken i strid med åndsverkloven eller avtaler om kopiering inngått med KOPINOR, Interesseorgan for rettighetshavere til åndsverk. Kopiering i strid med lov eller avtale kan medføre erstatningsansvar og inndragning og kan straffes med bøter eller fengsel.

e-mail: cafinfo@cappelen.no
http://www.cappelen.no

Contents

FOREWORD 7

INTRODUCTION TO PART I.
MANAGEMENT CONSULTING – OPPORTUNITIES
AND THREATS 13

1   Göran Roos
    **Management consulting: Heading towards a
    scientific approach** 23

2   Flemming Poulfelt
    Thought consultancy – In action 56

3   Göran Roos
    Experience with Scandinavian consultants ... 79

INTRODUCTION TO PART II.
METHODOLOGY AS A SOURCE OF COMPETITIVENESS   93

4   Carl Erik Grenness
    Consultants: A critical perspective 101

5   Andreas Werr
    **The roles of popular management concepts in
    management consulting** 126

6   Mats Alvesson og Hugh Willmott
    The power of science and the science of power 146

INTRODUCTION TO PART III.
CONSULTING IN A POLITICAL LANDSCAPE 181

7   STEINAR BJARTVEIT
    In the realm of Fortuna 189

8   STEINAR BJARTVEIT AND GÖRAN ROOS
    Hidden agendas 207

9   HEIDI VON WELTZIEN HØIVIK
    **Consultants as destructive confidants and the unethical
    'games that people play'** 229

INTRODUCTION TO PART IV.
THE CONSULTEE 253

10 CARL REINHOLD BRÅKENHIELM AND BENGT HANSSON
    View of human nature, leadership, and consulting 259

11 STEINAR BJARTVEIT AND KJETIL EIKESET
    Dante's journey 277

12 OLE FOGH KIRKEBY
    Leadership as a possible mode of existence 304

About the contributors 324

Hip, hip, hurra!

Take a close look at the cover illustration – it's *Hip, hip, Hurra*, painted by P.S. Krøyer during 1848–1888. They're all here: Michael and Anne Archer with daughter Helga on Anne's lap; the somewhat boisterous Norwegian Christian Krohg; the Swede Oscar Björck sporting a beret; and of course there's Krøyer himself with his straw hat pushed all the way back. Captured, almost snapshot-like by that unique Skagen summer light trickling down through the canopy of leaves, as they raise their glasses in a toast to brotherhood. Hip, hip, hurra! The painting is a tribute to the artistic colony that emerged at Skagen – a milieu that attracted painters, authors, and composers, and that would leave a lasting impression on Scandinavia.

They came together at Skagen, on the northernmost tip of Jutland – the peninsula of Denmark that stretches out in to the sea as though trying to bridge the distance between Denmark, Norway, and Sweden. Inspired by the endless waves playing with the sand on the long, winding beaches that glow in the warm, northern sunlight unique to Skagen, these artists would paint, create poetry, and make merry. Skagen cast its spell on many. It influenced the great composers Hugo Alfven and Carl Nielsen; the authors Georg Brandes and Henrik Pontoppidan; and through Christian Krohg it also influenced the bohemian painters Edvard Munch and Oda Krohg. They worked hard and played hard, and through a creative process that often included fierce disagreements they would push each other and eventually succeed in creating something new, and distinctly Scandinavian – as opposed to the mainstream influences from the continent. They put Scandinavia on the map. Just look at the intense joy of life captured in this unique work of art. In this instant, so wonderfully captured on canvas, new bonds are formed, and barriers are smashed. It is astonishing that so much life can be captured in a single painting.

In this book we have attempted to bring together some of the foremost thinkers on consulting in Scandinavia. We could hardly measure up to the creative genius of the artistic milieu of Skagen of old. To do that, we would need large amounts of absinth and some of that magical sunlight. But we would like to provide a perspective on consulting that is more suited to the Scandinavian business climate than the mainstream view that is chiefly predicated on the Anglo-Saxon business mindset. For what term could possibly be more remote from the natural splendor of Skagen than *management consulting*? A term that oozes of cut-and-dried methodology, 2-by-2 matrixes, and pin-striped MBAs. Hardly the backdrop for a celebratory toast or even a nervous little hip! Management consulting is the realm of American business schools and global consultancies. But despite this American dominance, or perhaps as a result of it, some distinctly Scandinavian perspectives on consulting have emerged in recent years. So far, there is no single unifying position based on any common theoretical framework. In fact the views are often as disparate as those of the Skagen artists more than a century ago. Some of the views might seem to dovetail with the extant American view on consulting, while others embrace the more critical European tradition, and there are even some perspectives that adopt literary and humanistic approaches. In other words, the same colorful variety you would expect to see on a Skagen meadow at the height of summer. However, they are unified by one common theme, and that is that they all approach consulting from a somewhat different point of departure than is customary. They are somewhat at odds with the prevailing views and models that define the consulting industry, and they draw attention to some interesting, though not mainstream, topics. These perspectives on consulting are influenced by that which is unique to Scandinavian history and culture and are set against the historical sociopolitical backdrop of these countries. These are quite simply Scandinavian perspectives on management consulting.

The different contributions can be grouped under four themes. The first concerns the future of the consulting industry in Scandinavia – as seen through the eyes of professionals, both consultants and clients. It seems clear that some of the developments that became evident in the international consulting environment following the collapse of Enron and the recent decline in demand for consulting services have also played out in Scandinavia. Consultants find themselves, justifiably so, coming under increasing criticism from clients – who question their consultants' professional integrity and expertise. When the client is forced to ask him- or herself whether the consultant is really providing valuable assistance or just prolonging the assignment to ensure a good source of revenue, the consultant faces a serious integrity crisis. The fact that consultants' professional expertise is often questioned may come as result of their propensity to latch on to a particular model or perspective. There has been growing scepticism towards the generic models employed by most global consultancies. In this part of the world, where egalitarian values play a major role in society, questions have arisen concerning the authoritarian style and princely fees typical of large consultancies. Despite this, Scandinavians have historically stood meekly by, hats in their hands, and allowed themselves to be swayed by the rosy representation of accomplishments from "over there". However, following the recent downturn in business and the ensuing crisis in the consultancy industry, it would seem that clients have learned to require of consultants that these should provide immediate results. At the same time, clients also seem more willing to form closer and more long-term relationships with their consultants. Thus, such key concepts as real benefits and relationship quality will play an important role in the future.

The second theme concerns consultants' methodological aptitude and expertise. It should come as no surprise that the cultural environment that formed the backdrop for *The Emperor's New Clothes* is somewhat wary of anything that smacks of witchdoctors and miracle cures. H.C. Andersen playfully illuminated our dread of asking what may seem like simple or even naive questions by showing how we tend to blindly trust the expertise that weaves a tale of exquisite elegance – from fabrics that don't really exist. A good tailor knows how to weave magic, and ignorance and gullibility are often brought to the fore when those of similar disposition flock together. Sometimes we do need drunks and children to set us straight. Does the medicine prescribed by consultants really work, or are we simply overwhelmed by placebo effects, management fads, and social anxiety – a dread of standing apart from that which the rest of the business community is doing? Judging by the life expectancy of most management models, there is every reason to question the methodological and scientific basis for many of the models in the consultant's toolkit. Consultants cannot usually rely on their experience or on their latest standardized model as a source of competitive advantage. Fortunately, Scandinavian managers seem, historically and at least for the time being, less inclined to believe in the existence of silver bullets than their Anglo-Saxon colleagues, and this increases the pressure on consultants to verify that the assumptions underpinning their models are truly valid, that the models are firmly grounded in knowledge, and that their experience truly is transferable. There is simply no substitute for well-founded knowledge and a scientific approach – and in their absence we should expect to hear a child cry out: "But he has nothing on at all!"

As such, the reality facing the consultant extends far beyond the scope of simplistic toolkits and crude roadmaps. And this is the theme for the third section in this book: if an organization, any organization, is in effect a highly complex political reality where opposing interests clash against each other, we should hardly expect to find causal relationships that are straightforward or processes that flow uninterrupted from start to finish. Nor should we expect to find that the interests of all those involved magically dovetail with the strategic plans for the next five-year period, as laid out by senior management. The consultant should be prepared for some rough terrain. Rather than a new stretch of a four-lane highway, the consultant should expect to find deep forests, windswept moors, and the deep shadows cast by unyielding mountains during the long darkness of winter. Working in such an environment, the consultant needs to understand power and influence, and be able to work with open as well as concealed agendas. Some of the new perspectives in chaos theory and theories of complexity have gained ground in Scandinavia. When these relatively novel perspectives are merged with the classical theories of power and influence described by Machiavelli and Shakespeare, there is great potential for astounding new insights.

The final theme deals with the human aspects of leadership – a topic of long-standing tradition in Scandinavia. The focus here is on the leader as a human being, not necessarily in terms of psychological insight and knowing your strong versus your weak traits – it is more an existential question of deciding who you are and what you represent. We can trace this issue from Søren Kierkegaard to Henrik Ibsen. One must eschew all that is escapism and cowardice, that which is merely superficial and conforming – and dare to assume one's true character. This issue resonates through literature; from the classics to modern management literature. Using the terminology of contemporary management consulting, this issue is the concern of coaching. The Socratic approach to giving counsel requires that the consultant refrains from offering personal expertise, and rather attempts to bring forth that which may be locked up within the leader, and encourage the leader to realize his or her own potential. This is the main challenge faced by leaders, and their counsel, if they seek to go beyond the most easily attainable goals of personal development. For the path of least resistance will always circumvent the toughest issues, and both conviction and determination are required when addressing these existential issues. In the words of Ibsen's infamous anti-hero Peer Gynt: "Think of it, wish it be done, will it to boot, but do it!"

We sincerely believe that consultants can play a major role in the business environment and be an important factor in the success of their business clients. However, at times, consultants may be merely an expensive distraction, or – even worse, a destructive force within the organisation. And this places a great deal of responsibility on those who provide consultancy services as well as on those who procure these services. We hope that this book will provide insight for professionals on both sides of the table. The book covers the themes we have outlined here, and for each section we have provided an introduction that should help to clarify the key issues for both clients and consultants.

The contributors do not represent a unified body – rather we have sought to keep the tradition of Skagen alive, and have brought together a broad range of perspectives on consulting. We hope that the book can provide new insight into the field of management consulting, and that it may serve as a catalyst for innovative thinking within this area. This constitutes our contribution to the further development of this multifaceted field. Hip, hip, hurra!

INTRODUCTION TO PART I

Management consulting – opportunities and threats

GÖRAN ROOS

The burst of the IT bubble at the end of the nineties – following years of unchecked glory and the terrorist attack on the World Trade Center are among factors that led to a severe downturn for the consulting industry. The top quartile of consulting firms, in terms of performance, certainly made it through the economic crisis of 2001 and 2002, and even the middle half weathered these difficult times, but the lower quartile experienced steep downturns that often ended in bankruptcy or other forms of failure.

According to an article in the Danish news magazine *Berlingske Nyhedsmagasin*, 2005 will be the best year for the consulting industry since the advent of the new millennium. The article is based on research conducted among the people that hire consultants – who seem to have retained their faith in consultants and now feel that they once again can afford the services of consultants. Thus it would seem that the consulting industry is in for some positive growth.

Consulting in numbers?

Despite recent difficulties, the consulting industry thus seems to be growing. Being a relatively new and somewhat loosely-defined business sector, there is a dearth of reliable statistics on the consulting industry. There are many different countries trying to establish definitions and routines for data gathering in order to define and measure the industry in numerical terms. So far, the most reliable and complete source is The European Federation of Management Consultancies Associations (FEACO), and this is the primary source for the following review.

A quick look at Europe

Before we focus specifically on the consulting industry in Scandinavia, it might be interesting to take a brief look at the business climate in some European countries.[1]

	2001	2002	2003	2004
Market Size	€ 47,5 bill.	€ 47,5 bill.	€ 47,5 bill.	€ 47,5 bill.
Growth Rate	11,5%	-2.0%	3.5%	3.7%
Management Consulting Firms	60,000	57,000	58,000	60,000
Management Consultants	300,000	300,000	310,000	315,000
Key Service Lines	IT: 33.2% OM: 24.1% Strategy: 25.8% Outsourcing: 12.4% HR: 4.5%	IT: 28.5% OM: 28.2% Strategy: 19.9% Outsourcing: 12.7% HR: 10.7%	IT: 28.1% OM: 26.9% Strategy: 17.4% Outsourcing: 17.4% HR: 10.2%	IT: 27.3% OM: 25.8% Strategy: 17.1% Outsourcing: 19.0% HR: 10.8%
Management Consulting Markets (Total Turnover in € bill.)	UK: 12.9 Germany: 12.9 France: 6.3 Netherlands: 2.4 Spain: 2.4	UK: 13.6 Germany: 13.0 France: 6.2 Spain: 2.4 Italy: 2.2	UK: 14.8 Germany: 13.1 France: 5.6 Spain: 2.6 Italy: 2.0	UK: 14.2 Germany: 13.3 France: 5.9 Spain: 2.8 Netherlands: 2.0

Key figures 2001-2004 in Europe (FEACO)

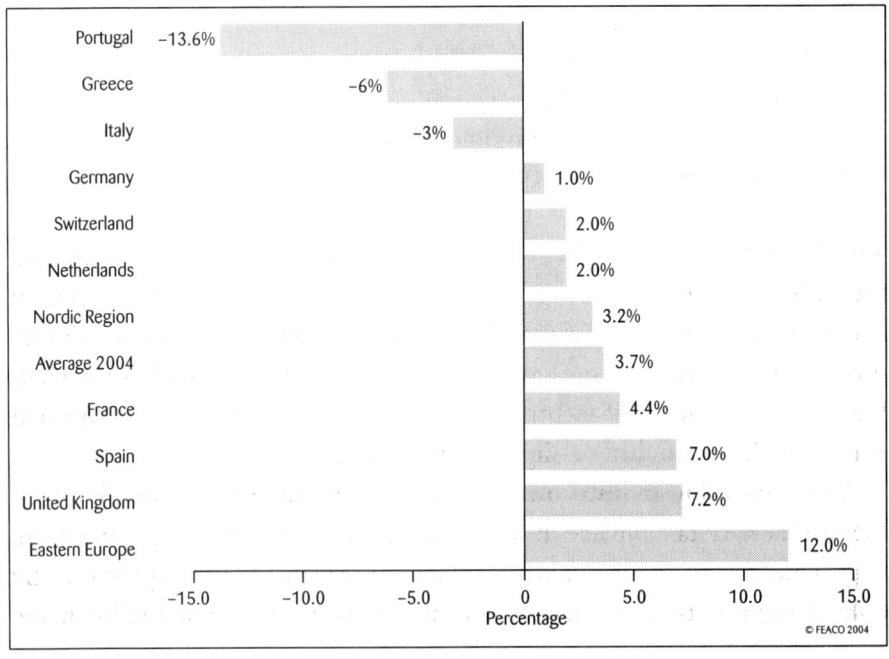

Country	Growth Rate
Portugal	-13.6%
Greece	-6%
Italy	-3%
Germany	1.0%
Switzerland	2.0%
Netherlands	2.0%
Nordic Region	3.2%
Average 2004	3.7%
France	4.4%
Spain	7.0%
United Kingdom	7.2%
Eastern Europe	12.0%

Growth rate in selected European Countries (FEACO, 2004)

---

[1] FEACO, 2003

In 2003, the consulting industry in the Nordic region had a negative (11.6%) growth rate, which swung around to a positive growth of 3.2% in 2004. These numbers illustrate the strength of the recent turnaround, and also serve to highlight the fact that the consulting industry is very sensitive to changes in the general economic climate.[2]

Let's take a closer look at the situation for the Nordic countries, country by country.

Sweden[3]

The latest numbers on the Swedish consulting industry are from FEACO's 2003 survey. This survey estimates that the number of management consulting firms in Sweden was down to 650 from 700 the previous year and that the number of management consultants declined from 6,000 to 4,000 during the same period. As mentioned above, 2003 marked the turnaround following a period of several difficult years – and current figures indicate strong growth that is expected to continue. The key client industry sectors for Swedish consultants were in 2003:

- Non-profit & government (24,0%)
- Consumer Goods (10,0%)
- Communication/media/entertainment (10,0%)
- Personal & Business Services (10,0%)

The 2003 survey shows that cost reduction, IT/telecommunications, and the public sector increased in importance, whereas Project Management and Marketing declined. Demand from the financial sector, large manufacturing companies, telecom, and real estate clients increased somewhat. Demand from the retail sector declined, whilst the public sector remained almost stable – with only a slight decrease in demand.

The consulting industry in Sweden is experiencing the same developments that have taken place in other countries, with clients requiring more experienced consultants for what are often more limited and quite specific tasks. Assignments are often more limited in scope and require tailor-made

---

[2] FEACO, 2003
[3] FEACO, 2003

solutions. There is also an increased focus on costs, cash flow, and on swift and reliable results. There has been an increase in demand for consultants that can provide assistance in the areas of senior management and on boardroom issues and, in this ever-changing world, analysis of culture/people issues.

"Growth is once again the number one issue for many managers, which leads to more projects concerning strategy and business development, mergers etc." As a result, the demand for expertise in cost cutting, streamlining production, downsizing and lay-offs, and even marketing, is likely to decline. Current growth areas include Strategic Planning, HR Management, Operations Management, Organization development in sales and service functions, IT/Communication services, mobile communications, and production-oriented assignments.[4] Most sectors seem likely to increase demand for consultants' services, but the consumer goods industry, banking, energy, transportation, real estate, and heavy industry sectors are expected to show a particularly strong growth in demand. The demand from the public sector is likely to decline, as a result of budget cuts, as is the case for the retail sector.[5]

Norway[6]

Norway is the Nordic country covered in most detail in the most recent FEACO surveys.

As was the case for other countries, the demand for consulting services in 2004 in Norway showed promise – with discernible growth compared to the recent period of recession. The moderate growth evident during the latter part of 2004 is expected to continue, but this demand will be easily covered by available capacity. There is good reason to be optimistic as the current underlying economic factors in Norway are solid.

There was a general decline in the demand for consulting services from the private sector during 2004, but the public sector remains a very important customer. Most large public-sector projects tended to go to multinationals. In the latter part of 2004 both sectors showed a slight increase. The authorities have indicated that they will be looking into this

---

[4] FEACO, 2003
[5] FEACO, 2003
[6] FEACO, 2004

issue, as it would seem to require a great deal of effort – without providing any real benefit for either party. There has been a trend towards smaller and more limited projects with clients being more specific in terms of what they require from consultants and what they intend to do on their own. There is still considerable competition from managers who suffered redundancy during the recent decline and who continue to proffer their services at comparatively low rates, due to low overhead costs.

FEACO's estimates for 2005 are that demand for all types of consulting services will increase. Demand will continue to be dominated by innovation, increased focus on short term gains, and smaller projects, and a decline in the number of long-term strategy projects. Within IT consulting the trend towards close bonds between suppliers and consultants is expected to continue, but we should also expect to see an increase in demand for independent consultants, as well as increased demand from the public sector. The size of IT consulting projects tends to be increasing. In HR consulting the main focus is on coaching and coach-training. There is an abundance of firms providing these services, many of whom are newcomers, and as a result there are few, if any, firms currently showing a profit. Not surprisingly, the traditional consultancies have shown little interest in this market segment. There is an increase in demand for advice on outsourcing of logistics and Supply Chain Management activities. In general the attitude is positive, and moderate growth is expected due to more optimism in the business climate. Demand is expected to be solid in all sectors and particularly strong from the consumer goods, healthcare, and pharmaceutical sectors.

Denmark

Like most other countries, Denmark has no established system for measuring the consulting industry. The Danish Management Council (Dansk Management Rad) estimates that there are approximately 2000–3000 consulting firms in Denmark, but they are unable to specify how many of these are management consultancies. The official statistics do not provide much information since firms are not required to declare actual consulting activities. Dansk Management Rad itself has 140 members (companies), employing approximately 1,600 management consultants.[7]

---
[7] Dansk Management Rad, 2005

I. Management consulting – opportunities and threats

Dansk Management Rad says that the vast majority of consulting companies are very small (1–10 employees), and estimates that 80% of the companies have less than 5 consultants. In general, the market is showing positive signs, with an increase in demand across the board and especially within general management consultancy and IT governance. An upcoming public sector structural reform has resulted in a "boom" for consulting services. In the private sector the demand for traditional management consulting and for lean-production consulting has increased. Dansk Management Rad also says that there are signs that consultancies are experiencing difficulties in recruiting personnel with relevant skills.[8]

Berlingske Nyhedsmagasin has provided the following tables, which suggest a strong belief in a bright future for consulting.

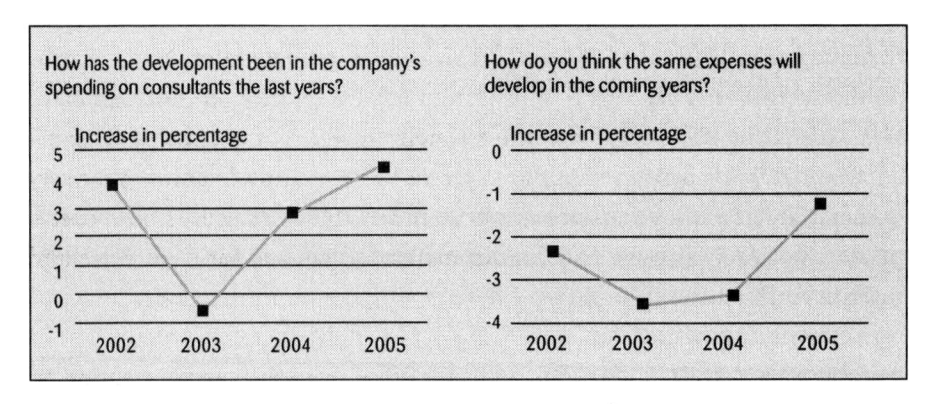

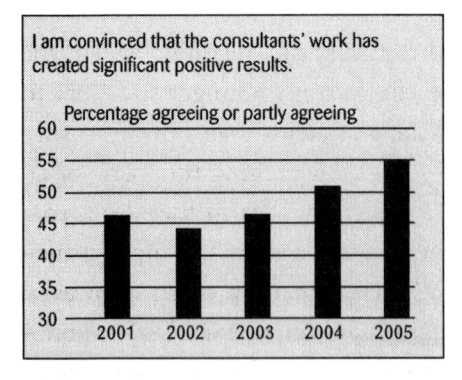

How has the development been in the company's spending on consultants the last years?

Increase in percentage

Year	2002	2003	2004	2005
%	4	-1	3	5

How do you think the same expenses will develop in the coming years?

Increase in percentage

Year	2002	2003	2004	2005
%	-2	-3	-3	-1

I am convinced that the consultants' work has created significant positive results.

Percentage agreeing or partly agreeing

Year	2001	2002	2003	2004	2005
%	46	44	46	51	56

(Based on *Berlingske Nyhedsmagasin*, p. 31, No 5, Feb 2005)

---

[8] Dansk Management Rad, 2005.

Current issues and new approaches

From a European perspective, management consulting is an industry facing adverse economic conditions. The ability to offer implementation as part of the service package is no longer a source of differentiation. The market is dynamic and has changed a lot since the mid 1990's, and these changes call for an innovative approach to consulting. *INSEAD Quarterly*[9] has identified the main drivers of changes as [The comments under each heading are those of the editors]:

1) **Clients are becoming much savvier when hiring**
   Today, most business managers have attended the same business schools as the consultants they hire. In addition, in order to succeed, managers now have to keep abreast of the latest developments in many fields, and this serves to reduce the knowledge advantage that consultants have traditionally enjoyed in relation to their clients. As a result today's managers are more knowledgeable in terms of being able to define precisely what services they require, and how much these services should cost – thereby placing consultants under increased pressure for both price and deliverables.

2) **The value of 'top-level' strategy-only projects seems harder to justify**
   "The proof of the pudding is in the eating", or in other words, the value must be readily evident to the client. It is no longer sufficient to provide solutions that look good. A new strategy is an option to succeed, but today companies will hold back on judging the value of an option until it has been successfully exercised. This in turn leads to a lower value being placed on an unexercised option – which in turn leads to lower willingness to pay for pure strategy projects. However, this also leads to a higher value being placed on an exercised option – resulting in more pressure from clients for success fees and shared risk.

---

[9] *INSEAD Quarterly*, August–October 2005.

3) Competition from niche consultancies, networks, the Big Five, investment banks and research houses is increasing

Like all industries, management consulting is vulnerable to industry boundaries becoming blurred, which tends to lead to increased competition. In addition, and as a consequence, the industry is forced to restructure, and one of the frequent outcomes of restructuring is that staff is laid off. However, in the consulting industry, many of these redundant consultants immediately start their own consulting firms – further increasing the level of competition within the industry.

4) The market and the economy are becoming more dynamic, and volatility is increasing.

So where are these driving forces converging? Various new strategic consulting business models are emerging in answer to changing demands.[10] But the fact remains that consulting is all about talent; people who can observe, analyze, reflect, communicate, and motivate other people to solve issues. Relationship skills and political understanding are rapidly becoming crucial skills for consultants – an issue that will be dealt with in some detail in this book.

Chapter one will take the reader through new approaches that are emerging as a result of the changing business climate and describe some of the new challenges facing both consultant and client. The first chapter will review different perspectives on value creation and provide a perspective on past developments and possible future areas of conflict. The second chapter will further develop this discussion by reviewing the consultancy sector and some of the challenges it faces in more depth and look at the industry developments: When are consultants used? What value can they add to the organization? And how are the stakeholders interacting? The third and final chapter in the first section is a summary of interviews conducted with a group of Scandinavian executives, who frequently use consultants. The reader will gain some real-life insight into the client side of consulting, based on the responses from these business leaders and their experience with consulting services.

---

[10] *INSEAD Quarterly*, August–October 2005.

References

Baden, M. (2004). Det går sindssygd godt. *Berlingske Nyhedsmagasin*, pp. 30–33. February 2004.

FEACO Survey of European Management Consultancy Market, 31 December, 2003.

FEACO Survey of European Management Consultancy Market, 31 December, 2004.

INSEAD Quarterly. August – October 2005.

Phone Conversation with LJK, the Association of the Finnish Management Consultants, September 2005.

E-mail-conversation with Dansk Management Rad, the Association for Danish Management Consultants, September 2005.

Chapter 1 | Management consulting: Heading towards a scientific approach

GÖRAN ROOS

About management consulting

The issue of what constitutes a management consultant is fraught with difficulties, among other things because the sector itself is being constantly reinvented. Nevertheless, definitions for consulting abound, and given the evolving nature of the field, are subject to constant review and reformulation. Over the last decade, there has been an increasing trend towards definitions that apply to the entirety of the management consulting sector. Examples include:

International Labour Office, 1996, p.8:
"Management consulting is an independent professional advisory service assisting managers and organizations in achieving organizational purposes and objectives by solving management and business problems, identifying and seizing new opportunities, enhancing learning, and implementing changes."

Management Consultancies Association Annual Report, 2001:
"The rendering of independent advice and assistance on management issues. This typically includes identifying and investigating problems and/or opportunities, recommending appropriate action, and helping to implement those solutions."

Institute of Management Consultancy, 2002:
"Management consultants are used first to provide wider additional expertise than is available within a single organization. Thus a change in production or marketing may require expertise in designing and imple-

menting a new system. Secondly, management consultants are used to provide objective appraisals where it is often easier for the expert outsider to see the broader picture and recognize the long-term requirements. Thirdly, the management consultant may be needed to provide additional assistance where there is a temporary increase in the management workload. This may be to cope with a major change or new development in any area of management responsibility."

Management Consultancies Association, 2004:
"Management consultancy is the provision to management of objective advice and assistance relating to the strategy, structure, management and operations of an organization in pursuit of its long-term purposes and objectives. Such assistance may include the identification of options with recommendations; the provision of an additional resource, and/or the implementation of solutions."

Such definitions have a number of threads in common. They are primarily concerned with the solving of a significant, although not necessarily always strategic, management *problem* facing a client or customer. In the broadest sense problems can be defined as differences between an existing state and an aspired or desired state[1]. Problems involve situations requiring remedial action and situations where there are improvement opportunities.

A second common thread is concerned with the role of the consultant as an expert outsider with regards to the provision of advice. Problem-solving, the value provided by consultants, involves bringing about change from an existing to a more desired state. Clients provide the context and some facts, and consultants are employed to identify the missing facts and use analysis and their practical experience to identify solutions.

A third common thread involves the extension of the role of management consultants beyond the mere provision of advice, and into the actual implementation of solutions. In this capacity, the management consultant schedules activities and applies resources that suit the needs of the client's problem. The complexity of the management problem to be solved determines the intensity of the management consultant's activities. In each dif-

---

[1] Simon, 1977.

ferent case, the selection, combination, and application of resources and methodologies is performed according to the requirements of the problem at hand.

It has long been accepted that management consulting can be viewed both as a professional service operated by specialists and experts, and as a method of providing practical advice and help[2]. In today's knowledge-based economies, professional services are particularly defined by their knowledge specialization and applied methodology[3]. Put differently, management consulting firms are professional services that rely on intensive knowledge specialization and on methodologies to solve problems and create value for their clients. There are two important aspects to this statement, one concerning knowledge specialization and the other concerning methodologies:

Knowledge specialization. Corporate clients can perform many functions with their own capabilities and expertise, but increasingly they need to access highly specialised knowledge from external sources for a host of problem-solving reasons including outsourcing functions and improving their own processes. Management consultants have the opportunity to focus their resources on very narrow fields of expertise, to gain experience from a wide range of clients, and to innovate in the course of their efforts to help solve a client's problem. As both individuals and organizations they are able to develop a far greater depth of knowledge and expertise within highly specialised areas than their clients.

Methodologies. A methodology encompasses a set of working methods and body of practices, procedures, and rules used by those who work in a discipline or engage in an inquiry. For a consultant, methodologies are to be viewed as a pieced-together, close-knit set of practices that s/he uses to provide solutions to the customer's problems. We view the concept of consulting methodologies as relatively broad-reaching. From a theoretical standpoint, methodologies bridge disciplines, fields and subject matters, and a complex, interconnected family of related terms, concepts and assumptions surround the term 'methodology' itself. Having said this, a

---

[2] Kubr, M. (1996). *Management Consulting.* Geneva: International Labour Office.
[3] Abbott (1988).

core argument of this book is that in the future consulting will have to rely more and more on methodologies as an avenue of differentiation and competitive advantage.

Value creation in consulting

In practice consultants are known to provide value for their customers in two areas. The first area is not directly related to consultants solving clients' problems. Here consultants may provide legitimacy and/or a reduction in cognitive uncertainty for clients. In this light, consultants may also present themselves as a useful resource in political battles in organizations – the outcome of which might be beneficial for the client hiring the consultants.

The second and predominant perspective on the value provided by consultants is the one we chose to follow in this book. This perspective assumes a certain level of rationality and sees 'value creation' as a key element in normal consultancy work as per the definitions introduced above. This implicit assumption involves consultants as being capable of delivering something valuable through rational interventions based on their sophisticated knowledge, and thereby creating value through deep expertise-based problem-solving – a professional helper aiding those in need of help. An important characteristic of this view of consulting is the large asymmetry in knowledge that is assumed to exist between the consultant and the client – the asymmetry in knowledge specialization being the reason the client approaches the consultant. Traditionally this has meant that consultants are approached by clients seeking the consultants' specialist knowledge in different domains where consultants can provide value, including[4]:

- Providing information
- Providing specialist resources
- Establishing business contacts and linkages
- Providing expert opinion
- Doing diagnostic work
- Developing action proposals

---

[4] Kubr, M. (1996). *Management Consulting.* Geneva: International Labour Office.

- Improving systems and methods
- Planning and managing organizational changes
- Training and developing management and staff
- Providing counselling

In a typical consulting scenario the customer provides the context and some facts, and the consultant uses his or her methodologies to pursue missing facts and uses analysis and interpretation to identify solutions. The management consultant may even deliver value by determining that the client has no problem to solve. The consultant uses the tools of his or her methodological specialization, deploying whatever strategies, methods, or empirical materials are at hand. If a solution requires that new tools be developed or pieced together, then the consultant will do this. In the end the solution is the result of the consultant's methodology.

Management consulting firms are human resource intensive value constellations with professionals and specialists at the heart of the value creating model. In order to both generate maximum value and limit overall costs, it is not enough to scale an operation as a collection of independently performing professionals. For example, every consulting firm attempts to leverage the expertise available in-house and to justify the maximum internal transfer of knowledge to clients. In order to do so, experienced senior consultants and partners may be leveraged with more junior and less experienced colleagues.

Consultants also leverage expertise from other sources. For such purposes the consultant will use a standard information and knowledge acquisition procedure to make sure that the problem has been correctly framed. The standardization of information and knowledge acquisition activities within knowledge management initiatives provides value and serves to limit overall costs, in part because it provides the basis for early anticipation of ensuing activities. New kinds of information systems provide the opportunity to capture and store information and knowledge from previous problem-solving cases in the form of collective experiences, organizational practices, improved expertise, more or less formal documentation, and explicit information, in global databases.

---

[5] For an in-depth discussion of different value constellation models, see: Stabell, C.B. and O.D. Fjeldstad (1998). On Chains, Shops and Networks. *Strategic Management Journal*, Vol. 19, 413–437.

Given the basic value creating nature of consulting, the way in which consultants assure that their clients are getting the appropriate professional expertise and problem-solving effort at all times, is subject to the specific value constellation model adopted. Consultants operate according to two primary value constellation models: the *value chain* and the *value shop*[5]. Differences in consulting value constellations are justified partly by the need to address various types of problem situations within the clients' organizations and partly by the need to provide different problem solving approaches.

Value chain

The value chain mode of consulting is based on Porter's[6] conventional value chain model. Here the output alone is what brings value to the customer. This type of value creation relies on standardised processes and repetition (economies of learning) and mass production (economies of scale). Consulting firms organized as such are all about selling packaged and standardized solutions. This is the predominant model associated with most of today's ma-

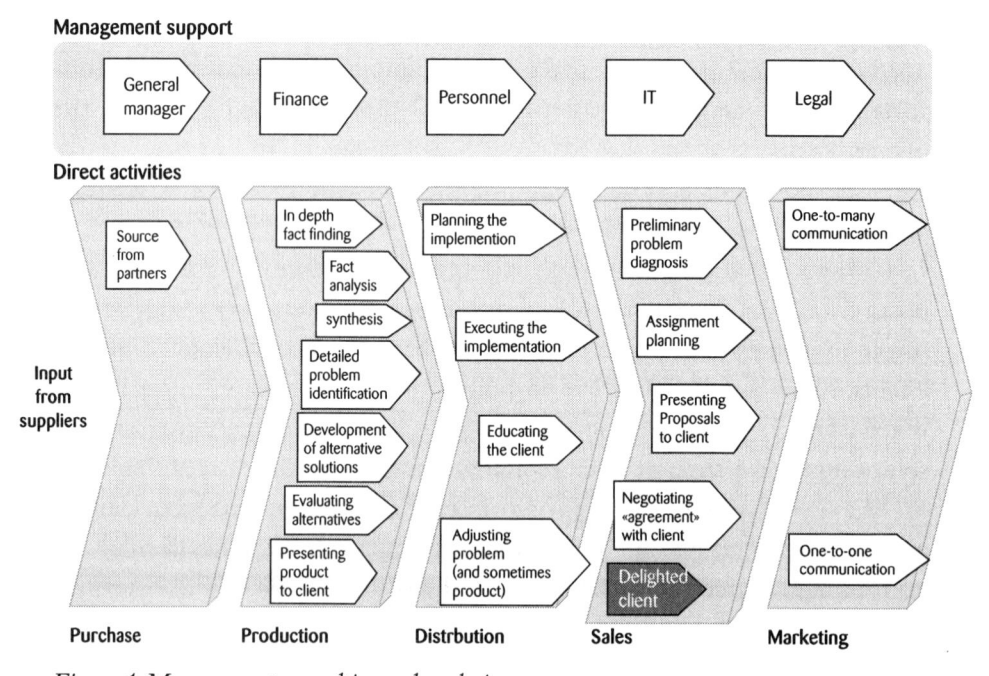

Figure 1 Management consulting value chain

---

[6] Porter, Michael E. (1985). *Competitive Advantage: Creating and Sustaining Superior Performance.* New York: The Free Press.

jor professional service brands including the leading technology consulting giants such as IBM, HP, and Dell, and global accountancy firms such as KPMG, Ernst & Young and Deloitte. Figure 1 depicts the generic representation of value creation activities within a value chain.

Firms such as these produce very good, albeit standardized solutions. By leveraging excellent organizational resources and pushing for a high degree of standardization, firms such as these may increase the efficiency of their service provision, but they may also reduce the effectiveness of their solutions. From a resource perspective, it is their organizational resources such as processes, manuals, systems, brands, and intellectual property that allow them to use average human resources to provide good solutions. Generally speaking, however, the solution the client is investing in is being prepared and delivered with a relatively low proportion of man-hours. As a consequence, such firms struggle in justifying and charging very high rates for their man-hours and therefore depend on high volumes of business. When organized along the value chain, such professional service firms can grow easily by hiring some more people and leveraging them throughout the system. On the other hand, these types of organizations are not very flexible because it takes a long time for a new idea to be converted into a standardized offering that can be leveraged throughout the organization.

Value Shop

In a value shop, the main focus is on problem solving. Contrary to value chain thinking where standardized output is assumed to provide value to a client, the main focus of the value shop lies in solving unique problems for clients. The value in a value shop resides not only in the solution itself – the output – but also in the way the individuals who came up with the solution reached their problem-solving conclusions.

The value created resides in two inseparable components: the solution and the way in which the individuals come up with the solution.

From a resource-based perspective[7], the primary sources of competitive

---

[7] See Wernerfelt, B. (1984). A resource-based view of the firm. *Strategic Management Journal*, 5: 171–180. Barney, J. B. (1986). Strategic factor markets, expectations, luck, and business strategy. *Management Science*, 32(10): 1231–1241. Barney, J. B. (198b). Type of competition and the theory of strategy: Toward an integrative framework. *Academy of Management Review*, 11(4): 791–800. Barney, J. (1991). Firm resources and sustained competitive advantage. *Journal of Management*, 17(1): 99–120.

advantage in a consulting value shop are most definitely human resources, but this can also be complemented by organizational or relational resources. The totality of these resources form what is commonly termed the intellectual capital[8] of the firm, and for management consulting firms the source of competitive advantage in their value shop can therefore never be physical or monetary resources.

Management support

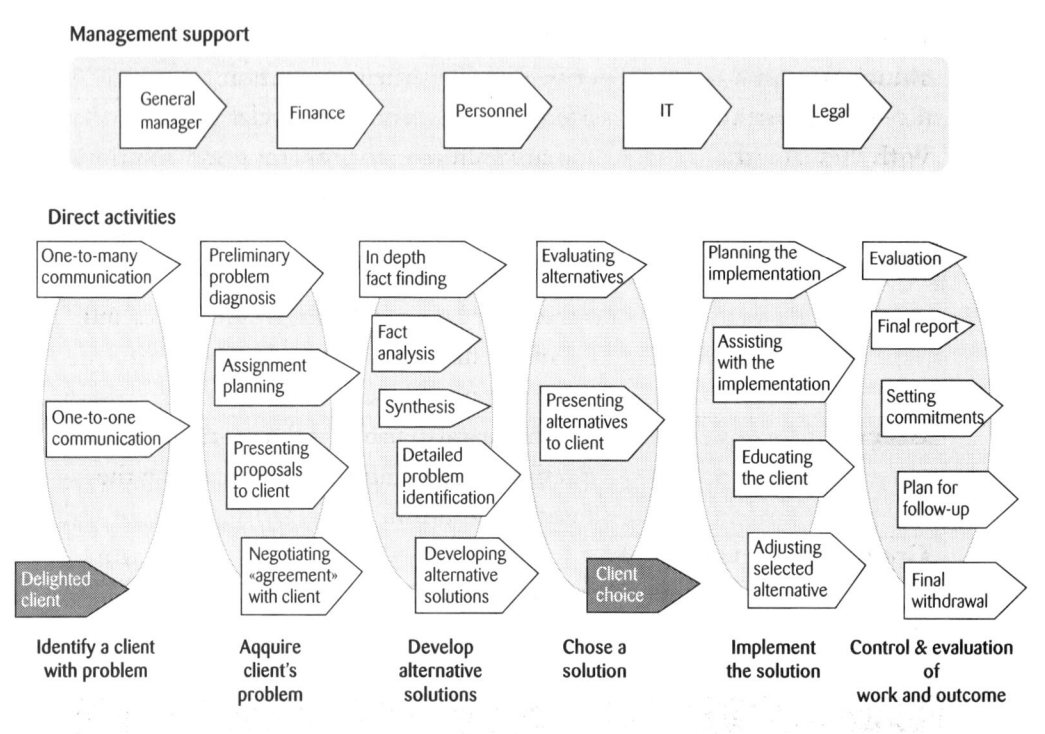

General manager → Finance → Personnel → IT → Legal

Direct activities

One-to-many communication → Preliminary problem diagnosis → In depth fact finding → Evaluating alternatives → Planning the implementation → Evaluation

Assignment planning → Fact analysis → Assisting with the implementation → Final report

One-to-one communication → Presenting proposals to client → Synthesis → Presenting alternatives to client → Educating the client → Setting commitments

Negotiating «agreement» with client → Detailed problem identification → Plan for follow-up

Delighted client → Developing alternative solutions → Client choice → Adjusting selected alternative → Final withdrawal

Identify a client with problem | Aqquire client's problem | Develop alternative solutions | Chose a solution | Implement the solution | Control & evaluation of work and outcome

Figure 2 Management consulting value shop[9]

With the value shop the basis of competitive advantage can be understood by disaggregating the value creation process of the firm into discrete activities that contribute to the firm's relative cost position and create a basis for competitive advantage. Figure 4 depicts the generic representation of value

---

[8] The value and importance of intellectual capital is emphasized by Sveiby, 1997; Edvinsson & Malone, 1997; Roos et al., 1997. This perspective emphasizes the economic value of human capital, knowledge and other kinds of intangible resources for a firm. For more on this, see: Roos, G., Pike, S. and Fernström, L. (2005). *Intellectual capital in practice*. Elsevier.

[9] adapted from Chatzkel, J. (2002). A conversation with Göran Roos. *Journal of Intellectual Capital*, Vol. 3 No. 2, pp. 96–117.

PRIMARY ACTIVITIES	
Find someone with a problem:	Activities associated with the marketing of problem-solving capabilities.
Acquire the right to address the problem:	Activities associated with the bidding and procurement of the right to solve a problem.
Develop alternative solutions:	Activities associated with generating and evaluating alternative solutions.
Co-select the solution with the client:	Activities associated with choosing among alternative problem solutions. This activity has limited importance in terms of effort and time, but is important in terms of value. It also represents the interface between different specialties and a major discontinuity in the problem-solving cycle.
Execute:	Activities associated with communicating, organizing and implementing the chosen solution.
Control and evaluation:	Activities associated with measuring and evaluating to what extent implementation has solved the initial problem.
SUPPORT ACTIVITIES	
Infrastructure **Human resource management** **Technology development** **Procurement**	Support activities that are co-performed with the primary activities. These functions are often neglected because they are not distinct, but they are crucial to competitive advantage.

Figure 3 Description of value shop activities[10]

---

[10] adapted from Stabell, C.B. and O.D. Fjeldstad (1998). On Chains, Shops and Networks. *Strategic Management Journal*, Vol. 19, 413–437.

creation within a problem-solving value shop. Thinking exactly along the lines of value-chains, the activities in a value shop can be differentiated into primary and support activities. Whereas primary activities are directly involved in creating and bringing value to the customer, support activities enable and improve the performance of the primary activities[11].

Consulting value shops differ from consulting value chains in a number of ways, and the most distinctive differences are:
1. Consultants must be configured to deal with unique problems;
2. Consulting involves iterative, cyclical, interdependent and interruptible problem-solving activities;
3. The co-performance of primary and support activities.

Value shops are configured to deal with unique problems

Consulting value shops are distinguished by their ability to solve unique problems and cases. Although client problems may also involve more-or-less standardized methodologies and solutions, the value creation process set in motion by value shop consultants is organized to deal with uncommon and even unique cases. It is therefore necessary for the consultant to always be able to recognize and deal with the limited number of cases that require their expertise for innovative solutions and problem-solving methodologies.

Value shops rely on iterative, cyclical, and interdependent problem-solving activities

In a consulting value shop the flow and creation of value is not linear as is common in a manufacturing value chain, but rather iterative involving activities that span the entire value shop activity set. The iterative nature of a value shop means that when consultants go about solving problems, their diagnosis moves back and forth between defining assumptions and collecting new data that confirm, reject, or lead to a reformulation of the diagnosis. A solution may result in the resolution of the client's problem, but it can also lead to a new and perhaps different sequence of activities. This process is not only iterative; it may also be interrupted at any stage.

The cyclical nature of the consulting value shop means that when a particular customer problem is solved, a new set of issues may arise and the con-

---

[11] for a similar two-level activity categorization see also Kornai (1971); de Chalvron and Curien (1978); Stabell (1982).

sultants may be required to find a further refined solution. In the course of developing solutions to customer problems, there is a basic problem-solving cycle where each cycle implements the solutions selected by the previous cycle or deals with a new problem that has resulted from the resolution of the initial problem. The process also evolves in terms of the main objective.

The iterative and cyclical nature of problem-solving means that a high degree of coordination and management is required between these interdependent problem-solving activities. In large consulting projects the huge demands for coordination across activities are dealt with by assigning this responsibility to a project manager who follows the problem to resolution and uses lateral integration mechanisms that facilitate information exchange while maintaining professional commitment and accountability. In more demanding cases that require interaction between multiple consulting disciplines and expertise, the need for coordination is often addressed by assigning a full-time cross-functional team. In all cases the coordination needs are addressed by reducing the coordination across the problems and clients to simple pooled interdependence.

In a consulting value shop approach, the choice of which practices and tools are to be used is not predetermined. Instead, the choice of practices

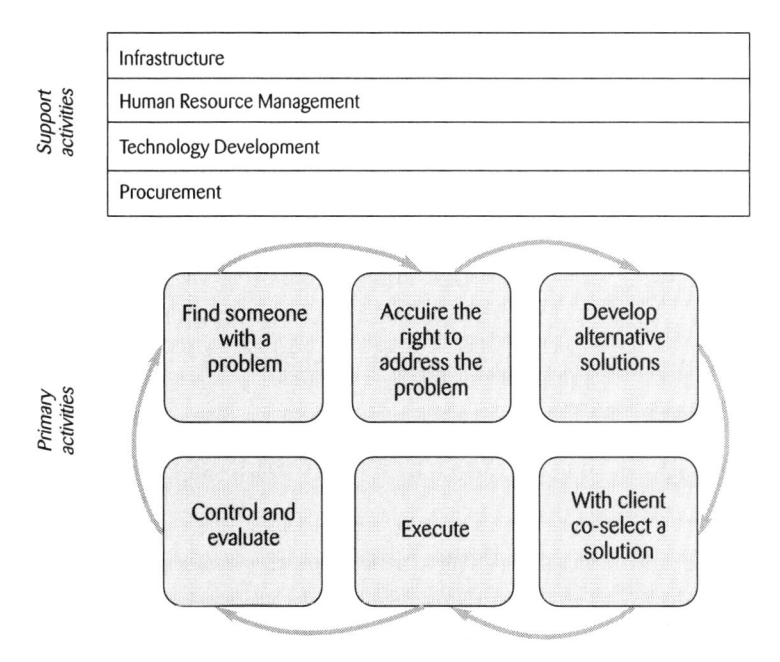

Figure 4 Cyclical nature of the consulting value shop activities

depends on the situational context of the customer's problem, what is available or *allowed* within the context of the problem-solving right acquired by the consultant, and what the consultant can accomplish in that setting. The consultant uses the tools of his or her methodological specialization, deploying whatever strategies, methods, or empirical materials are at hand. If a solution requires that new tools be developed or pieced together, then the consultant will do this. In the end, the solution is the result of the consultant's methodology.

The cyclical nature of the consulting value shop means that when a particular customer problem is solved, a new set of issues may arise and the consultants may be required to address these as well. No solution is final, but rather it may evolve and take new forms, as new facts and different tools, methods and techniques are added to the puzzle.

Value shops rely on the mutual performance of both primary and support activities

A successful consulting value shop requires the mutual performance of both the primary and support activities. This is important because in a consulting value shop, support activities such as human resource (HR) management (recruiting, developing and retaining good professionals) must be carried out by the consultants themselves, in part because consulting is in itself a profession that needs to be managed. And because HR activities are limited, as the recruiting and retention capability of the specialized firm depends primarily on the reputation and quality of the consultants. Similarly, other support activities such as finance, IT and general management administration are rarely performed by dedicated functions in all but the largest consulting firms. Regardless of firm size, these activities are dependent on and therefore, to a varying degree, carried out by consultants in the course of solving client problems.

A brief recap on the development of management consulting

Often branded as the world's newest profession, the establishment of management consulting as a recognized and legitimate carrier of knowledge has been a conflictual process. There are several perspectives on the structural origins of the professional business known to have a fragmented and uneven history. A mainstream perspective suggests the industry's origins stem from scientific management and the established historiography of Taylorism[12] which came into vogue with the advent of the Industrial Revolution, the modern factory and the related institutional and social transformations that have taken place since the end of the 19th century. Consulting that emerged from the scientific management movement focused mainly on factory and shop-floor productivity, the rational organization of work, time and motion studies, and eliminating waste, and reducing production costs[13]. According to this historical account, the consulting industry evolved as a logical consequence of organizations' attempts to minimise their transaction costs[14] through the use of "efficiency experts". Over the following century new areas of management and new types of problems were addressed, and these practices becoming a regular part of the consulting business. Thus, it follows that, today, consultants are regarded as experts at finding new ways of increasing productivity and at making the most of resources, even when others see no such opportunities – thereby offering "economies of problem-solving" that clients cannot match internally.

A contrasting perspective proposes that scientific management did not actually provide the structural origins of the industry, but rather that management consulting can be traced back to the United States at the beginning of the 20th century when regulatory changes inspired the amalgamation of three professions (professions-engineering, law, and accounting) combined with the consultative role of investment bankers[15]. The large consulting firms like Booz, Allen & Hamilton, and McKinsey & Company, that have dominated the field since the 1920s and 1930s, were originally partnerships

---

[12] William B. Wolf (1978). *Management and consulting: An introduction to James O. McKinsey.* Ithaca, N.Y. Popular accounts of management consulting include Hal Higdon (1969). *The Business Healers* (New York); Daniel Guttman and Barry Willner (1976). *The Shadow Government* (New York); John Micklethwaite and Adrian Wooldridge (1996). *The Witch Doctors: Making Sense of the Management Gurus.* (New York); James O'Shea and Charles Madigan (1997). *Dangerous Company: The Consulting Powerhouses and the Businesses they Save and Ruin* (New York). Firm-sponsored histories include Jim Bowman, Booz, Alien G- Hamilton (1984). *Seventy Years of Client Service, 1914-1984* (Chicago); Marvin A. Bower (1979), *Perspective on McKinsey* (New York); David Neal Keller, Stone fr Webster (1989), *1889–1989. A Century of Integrity and Service* (New York); E.J. Kahn, Jr. (1986). *The Problem Solvers: A History of Arthur D. Little, Inc.* (New York).

[13] Kubr, M. (1996). *Management consulting.* Geneva: International Labour Office.

[14] McKenna, C.D. (1995). The origins of modern management consulting. *Business and Economic History.* Vol 24, No. 1, pp. 51–58.

[15] McKenna, C.D. (1995). The origins of modern management consulting. *Business and Economic History.* Vol 24, No. 1, pp. 51–58.

of professional accountants, lawyers, and engineers. At first, "management engineers" within these firms promoted themselves to corporate executives as experts in bureaucratic organization, operational techniques, and strategic planning, and they were hired to analyze specific departmental problems. By the 1930s, hundreds of large corporations including Armour, Union Carbide, Kroger, Borden, Upjohn, and Johnson Wax routinely hired consultants to improve the most fundamental aspects of their organizations, including their strategy, structure, and financial performance.

Even from a geographical viewpoint, there are uneven historical developments. Although much of the industry's history can be traced to developments that have taken place in the United States, some incidental but historically significant, developments could also be observed in the nascent and heterogeneous European consulting industry. In Great Britain the origins of consulting can be traced back to the second half of the 19th century when Great Britain was bogged down by laissez-faire paternalism and self-help economics and was losing the competitive advantage the industrial revolution had given it. In Sweden, the development of consulting was particularly fostered through the symbiotic relationship between consulting firms and academia setting a pattern for what continues to be one of the most "intellectual" consulting markets today. In Finland the growth of consulting was aided by a "few great men", drawn together by their common experience in resisting Nazi Germany and the Soviet Union in the Second World War, and who developed a "specifically Finnish rhetoric of management". Despite these trends and consulting gaining ground in most of the European industrialized countries by the 1920s and 1930s, the volume and scope of the industry remained limited. There were only a few firms, prestigious but relatively small, and their services were mainly used by the larger business corporations.

Back in the United States, the middle of the twentieth century boasted a distinct hierarchy of management consulting firms led by three companies: McKinsey & Company; Booz, Allen & Hamilton; and Cresap, McCormick & Paget. After growing rapidly during the postwar boom, consulting firms such as these found themselves venturing into Western Europe, Asia and other countries undergoing "modernization" where they faced little or no institutional counterparts. In doing so, management consultants acted as disseminators of American organizational models throughout the world. By the mid-1960s, a handful of leading US consulting firms dominated the world market for organizational consulting, encountering little competition and only extraordinary demand in these new markets.

In the late 1960s, however, this comfortable oligopolistic structure began to deteriorate. Accounting firms, like Arthur Andersen & Company, and "strategy" consulting firms, like the Boston Consulting Group, started to move into the market for consulting services. The strategy firms began to steal business from the top, while the accounting firms won routine assignments from the bottom. By the 1970s, although McKinsey & Company, Booz, Allen & Hamilton, and Cresap, McCormick & Paget no longer dominated the market for management consulting services, the model of the professional firm with its concomitant system of rewards remained the central organizational form among management consulting firms. Only recently have large, publicly owned, technology-based corporations like EDS, IBM, and AT&T built consulting divisions that rival the older consulting firms in size, if not in their profitability per consultant.

Also interesting to recap is the development of the role of the consultant over the last 50 years. In the 1950s and 1960s the consultant's role was still reminiscent of a style of consultancy based on the techniques and rationality originating from scientific management and on the expert society. However, a kind of combined evolution and revolution happened during the 1960s and 1970s in the perception of the consultant's role. A new set of values and novelle theories from the behavioural field were included in the universe of management consultants, and more emphasis was placed on processes. Since then the role of consultants has been further refined, both in theory and practice, up through the 1980s and 1990s.

Much of the source of business for today's management consulting practices and methodologies are based on the changing nature of modern management. Wide-reaching trends, including globalisation, rapid developments in information and communication technologies, development of regional economic groupings, and privatization are primary examples of change that have significantly changed the content and quality of consulting[16]. The other major source of growth for consulting practices and methodologies can be traced to the research, entrepreneurship, and strategic decisions of both consulting firms and their customers. Consultants are

---

[16] Examples include the opening of Eastern European markets, following the collapse of communism and the resulting rush by major companies for market entry, thereby calling on the expertise of consultants and audit firms already familiar with the ways of working in these countries.

known for inventing and creating their own markets and their own future, probably more so than other professionals. The nature of demand for many current consulting services and products (i.e. Business Process Reengineering, Balanced Scorecard, Knowledge Management, and e-business initiatives) was brought about by innovative consultants who invented, structured, packaged, sold, and delivered such services to their clients. By doing so, they stimulated other clients' appetite and incited fellow consultants to renew these services, often creating "management fads". In a similar vein, the current trend towards outsourcing is largely being shaped by IT and management service providers working on software for related activities and processes and for systems integration.

As it stands today and as indicated by the importance of new concepts and methodologies in the corporate world, the management consulting industry has evolved into one of the most important conducts for new managerial knowledge and methodologies. With the industry expanding both in scale and scope through the development of a wide array of new services and methodologies, consultants can now be found in all areas of strategic and general management. For the industry as a whole, however, its developments over the last decades can best be considered from the perspective of the fundamental forces of change.

Driving forces of change in the consulting industry

The question facing consultants and managers is not just: "What is driving change in the industry today?" It is: "What should be *done* to respond to all these changes?" This book is intended to help answer the latter question. But before doing so, we briefly review the forces of change that have fostered the developments that have made the industry what it is today. These changes have already had a substantial impact on the industry, but they are likely to bring about even more dramatic changes.

The fundamental forces driving change in the industry can be synthesized as *convergence* and *unbundling*. Together with other factors, these trends are leading to *commoditization,* making it increasingly difficult for management consultants to *differentiate* themselves[17].

---

[17] For a further discussion on the developments and trends observed within professional services industries, see Dawson, R. (2000). *Developing Knowledge-Based Client Relationships: The Future of Professional Services*. Boston: Butterworth-Heinemann.

Convergence of problem-solvers

One long-term development that has generated significant upheaval in the consulting industry has been the trend towards *convergence*. By convergence we refer to the blurring of boundaries between the services provided by traditionally "pure-play" management consultancies and other professional service firms from sectors such as accounting, information technology, law, and advertising.

The evolution of the top tier global accounting firms in the period from 1989 to 1998 is an example of the forces of convergence at work. The effects of convergence started to emerge in the 1990s when the Big Five (KPMG, Arthur Andersen, PricewaterhouseCoopers, Ernst & Young, and Deloitte & Touche) began to realize that there was a significant demand from clients for consulting services on business processes, enterprise resource planning, IT systems implementations (particularly SAP), and management practices. The shift in emphasis reflected the recognition of the fact that a large proportion of their business had become consulting across a wide variety of disciplines, and as a result of this, they proclaimed that they were no longer just accounting firms, but actually integrated consulting firms. In response, consulting practices and non-auditing services that they could cross-sell to their accounting clients, were developed.

The trend is being reinforced by both the "pure-play" management consultancies and other traditionally non-consulting professional service firms. For management consultants this has meant moving into new service areas, which may be emerging areas of management consulting, but also areas outside the management consulting field. For other professional service firms, the trend of convergence has meant that these providers of professional and business services are increasingly doing more and more management consulting. With convergence, niche professions no longer enjoy distinct boundaries and absolute protection against market entrants from previously unrelated industries. As a result, there are more and more new entrants to each market. While these new entrants often may not have exhaustive experience in the industry itself, they bring a high degree of competitiveness through existing relationships with the major clients, knowledge of the common methodologies of professional services, and often extensive resources.

Within the management consulting industry, convergence has largely been driven by the technology and e-business booms witnessed over the last two decades. However, what started off as the logical way forward for consulting firms to begin offering services outside their traditional core competences, ultimately turned into a liability for the entire industry. For example, the explosion in internet usage in the late '90s gave rise to a large number of new "internet" consultancies, such as Viant, Razorfish and Sapient, all competing heavily for work traditionally reserved for the established consulting firms. However, the excesses of the dot-com boom attracted such an inflow of new consulting firms that the consulting market suffered from a temporal overcapacity. The result was downward pressures on pricing with several consultancies having offered services to clients for free in order to maintain the relationships in anticipation of better times.

Unbundling of services

Going hand-in-hand with the trend of convergence has been the trend of unbundling. Unbundling refers to the practice by management consultants of separating and billing for services that had previously only been available as a combined package, such as technology and strategic advice. In our example of the bundled services offered by the Big Five during the early 1990s, the customer's choice was limited to taking either the entire package or nothing at all, leaving them with no knowledge of the relative value or pricing of the offering's components.

Rather than competing head-to-head with existing firms on a full range of services, new competitors in management consulting have often selected a narrow range of services in which to offer specialized competition. The competition from these focused offerings has left established service providers with little choice but to unbundle their offerings. Pressure has come from clients seeking more specialized knowledge and greater value, and who now have the opportunity to make direct comparisons of the offering's various elements. This has been particularly evident in separation of the knowledge-based components from other components of client offerings. Figure 5 illustrates a common occurrence in management consulting, how a single bundled service, that is traditionally offered to clients, has now been broken into several components, and it shows how actual client offerings are becoming more specifically targeted, in response to the current nature of competition between different consulting fields.

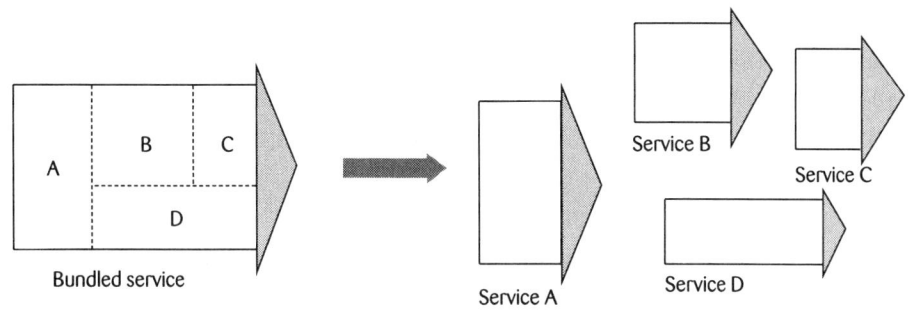

Figure 5

Commoditization

Whereas the twin forces of convergence and unbundling have each had a significant impact on the management consulting industry, the emerging dynamics of increased competition, digitization, rapid diffusion of innovations, and lower industry barriers to entry have pushed consulting and other professional service industries toward a rapidly increasing trend of commoditization. In a commoditized market clients perceive little or no difference between product or service offerings, as these have become indistinguishable commodities. In this situation market segments become price and cost-driven: price is the only way clients differentiate between offerings, and the only sustainable competitive advantage is having the lowest cost base. When freed with this type of market pressure, an industry will usually be driven by volume business, supported by technology and sometimes by international production, and by outsourcing, as a means of controlling production costs. In the consulting industry, the competitive actions of new entrants, who identify separate parts of an overall package – for which they then compete on price, has led to commoditization.

The challenges for management consulting today

The transformations brought about by convergence, unbundling, and commoditization have significantly influenced the evolution of management consulting, its relationships, and its methods of work. Today, the consulting industry is faced with challenging market conditions that are signified by an intensely competitive landscape that is significantly different from anything it has ever experienced before. Some of the most demanding issues that must be resolved include choice of value constellation; the increasing sophistication of buyers of consulting services; the shrinking half-life of useful knowledge; the consulting innovation paradox; the complexities involved in leveraging expertise, and pressures toward professionalization.

Choice of value constellation

What we find in today's consulting competitive landscape is a range of confused consulting firms trying to be everything to everyone. By attempting to please everybody, they are not allowing themselves to be true value shops or value chains. For both consulting value chains and value shops, it is a basic requirement that each activity in the value constellation is executed properly, so that clients receive trust-rate solutions. To carry out these activities, requires the ability to transform different types of resources effectively and efficiently. It is therefore the methodological responsibility of the consultant not only to provide the right advice, but also give it in the right way. It does not matter whether a value chain or value shop philosophy is being used – provided it is being done properly. It is therefore reasonable that consulting value chains and consulting value shops will achieve similar performance characteristics. If both firms are managed well and according to the specifications of their respective models, it is possible for both to score equally well on financial results (turnover, margin, and balance sheet), client satisfaction (customer satisfaction level, and retention ratio levels) and even on competencies (e.g. the type of processes, structures, IP, and brands). It would be incorrect to claim that one model is inherently better than the other – provided each is managed the way it is supposed to be, as both models operate under very different economics and competitive strategies.

Without doubt this strategic confusion has been brought about by the forces of convergence, unbundling, and commoditization. To ensure future success and the ability to develop sustainable competitive advantages, these confused firms will find it imperative to move toward either end of the value chain or the value shop models. Consulting firms will find they are unable to continue to portray themselves as being both a value chain and value shop and accept the fact that it is not possible to be both equally well. This is due to the high coordination costs involved in trying to be both. In particular, consulting firms still operating around a predominantly value chain model, but behaving like a value shop, will find it imperative to rethink their business model. They will either need to focus entirely on being a very efficient value chain (low cost, commodity business) or give up most of their economies of scale and move toward a true consulting value shop model.

Increasing buyer sophistication

There has been a marked shift in the distribution of the powerbase between clients and consultants in recent years. Consultants have begun to realize that as part of a continually evolving trend, buyers are becoming more sophisticated in their procurement of consulting services. Clients have become more demanding of client managers and become more knowledgeable about the providers of consulting services. Even client organizations that traditionally have not used management consultants (such as small- and medium-sized enterprises, non-profit organizations, and the public sector) now have substantial experience in dealing with consultants.

Shrinking knowledge asymmetry

Due to the steady flow of consultants that join their client organizations as practicing managers, and the fact that existing client managers are becoming increasingly familiar with consulting methodologies and frameworks through MBA hires, executive training, and ready access to information, consultants are finding it more difficult to justify their services.

Shortening half-life of useful knowledge

The business of consulting is burdened by the ever shrinking half-life of useful knowledge and relevant consulting skills. Clients expect their consultants to be up to date with industry trends and to have sound knowledge bases in areas such as operations, human resources, and the like. Therefore, knowledge and skills need to be updated frequently. However, the now steadily diminishing half-life of knowledge drives consultants to distraction. Firms must update institutional memory more frequently than was previously necessary to remain current on consulting techniques.

Consulting innovation paradox

Although consulting firms like to believe that their competitive edge lies in creating and implementing innovative solutions, a more critical eye reveals a rather different picture. In reality, most consulting firms do business by applying commonly known analytical methodologies to one of several established business problem domains in which they have experience. To solve the problem they then reach into their tool kit for one of several known solutions, because that solution is considered to be tested, costed, tried, and true.

Therein exists the innovation paradox most consulting firms suffer from but few wish to acknowledge. Generally, the more a firm innovates, the more brand-recognition it gets, and that helps to develop more business. Yet the more a firm implements well-known and well-practiced methodologies, the more value it may deliver to clients for the money they spend, and the more profit it may make on its assignments. For management consulting, innovation is almost an anathema. The innovation that has taken place within consulting can largely be summed up as a series of improvements in process efficiency enabled by greater use of IT and the occasional theory development interpreted and implemented by management gurus (i.e. the movements of Balanced Scorecard and Intellectual Capital are recent examples). If these are stripped away, it is hard to find many significant examples of real innovation occurring across the consulting arena.

It can be argued that true innovation is expensive – it costs time and financial and human resources that managing partners don't want to give away. And they have sound business reasons for not doing so. How many clients would pay for consultants who claim not to have "the answer" but rather to have an untested innovation that might be an answer? There is also the issue of how the majority of consulting firms are managed on the basis of maximizing individual utilization and realization. Based on the premise that time is money, most consultants are expected to fulfill 'average realization and utilization' targets by billing clients a certain amount of hours or days. In a 100% utilization culture there is little room for thinking, questioning and developing new approaches, perspectives and services. Some more evolved firms reward employees on the basis of total contribution to the business which includes an element of innovation – but not many.

When taking a closer look at the innovative performance of consulting – and the professional services sector as a whole – and comparing this to the manufacturing sector and the likes of Sony, BMW, and 3M, the manner in which innovation is stimulated and delivered internally within professional service firms is in reality decades behind the times. In consulting, accounting, advertising and law the prevailing issues of convergence, unbundling and commoditization are three themes that manufacturing companies had been pursuing for well over a decade – and from which they have now moved on. Even with today's consulting boom, evident in outsourcing by larger IT companies such as Accenture, IBM, and HP, the value proposition offered to clients is all about using economies of scale and lower cost of supply as the main drivers of value creation – nothing that would be considered new to the likes of Nokia, Ford, or Wal-Mart. Whilst other sectors have questioned the mechanics of their value chains and revised the way they create value in order to actively encourage and foster innovation, most consulting firms tend to cling to traditional approaches that may actually discourage change.

Complexities in leveraging expertise

Despite the commendable advances in knowledge management and information technologies at the disposal of consultants today, and the increasing use of modern organizational structures, the issue of leveraging expertise and organization knowledge is one that will continue be of importance, even though it continues to be fraught with difficulties.

Knowledge management is essential for consultants in their quest to keep up-to-date with relevant consulting knowledge and skills. However, knowledge management within consulting is notoriously difficult to master, with most implementations giving unsatisfactory results due to their central focus on standardized and often inappropriate IT approaches. Little consideration is given to the alignment of epistemological and knowledge development preferences between consultants and KM systems. Such misalignment does little to help consultants create and capture knowledge, and to gain access to the existing knowledge amassed within the organization.[18]

Consultants face the continuing problem of leveraging internal human resources. Many consulting firms remain stuck in traditional organizational models and strong supporting cultures that use pyramidal partnership silos

---

[18] See e.g. Roos, G. (2005). An epistemology perspective on intellectual capital. In Marr, B. (Ed.), *Perspectives on intellectual capital: Multidisciplinary insights into management, measurement and reporting*. London: Butterworth–Heinemann.

to maintain differential margins and drive up maximum return for their leaders, who largely shy away from the operational coalface. The result is often a dilution of quality of advice through an enthusiastic but presumably somewhat naive intermediary consultant. In effect, the internal structure of so many consulting firms acts as barrier to the effective leverage of expertise.

The ability to leverage external expertise – or rather the lack thereof – is another cause of concern for consulting. Previously we mentioned the lack of innovation evident in the management consulting sector as compared to the level of innovation witnessed in manufacturing sectors. Herein lies a further opportunity for consulting, for it is surprising to what extent the consulting sector refuses to learn from other industries. Manufacturing companies across the board, from BP to Honda and Dell, are constantly looking for lessons from others sectors and transferring and incorporating best practices in value delivery – allowing them to stay at the forefront of competition. No such effort is evident in consulting.

Improving the management of consulting firms

Despite the fact that consultants are respected as experts in management issues, they are notoriously poor at managing their own firms. Traditionally, management in consulting firms has been much less formal and less apparent than in other industries. There are many reasons for this phenomenon. First, it is only in recent years that large-scale consulting firms have emerged, and average firm size in this industry is still small when compared with the manufacturing sector or even some service sectors, such as insurance. Second, many consulting firms are run by consultants who tend to despise full-time management and administration. Even in areas that are managed by non-consultants, decision-making power tends to remain concentrated in the hands of the consultants. Third, and most important, as long as conditions in the consulting industry remained favorable, the need for formal and explicit management seemed to be limited. For example, the incentives for junior consultants to work hard stemmed primarily from the motivation to become a partner. Similarly, the apprenticeship model – with junior staff working alongside more experienced colleagues – ensured that the primary mode of training was provided by consultants rather than by designated HR specialists. Overall, in classical consulting firms, many aspects of "good management" were embedded in the organizational structure of the firms themselves.

It might be appropriate to question the functioning of the typical consulting organizational structure; while other sectors have moved on to lean organizations to minimize the variable costs of human resources, enable profitable workforce, outsource non-core activities, form expert collaborative partnerships, and ensure high levels of multi-tasking, few consulting firms made any effort to adopt such changes.

Pressures toward professionalization

There is a pressing need for management consultancy to score better on 'professionalism'. In a profession where the working environment is often characterized by ambiguity, ignorance and uncertainty, there has been an increased focus on moral standards and ethical behavior for management consultants. Notwithstanding the battering the industry's claim to professionalism took, during and after, the collapse of Enron and other major corporations, in part due to the advice received from professional advisors, consultants have always been looked upon by some clients with a wary eye. The general image of management consultants in contemporary society can be, for different groups both provocative and appealing. Some of the provocative issues cited by clients include excessive charging, untested panaceas and universal solutions, superficial promises, unfulfilled commitments, unwanted results, and the fact that customers may simply be overwhelmed by the consultants' approach. In addition, consultants are often linked to questionable management fads (e.g. TQM, Business Process Engineering, and Balanced Scorecard), that trigger quick and superficial change initiatives that are not implemented seriously.

Professionalization issues are compounded in that consulting markets are not perfect. In view of the fact that consultants create value through rational interventions based on sophisticated knowledge, one might interpret the exorbitant fees charged by consultants, and the rate of growth in the consulting industry as evidence of value creation. However, the 'market knows best' – argument may not yet apply to consulting. In reality, the markets for most professional services are highly inefficient due to their diversity, fragmentation and the intangible nature of their output. Consequently, it is difficult for clients to assess quality of services provided, and since there is seldom any communication between clients where experiences with different consultants might be exchanged, it is difficult for the market to react 'rationally' (as would be the case in a perfect market). As clients will tend to be uncertain about what they expect from consultants, the consultants rely on factors that build mental proximity with clients, and as such, reputation, image and personal relations matter more than quality of services. In order to address this, management consultants are coming under pressure to adopt a more professional approach, by establishing closer ties to 'science' and/or other formal knowledge, regulating entry, restricting variation in competence and practice, emphasizing independence, etc. The requirements that consulting firms must meet in order to take on an assignment and ensure the quality of advice provided are increasingly being prescribed – though not yet enforced – by the codes of conduct and ethics of an increasing number of management consulting associations.

The way forward

The reappearance of the individual consulting firm, and not the industry, as the key determinant of profitability is based on the view that superior performance and a sustainable competitive position depends primarily on the human resources of the firm.

By adopting the value shop as an alternative value constellation to the value chain we have already started to see how the shape of the business world has changed dramatically since Michael Porter first propounded that essentially only two competitive business strategies exist: price-based competition and value-based competition. Following this line of reasoning, the key drivers of firm profitability are the characteristics of the industry in question. This led to the prevailing belief that the key challenge to achieving profitability is managing the fit between the firm and the external environment. As could be observed by the growth of Big 5 consulting organizations during the 1980s, the goal was to achieve a competitive position and superior performance with the intention of obtaining a monopoly position and earning monopoly rents in the long run. Here barriers to entry and exit are important features of the competitive landscape. Furthermore, the consulting industry could be subdivided into different strategic groups with mobility barriers constraining movement across groups.

The nature of consulting is changing and will continue to do so in the future. We have reached an era where the trends towards convergence and unbundling have greatly moderated the impact of traditional industry factors such as entry barriers, industry concentration, market share power, and strategic group membership. Instead, we need to shift the emphasis on competitive advantage back to the consulting firms. This is best done through the resource-based view (RBV) of strategy. The RBV provides a perspective on the nature of competition that is more in line with the future of consulting.

From the RBV point of view, the key challenge for consultants is to transform basic resources into core competencies, which form the basis for superior competitive positions in specific market segments. Resources can be both tangible and intangible, and may encompass the entirety of a firm's intellectual capital. The basic idea is that the basis for superior performance is made up of those resources that are difficult to *imitate* and *substitute*. These resources are embedded as core competencies within the firm. They are developed, not acquired, and hence have low tradability. As core competencies improve with use, and are less subject to depreciation, they can become a fundamental source of sustainable advantage. What is important here is the firm's ability to develop core competencies that are so embedded in the organization that they are causally ambiguous, inimitable, not tradable, not easily substitutable, and important to specific customer segments. This is the key secret to sustainable competitive advantage and can be achieved if:

- Consulting firms continue to invest and accumulate the resources that led to an advantage and,
- Rivals are unable to imitate these resources, either because they are protected by patent and/or are causally ambiguous and socially complex in nature.

In the future competitive landscape of consulting, competition may well be viewed as a process that focuses on marketplace positions of competitive advantage. If this turns out to be the case, the function of the competitive landscape will not be to create barriers to entry, but rather to ensure the proper allocation of rewards to those firms that create strategic value for their clients. So, with the challenge of sustainability in the face of imitation, substitution, and constant change as the key to survival, what should consultants do differently?

There is no straightforward answer to this question. There are many avenues for change available to consultants, based on the trends and issues that we have highlighted. One such avenue offering considerable scope in terms of building a causally ambiguous and inimitable competitive advantage lies in the increased use of scientific procedures and research in the entirety of the consulting value constellation. We find that many of the issues faced by consultants today are compounded by the lack of any scientific approach in consulting, and this is partially to blame for the unfavorable opinion of management consulting. In particular the lack of innovation in consulting methodologies, the shrinking knowledge asymmetry vis-à-vis clients, and the shifting powerbase toward clients, necessitate that consultants align themselves more closely to 'science', formal knowledge, and research.

Competitive advantage of a scientific approach

A scientific approach to management consulting involves problem solving through methodological activity and study complemented by knowledge gained through experience. It has already been established that adopting a scientific approach in management is a source of competitive advantage which, under the right conditions, can be sustainable over a long period of time. In its essence, a scientific approach to consulting is multifaceted. It should not be considered a project or a set of techniques; rather it should be viewed as a process, way of thinking, and managing.

A scientific approach has the potential to validate all substantive aspects of consulting in that it facilitates the collection, analysis, and interpretation of primary and secondary data. By introducing scientific rigor into the consultant's realm, the ability to conduct and apply research may become a competitive advantage.

Using a scientific approach in the context of consulting is a relatively new phenomenon and has been guided by rather conservative practices and perspectives. These are limited to the preparation and publication of white papers, reports, and case studies, of which many are mediocre and/or lack any substantial grounding. What is new, is the focus on research required to justify a scientific approach. There are consulting firms that have, to varying degrees, incorporated research into their approach by developing their own research programs, undertaking contract research, publishing books and articles based on their own research, or cooperating on research projects with universities and other researchers. Some consulting firms have gained the reputation of being firmly research based, most notably McKinsey & Co. for which it is reaping the rewards.

There are significant advantages to be gained by basing a competitive advantage on the scientific approach. Traditionally consultants brought personal credibility to the consulting process based on their experiences and skills; a scientific orientation provides additional credibility and justification to the consulting process. "We have researched and identified the critical factors determining the effectiveness of flexible production systems" is probably a more convincing marketing message than: "We have extensive experience with improving production systems". Certainly, not every issue or consultant intervention readily lends itself to this approach, but many do. In these cases, consultants will have an ethical responsibility to provide up-to-date, robust research in to the consulting process. Exchanging significant management research findings with the business community, potential clients, and other researchers, will help strengthen the consulting firm's competitive advantage.

The consultant/researcher

Consulting firms that wish to develop a competitive advantage based on a scientific approach will find that their consultants not only need to be informed about published results of management research, and keep in touch with on-going research projects and leading researchers, but also need to actively participate in research-creating a new breed of professional advisors that double as consultants and researchers. The consultant/researcher is capable of solving the customer's problems, and subsequently applying problem-solving methodologies based on intensive knowledge and a scientific approach. New capabilities are required from consultants. More importantly, the transition toward the consultant-researcher will mean adopting a new set of expectations and assumptions: The consultant/researcher is proficient at performing a large number of diverse tasks in the fields of research and consulting.

- The consultant/researcher studies a wide range of topics, is knowledgeable, and is capable of working between and within competing and overlapping perspectives and paradigms.

- The consultant/researcher will be required to understand that research is an interactive process shaped by his or her own personal history, biography, gender, social class, race, and ethnicity, as well as that of the people in the setting.
- The consultant/researcher will acknowledge that science involves power, for all research findings have political implications as there is no such thing as value-free science.
- In order to conduct excellent and insightful consulting, consultants/researchers need to be project managers, skilled negotiators, educators, co-workers, and collaborators as well as theorists, investigators, methodologists, and analysts. Further they must be able to organize and present their findings and output for maximum understanding and benefit to the client.

Methodologies of research and inquiry

When the scientific approach requires research, this may be conducted using quantitative and qualitative research methods or a combination of the two. Research methodology bears out all substantive aspects of consulting in that it facilitates the collection, analysis, and interpretation of primary and secondary data. Of particular relevance to the consulting field is the science and methodologies of qualitative research. The word qualitative suggests an emphasis on processes and meanings that are not rigorously investigated or measured in terms of quantity, amount, intensity, or frequency. Qualitative research places emphasis on the socially constructed nature of reality, the intimate relationship between the researcher and what is studied, and the situational constraints that shape the inquiry. Quantitative research, in contrast, emphasizes the measurement and analysis of causal relationships between variables, and is less concerned with processes where inquiry is purported to be conducted within a value-free framework[19]. The major differences in the basic assumptions between qualitative and quantitative resource approaches are summarized in Table 1[20].

---

[19] For a detailed discussion on the differences between qualitative and quantitative research approaches, see Denzin, N.K. and Y.S. Lincoln (1994). Entering the Field of Research. In Denzin, N.K. and Y.S. Lincoln, *Handbook of Qualitative Research*. London: Sage Publications.

[20] Although many qualitative researchers use statistical measures, methods, and documents as a way of locating a group of subjects within a larger population, they seldom report their findings in terms of the kind of complex statistical measures or methods to which quantitative researchers are drawn.

	Qualitative research	**Quantitative research**
Primary form of representation	Words and price descriptions	Numbers and statistical measures
Nature of enquiry	*Inductive.* Hypothesis not needed to begin research	*Deductive.* Hypothesis required before research can begin
Role of researcher	The researcher can gain knowledge about a situation by participating and/or being immersed in it	Ideally an objective observer that neither participates in nor influences what is being studied
Major drawback	Can focus too closely on individual results and may fail to make connections to a larger picture or possible causes of the results	Can "force" responses or people into categories that might not "fit" in order to make meaning

Table 1 Qualitative versus quantitative research

Table 2 presents some of the major research methodologies of inquiry available to the consultant-researcher. Each of these methodologies requires a study design which broadly speaking involves a clear focus on the research issue, the purpose of the study, what information will be most likely to answer specific research issues, and which strategies are most effective for obtaining this information. Each one of these research methodologies is lacked by an extensive body of literature; each has a separate history, exemplary works, and preferred ways of applying the methodology. It is beyond the scope of this chapter to discuss this in detail.

Research methodology	
• Ethnography	• Symbolic interactionist study
• Case study	• Interpretive research
• Participant observation	• Narrative research
• Field research and study	• Action and applied research
• Phenomenology, ethno methodology	• Literary review & criticism
• Naturalistic study	• Intervention research
• Phenomenological study	• Historiography
• Ecological descriptive study	• Clinical research
• Descriptive study	• Grounded theory

Table 2 Methodologies of research & inquiry

In addition, the consultant-researcher has several other methods for collecting data and knowledge as summarized in Table 3. These range from interviews to direct observations, to the analysis of artifacts, documents, and cultural records, to the use of visual materials or personal experiences. Different methods of reading and analyzing interviews or cultural texts include content, narrative, and semiotic approaches. Computer-assisted models and data management methods will aid the consultant in managing and interpreting these documents.

Methods of collection and analysis	
• Interviewing	• Personal experience methods
• Observational techniques	• Data management and analysis methods
• Interpretation of artifacts, documents, and records	• Computer-assisted methods
• Visual methods	• Narrative, content, and semiotic analysis

Table 3 Methods of collection and analysis

Assessing the validity of a scientific approach

The validity of adopting a scientific approach in the context of consulting is based on how well the research solves problems or exposes new problems, and its provision of value to the customer.

Conclusion

In conclusion, we recommend that consultants recognize the need for adopting a scientific approach as a step in developing sustainable competitive advantages for their specific firms. In a broader sense this perspective should contribute to further growth in the management consulting discipline and to increased relevance of management consulting for both theory and practice.

Some of the aims of this book are:
- To understand the rationale behind a scientific approach to consulting.
- To introduce the role, importance, and limitations of management research and the methods used in such research.
- To provide knowledge of qualitative and quantitative research methods.
- To provide an understanding of the process of management research through practical experience of conducting group research projects on selected managerial problems.
- To offer an overview of the nature of the research process.
- To contribute to a better understanding of the different modes of consultancy.
- To help readers develop a better understanding of the implications of the different theories of what constitutes effective consultancy.
- To introduce core methodologies used by consultants in problem-solving.

Chapter 2

Thought consultancy – In action

FLEMMING POULFELT

The landscape of driving forces

The role of a manager is neither more difficult nor easier today than it has been in the past. However, the role has changed, and this in itself provides significant motive to adjust and develop the foundation of the company on an ongoing basis. Therefore, change is a key concept in many organisations; the motto being: "change creates security, change creates freedom and change creates progress".

There are several major forces driving the development of organisations which are drawing particular attention to the need for change right now (Economist, 2002; Greiner & Poulfelt, 2004). These forces may affect different types of companies in different ways, and to varying degree, but they will all have an affect on most companies. It is the responsibility of management to consider how each of these driving forces will influence their organisation, and how the organisation should respond proactively to these forces.

Among the most dominant forces driving the competitive landscape today are:

1. The need to focus on more strategic activities while keeping up development and innovation.
2. Accelerating development of new products.
3. Outsourcing of production and internal services, e.g. IT facility management, recruitment, and the development and training of personnel.
4. Globalisation as an integral part of everyday life.
5. Focus on streamlining and cost minimisation.
6. Deregulation and outsourcing that have led to the need for restructuring.

7. Rapid developments in IT and the resulting requirements for new and often more integrated IT solutions.
8. The continuous need for the development of competences and leadership in many companies.
9. Increased uncertainty and complexity that have prompted many companies to include external consultants in the management process, both to provide inspiration and to assume the role of sparring partner. And finally,
10. The fashion phenomenon must not be ignored (Abrahamson, 1996). This implies the wish of most companies to adopt the most recent advances or concepts in management which can in itself provide the opportunity for making changes, provided it is possible to discern between good and bad. If not, a well-intended change could easily lead to increased organisational confusion.

The above mentioned factors apply to all types of companies, and consultants can play an active role in helping companies to deal with them. How this is being done with or without the assistance of consultants characterises the performance of management.

The term "Thought Leadership" reflects ambitions and even illusions. However, it has recently become a buzzword that is used to convey to others that one's thinking is widely recognised as being top-notch, and one's output excellent. In this article, the term "Thought Leadership" has been transformed to "Thought Consultancy" in order to embrace the concepts that should be an integral part of professional consultancy. As such, this article will focus on the most critical aspect of consulting, namely the cooperation between consultant and client and the manner in which they create mutual value.

The chapter is made up of four parts. It begins by touching on developments within the consulting industry and on some of the recent trends. Since the consultant-client relationship is the focus, part two of the article reflects on different motivations for using consultants and on the changes that are evident in motive structures. Part three explores some of the most important and critical elements of the cooperation between consultants and their clients, including the factors which may impede or advance the creation of optimal value. Finally, part four explores the challenges facing both consultant and client when solving future assignments.

The relevance of consulting

Over the years, the consulting industry has become increasingly more interesting (Clark & Fincham, 2002). In an age where the knowledge society has gained a strong foothold, consultants – as suppliers of knowledge – will play a major role in the further development of this society. However, the industry is relatively young and does not yet have any specific institutional characteristics or affiliations. In addition, our formal knowledge of the industry is limited (Kipping & Engwall, 2002).

Furthermore, consulting is an industry that has grown fairly significantly for a number of years (Greiner & Poulfelt, 2004; Czerniawska, 2002). A conservative estimate indicates that the growth rate in Europe and elsewhere during the nineties was in the 10–15% range. At one time, the growth rate seemed to be unstoppable, cf. "Growth and revenues seem to be unstoppable", which was the title of an article in the *Financial Times* in 1997 regarding developments in the consultancy industry. However, growth slowed down significantly when the IT bubble burst and, for some years, the consultancy industry has experienced leaner times. The growth rate increased once again from 2004. In addition to the fact that growth in the consultancy can be an indicator of the complexity and uncertainty that companies and managers face, it also illustrates that the consultant's raison d'être has been strengthened as growth is dependent on demand.

Finally, the consultancy industry is interesting from the perspective of value and effect, cf. "high-impact consulting" (Schaffer, 1997) which is based on the ability of the client to utilise the consultant's efforts, and, on the view of consultants as "the nurseries of the powerful" (which refers to the importance attributed to them). Many consulting assignments are strategic in nature, and may be concerned with the direction in which a company, or its management, is to grow, business process engineering (BPR), and quality development or outsourcing, to mention but a few of the areas in which consultants often are involved. As a consequence, consulting assignments are related to fundamental aspects of a company's operations and, therefore, development can be said to have a significant impact on decisions which follow in the wake of a consulting assignment. Factors such as relevance, trust, and credibility are therefore important for the success of any consulting project. As such, the consultant's interaction with management is crucial if the intended goals are to be realised and if the parties are to ensure that the intended results are achieved. Thus, implementation and learning are also important elements of the repertoire of the consultant.

Patterns in the use of consultants

The use of management consultants has been increasing for years. It can be suggested that the field of consulting, once marginal and insignificant, has developed into an independent, relevant, and useful business. It used to be the consultants who were called upon by companies in crisis, or if business was going badly. This perception has been replaced by a more progressive attitude. Thus, today, consultants are called in to assist in a wide range of activities: they are used as sparring partners on issues concerned with the strategic development of the company; as advisors when the company is in the process of recruiting a new managing director; to provide professional support during the development of quality systems; as advisors in connection with outsourcing; as a resource for the development of management competences; as an arbitrator in conflict situations; as project managers for large IT projects; or as specialists in performance improvement. One director put it this way: "The advantage of involving a consultant is that we avoid forcing a misguided concept on the whole organisation".

At the same time, there is a wide range of different motives for hiring a consultant; from a company with its back to the wall, to situations where management simply wishes to be on the cutting edge of development. Whereas consultants used to provide a reactive response to management, it has become more common for consultants to adopt a proactive approach to the way in which they can stimulate and strengthen the management process – both in the private and in the public sector. As one manager opined: "Consultants can be used to help prioritise and to increase the rate of change."

As a consequence of this development, the field has broadened significantly, and there have been major developments in the services provided by consultants. As the market for consulting services has matured, it has become more transparent. Current management fashion – for which consultants have, quite understandably, been advocates – has led to a continuous flow of new "leadership concepts", of which some have proved effective and viable, while others have been quickly shelved. In any case, the market for "management fashions" has seen tremendous growth and, for those involved, been very lucrative.

However, the increased usage of consultants – and thus also the increased costs linked to this use – also poses a number of fundamental questions related, to the practical value of consulting. The question might look simple, but the issue is highly complex, even though the obvious answer might be that good consultancy is almost priceless: "Good advice is expensive", whereas bad advice can lead a company astray if it is followed. The answer can sometimes be less than obvious, as illustrated by the fact that (O'Shea & Madigan, 1997) AT&T used around USD 1/2 billion on consultants between 1989 and 1994, primarily in connection with management and IT. The amount may not seem very large when seen in relation to an annual turnover of more than USD 50 billion, but when we consider that the effect was at best debatable, the amount is significant. A former AT&T manager claims that, despite the fact that AT&T lost market share, they did not take the advice given by the consultants seriously enough and, as a result, it was not implemented very well throughout the organisation.

Even though there has been a great deal of focus on "practical value" (expressed as "added value" in consultancy jargon) over the past few years (Czerniawska, 2002), this subject is still relevant. There is a limited amount of documentation on the subject, despite the fact that several studies on the use of consultants indicate that clients are satisfied with the services consultants provide. However, it can be claimed that the theory of "cognitive dissonance" (Festinger, 1957) can be a fly in the ointment of any such study, as a management team that has a great deal of resources on a specific consulting project might be a little reluctant to exercise "overt self-criticism", even if they are not entirely satisfied with the result.

However, regardless of this, if the intended value is to be created within the client organisation, the consultant (or the team) must be able to provide constructive input and support.

Thus, when using consultants, it is of critical importance to make sure their advice is implemented properly.

When consultants are used

The reasons offered for not employing consultants are usually that "we don't need to involve a consultant", "we can solve the problems ourselves", "we've had bad experience with consultants in the past", "they are too expensive", or "it won't be of any use", in other words, slightly defensive arguments. One manager expressed this in specific terms: "The reason for not using consultants is rooted in fear. If you open the door to these people, the results could be unpredictable." There is a grain of truth in this as, presumably, some companies have found that the results from consulting projects did not quite live up to expectations. However, the blame does not necessarily lie with the consultant. On the contrary, there are many examples of projects that have provided solutions that differ from the hopes or expectations of management. It is easy to see how this experience could be interpreted as dissatisfaction with the consultant, even though the solution may prove to be the right one. In this type of situation management needs to recognise that this is a constructive disagreement rather than insisting on being right. It is in this type of situation we often see that significant progress is made and developments take place.

On the other hand, a large number of companies see the employment of external consultants in a somewhat different light. One manager expressed it like this: "Consultants are a tool we can use to put pressure on midfield but, of course, we must take charge of the game ourselves."

Therefore, a basic question is: When is it advantageous to use consultants? Unfortunately, there is no universal answer to this. However, one answer might be that it can be wise to use consultants when there is no obvious answer to a current problem or when management does not have the skills required to deal with a specific challenge, e.g. in connection with recruitment, strategic activities, M&A, lean production, introduction of new IT systems, or management development.

However, regardless of the nature of the assignment, it should be noted that the consultant can never replace management, and the project is doomed to failure, if that is what is expected: "Consultants must not take on the role of management – the client must provide the managerial capacity."

Typical motives

Today, consultants are called upon for a great number of different reasons depending on the problem at hand and the situation in which the company finds itself. The typical motives for engaging a consultant are:

- New knowledge and new methods
- Extra capacity
- New perspectives
- Confirmation
- Independent evaluations
- Political legitimacy

It should be emphasised that there are several overlapping motives; a consultant may be called in because a company requires new knowledge as well as an external advisor who can stimulate development by looking at the situation from a new perspective.

Studies have shown that the motives for engaging external consultants are essentially the same for both the private sector and the public sector, although the political motive is slightly more pronounced in the public sector (Poulfelt & Payne, 1994). At least, clients in the public sector emphasise this motive more than clients in the private sector, but this could also be due to the fact that the public sector's concept of politics is different.

Therefore, an important task for the consultant at the beginning of any assignment is to identify the rationale for the client's request for assistance, based on the client's expressed motives and needs. This will enable the consultant to determine whether the basis for the potential assignment is sustainable and to outline the possible directions for the organisation of, and solution to, the assignment. In the process, the consultant will get a feeling for the client's actual requirements and interest in solving the problem at hand. In reality, where subjective truths often dominate, it is not always possible to presuppose that "reasonable people will do reasonable things". Another issue is that assignments are often reformulated along the way if there is mutual acceptance. However, if the consultant perceives that the basis for his or her presence is tenuous or uncertain, and there is little chance of making a significant change, it is obvious that the consultant should back out. One of the ground rules of professional consulting is: "If you can say 'no' to a proposal, you should not say 'yes'."

Therefore, some basic requirements must be met if a consultancy assignment is to be accepted. These are:

- There must be a real need for external assistance.
- The client must have relatively clear goals for the assignment's solution.
- The client must be motivated to reach the solution.
- The client must be willing to make changes.
- The client must be prepared to receive direct and indirect criticism.
- Resources must be in place to implement recommendations.

In reality, these requirements are simple, but experience shows that they are not always met in practice.

When collaborating with external consultants, management's agenda, will to change, motivation, and drive are crucial factors for success.

Value-added cooperation

When the authors of a recently published book on leadership were asked for their views on the value of consultants in large-scale change projects, their answer was clear: On the basis of their knowledge and position as external suppliers, consultants can add value (yes, they even claimed that consultants are, by definition, useful). However, they also stressed the importance of the client's role; if the client company is to achieve the desired effect, the client must take an active part in solving the assignment, and stay in control of relations to the consultants (Bauman, Jackson & Lawrence, 1997).

Therefore, the impact of a consultant's efforts is not only based on the consultant's knowledge base, it is also – to a very large extent – based on whether the company is able to develop a climate of cooperation with the consultant. In other words, neither the consultant nor the client bears the sole responsibility for a favourable result, it is a team effort. As such, it is this interaction that determines whether the solution will be labelled successful or unsuccessful. Only in very rare cases does one person – whether consultant or client – solve an assignment single-handedly.

From studies of companies that use consultants, a number of factors to which managers attach importance, and which contribute to the success of an assignment, may be identified (Poulfelt, 2000). If these elements are studied in more detail, it should be possible to achieve a better understanding of the rationale for the collaboration and, thus, what constitutes "Thought consultancy":

- The "clients first"-approach
- Customisation
- The process
- Involvement
- Stakeholders
- Competences
- Match between persons
- Trust
- Added value

The "clients first"-approach

The slogans "Clients' interests come first" or "Serving clients is the core of our business" have been predominant for many years. This illustrates that the consultant's idea of ideal service is to serve the clients in the best possible way and on their own terms. The point is that, in the mindset of consultants, clients should both come first and be the centre of the consultant's attention. As such, this can be said to be the general paradigm for "good consulting behaviour".

This is the guiding principle for many consultants. However, the way in which the client focus is developed within consulting firms, and the way in which it is put into practice, vary greatly. It is also a competitive parameter for consultants. But regardless of this, there are at least three critical criteria for success in consulting: Professionalism, authenticity, and commitment.

Customisation

Most companies that use consultants want or expect the consultant to attempt to customise the assignment's design and solution to meet the requirements of their own specific situation. However, studies (Danish

Agency for Trade and Industry, 1999) indicate that this is an area in which clients feel that consultants ought to make more of an effort. In many cases, consultants do not seem to tailor their services to the requirements of a specific situation despite the fact that many consultants emphasise this as an important characteristic of their services and working method. This behaviour is perhaps best explained by the increased conceptualisation and standardisation of services and methods in the consulting world. The danger that exaggerated standardisation also carries the risk of neglecting the need for customised solutions was emphasised at a global conference for consultants: "Watch out for productification of consultancy services" on the basis of the motto "Are we to be solution providers or problem solvers?" However, many consultancy companies are currently attempting to balance the need for the standardisation of services (with a view to achieving the advantages of large-scale operations) with a variety of methods, and an approach that is fully customised to suit the client.

It is not only the type of service that determines whether a project is perceived as having been customised to suit the client. It is as much a question of the way in which a consultant presents a project and the angle from which the consultant attacks the specific problem. As a manager in a large international insurance company said: "I feel a little uncomfortable when consultants present me with major pre-packaged programmes on how to solve key problems in our company before they know very much about the organisation", or as another manager expressed it: "It doesn't sound credible when a consultant can tell a manager what is good and bad about the organisation within half an hour." In addition to this, many clients have perhaps an unrealistically high expectation of what "customisation" involves in reality. Therefore, a better coordination of expectations, as well as a clarification of the added value expected by the client, can contribute to an improved and more realistic understanding of the process. Finally, it is, of course, important that the consultant lives up to his promises. This was illustrated by a senior manager with the following words: "Consultants sometimes forget that clients actually make note of promises."

There is a range of factors to which we ought to turn our attention in connection with the situation-oriented approach, the first being the actual "translation problem". This refers to the position of the company's problem in the consultant's frame of reference, and how we can ensure the client's understanding of this without ignoring the client's specific problem.

It is important to find a balance between the specific problem and the problem in a more abstract form. The motive for hiring a consultant is often the desire to use the consultant to move the company's specific problem up a level – but without affecting the way in which the problem is solved. Finding the optimal method is a balancing act, but it is vital if renewal is to be an integral part of the desired solution. Renewal is created in the abstraction process but it requires courage, cf. Søren Kierkegaard said: "To dare is to lose one's footing momentarily. Not to dare is to lose one self."

Thus, the client's expectations are that the consultant will be able to "read and understand" the company's specific situation and develop a solution accordingly. As one experienced consultant explained: "It is a question of the consultant's ability to 'identify himself with the company'." And it should be added that he must do this both in words and in deeds, as it is important that consultants live up to their promises. A shared understanding of the problem at hand is therefore a crucial element in consulting.

Focus on the process

The statement "the process is more important than the actual result" was marketed in consultancy circles for many years. It was later taken off the agenda. It was seen as being a travesty, and somewhat misleading, because the result of the consulting activity is significant – regardless of the type of activity involved! No competent manager would seek to initiate a management development project, a quality management project or an IT project without the probability of achieving specific results. Therefore, it can be claimed that the project is inadequate if it does not include specific criteria for success or other benchmarks standards. It is obvious that the process will be a project's most significant testimony if the consultant is lax on benchmarking. Another important element is the fact that the value of the process should not be underestimated.

Therefore, from a consultancy point of view, an understanding of the significance of the process is relevant, not in the least because most consulting projects include an element of change. Today, the majority of clients recognise that the classical interpretation of the role of a consultant – i.e. as an expert in the traditional sense – is a thing of the past. Rather, in most cases, the requirement is for a person or team that is able to design and run a consulting assignment as a process. Thus, it has been claimed that 75% of the problems experienced during a consulting project are not due to the change itself but are due to the process leading to the change.

Therefore, the consultant must be able to handle this type of process. Assignments that have gone awry can, in many cases, be attributed to the consultant's ability to handle this type of process, or to the fact that the process was too complicated.

However, it is one thing to share an understanding of the significance of the process, but understanding what the consequences mean for both consultant and client is something else altogether. For the consultant it is important to understand, manage, and time the development of the process in an environment that is full of contradictions, obscurity, and uncertainty. This means that although it may be easy enough for the consultant to plan the process, in most cases, the consultant will be required to revise, adjust, and intervene in the process along the way, due to new information, unforeseen wants, and the responses from clients.

In many cases, process management is more difficult than the actual technical planning and implementation of the assignment – although separating the technical aspect and the actual process may seem contrived – as the process itself is an integral part of the dynamics of the solution to the assignment and, thus, cannot be planned in advance.

Included in the process are a great number of factors that will contribute to the project's success or failure. First of all, there is the need for taking the temperature of the project regularly and responding accordingly. If, for example, it turns out that there is resistance to some activities, this ought to be dealt with immediately rather than postponed. The obligation to deal with any resistance lies with both consultant and client.

The ability to listen is important, and it is a question of listening with all senses and to all sources. Consultants who are able to listen to a client's needs and priorities, and who can respond to these, will promote problem-solving.

The ability to handle criticism is also important. Regardless of the type of assignment, it is common to take a critical look at existing methods and procedures – the desire to do things better is indeed the classic reason for calling in a consultant. Therefore, criticisms and critical evaluations will often be a natural part of the process. This is predictable, expected, and often explicitly required. However, this does not mean that it will be pleasant, and the client organisation should be made aware of this. However, neither individuals nor groups enjoy having their shortcomings paraded in public, and as such, criticism is bound to trigger defensive mechanisms. The consultant should be prepared for this, as handling issues like these is an important part of the process.

Finally, the need to maintain focus on the process is not just related to the issue of creating reasonable working conditions for the consulting project, it also sets the scene for implementing the solutions that, hopefully, will be a result of the process. Therefore, focus on the process and focus on change will often be two aspects of the same issue.

Active involvement

There has been a myth that the use of external consultants will free up time in the client's organisation. This was laid to rest long ago. On the contrary, consulting projects usually require increased internal resources. The point is that added value is not a commodity that can be purchased, but something that must be created. Therefore, excellent consultants do not work for their clients but with their clients (Thommen & Richter, 2004).

As a consequence, clients must be active participants in consulting projects in order to ensure progress, that the identity of the organisation is maintained, and that the assignment has a foundation in the organisation. This has become common knowledge, and it is typical of assignments that lead to a satisfactory result. On the other hand, experience shows that less successful assignments are often characterised by lack of client involvement. Leadership obligations and responsibilities still lie with the client. This can not and must not be changed. If the consultant makes an effort to assist with leadership tasks, this does not mean that the consultant has taken over the responsibilities of management.

Active involvement usually includes – apart from the support and visibility of management – the involvement of required staff, relatively well-defined goals, and a clear distinction between the roles of the client and the consultant. If not, there is a strong possibility that the project will be hampered by uncertainty and obscurity. At the same time, this cooperation provides the company with an opportunity to develop intellectual capital, and what is learned will be integrated into the organisation during the course of the project.

Active involvement from the client is usually necessary to ensure a favourable recommendation. This is also a matter of common knowledge, though there may be situations in which the implementation suffers due to the fact that other areas demand attention during the process. If this occurs, it is clearly the consultant's responsibility to keep the project on track or terminate it.

A crucial factor is the development of a sense of ownership within the client organisation. Without this, the probability of continued progress, once the consultant leaves the organisation, will be reduced.

Finally, it should be mentioned that the role of the consultant during implementation, and its significance for the success, is often debated. However, there are no definite indications that suggest that the success of a project depends on the extent to which the consultant takes part in the implementation phase, provided the project is integrated in the organisation. Therefore, although consultants often claim that they have contributed to the implementation of a project, this may be wishful thinking more than a specific requirement from the client. However, there is an ongoing debate amongst clients about whether consultants should be involved in the implementation phase. It is self evident that a consultant could contribute if the task is well defined, e.g. the consultant act as a professional guarantor, participate in solving partial challenges, or act as project leader.

Stakeholders

One of the classic questions asked when involving a consultant is: "Who is the client?" No matter how often this question is asked, it does not get any easier to answer. On one hand, the answer is "the person(s) who hired the consultant" and, on the other hand, the answer can be as broad as "the company that hired the consultant" without taking the actual person who commissioned the assignment or the main sponsor (if these are different) into account.

In order to make the concept of the client workable, clients can be divided into four classes (Schein, 1997):

- The contacting client: who contacts the consultant?
- The intermediate client: who is involved in the planning of contacts and meetings?
- The primary client: who has the problem and wants help?
- The ultimate client: what group is affected by the solution, regardless of whether they are actively involved?

Even though the configuration of the client concept is not always obvious, the idea behind the above frame of reference is to encourage greater awareness of the groups involved, and their role in solving the assignment. Thus, a number of other questions can be raised in connection with the client concept: "Who knows, who cares, and who can?"

In addition to the fact that it is important to identify the various stakeholders and their positions, there is also a political element involved. On one hand, the consultant must be able to deal with the various political agendas that are always present within an organisational environment and, on the other hand, be able to use the political system (pro)actively to solve the assignment and integrate it in the organisation – without, however, breaking any ethical or professional rules. And it is no secret that this raises a number of crucial dilemmas for both the consultant and the client. This is illustrated by a number of cases in the public sector.

Therefore, the consultant's power base is of great significance. Ultimately, it is a question of holding on to credibility in relation to the client organisation. This does not mean that consultants should remain neutral towards the situation and the persons involved, but that their behaviour and role should allow them to maintain their loyalty towards the assignment, the different parties involved, and the company. However, this also requires that the clients do not politicise the situation unnecessarily. If they do, the basis for a constructive solution to the assignment will be undermined.

Therefore, the consultant must ensure that s/he has political backing for his or her work. However, at the same time, the client should not try to use the consultant one-sidedly as a pawn in an internal political struggle. It would be unethical of the client to do so.

At the same time, it is necessary to bear in mind that while the consultant – mainly for professional reasons (e.g. confidentiality towards the client) – is prevented from responding to (un)justified criticism, the same rules do not apply to the client. This can be seen clearly in practice from time to time and, as a consequence, the reputation of the consultancy industry suffers correspondingly (Poulfelt, 1997).

Competency

When a client describes a consultant as particularly competent, in reality this covers several factors. It is an indication that the professional element of the assignment's results was satisfactory and also an indication that the client was satisfied with the way in which the assignment was handled. Both are significant when evaluating the assignment as a whole, cf. the previous interpretation of the concept of quality in the field of consultancy.

One of the characteristics of constructive collaboration is that the consultant must be qualified to contribute to the assignment's unique challenges. This may seem self-evident, but it is important that consultants ask themselves whether they have the right qualifications before they sign the contract. If this is not the case, there is a risk that the psychological bond may suffer – in addition to the fact that the results may be poor. The contract is a set of informal rules for the collaboration between consultant and client and it constitutes the basis for trust and, thus, professional reputation. As such, it is an extremely sensitive contract.

The demands on the consultant's competency and flexibility are great. At the same time, it could be argued that the more organic the collaboration is in nature, the greater the demands on both parties. As a consequence, the client must also be aware of his or her role and the competences s/he will be required to have on hand.

One type of competence that, in recent years, has gained a greater foothold and greater significance for the consultant's role as communicator and creator of change is "emotional intelligence". This constitutes a more explicit involvement of the emotional dimension of the organisation and of the individual. From an organisational point of view, it is a question of laying the myth of rational behaviour to rest, as parties within organisations often react somewhat less than rationally due to influences from other and less explicit sources.

Therefore, it is important that the emotional make up of the organisation is dealt with explicitly and openly in a consulting project. This is linked to the fact that the aim of consulting projects usually is change. Thus, one of the major standpoints of the consultancy world is that "change is the raison d'être of management consulting".

The emotional side of many consulting projects presents itself as uncertainty and resistance to change. The consultant must be aware of this and must be able to handle the situation. However, this requires special competences. Emotional intelligence consists of five main emotional competencies. These can be learned and developed. They are:

1. Self-awareness
2. Emotions
3. Motivation
4. Empathy, and
5. Social skills.

The common trait for all five competences is that they are qualifications that will promote successful collaboration if both consultant and client possess them – or are at least aware of them.

The point is that there is a range of significant aspects of competency which must be considered in connection with the collaboration between consultant and client if the best possible foundation is to be laid.

Match between persons

One of the important factors for success is the chemistry between consultant and client. This is confirmed by many studies that indicate that good chemistry is a common feature of successful assignments, whereas a mismatch is just as common in the less successful assignments. Furthermore, it is worth noting that when a project runs aground, the personal element is usually a comforting factor. It is also clear that the consultant's personal behaviour and style – and thus the "match" – have a significant influence on the form of management and the content of the process, as a consultant is typically viewed as a professional and personal role model. Therefore, the view is that a match between persons will promote the potential for the project's success. Added to this is the ability to interact at a personal level. Therefore, chemistry is a significant factor in assignments which require close partnership.

On the other hand, a match can also carry a risk that there will be too much socialisation, and this may restrict the problem-solving process, e.g. the consultants might ask less challenging questions and not be sufficiently reflective.

In addition to the above – i.e. competency and chemistry – initiative, perseverance, and courage are also characteristics that are important if the project is to succeed. It would be a pity if this client's experiences were to be repeated: "When the project ran aground, the consultant disappeared".

Trust

Trust is a key issue in consulting. As a client expressed it: "We chose Global Consulting, because we had confidence in their work." Often, trust is described as an issue related to the consultant. However, in practice trust is a two way phenomenon as trust also relates to the behaviour of the client.

Several elements contribute to trust. Among these are:

a) the consultant,
b) the process and
c) the solution or outcome of the consulting assignment. If the client has trust in the consultant and the process, and the outcomes are satisfactory, the trusted advisor will probably sustain. If neither the process nor the outcome turn out successfully, this can result in less confidence in the consultant.

To illustrate this, Maister, Green & Galford (2000) have developed a trust equation:

$$T = \frac{C + R + I}{S}$$

Where: T is trustworthiness, C stands for credibility, R for reliability, I for intimacy, and S for self-orientation. Without going into details, the equation can be used for mapping purposes when discussing trust factors for new clients and existing clients and when considering how to ensure balanced factors.

Added value

The ultimate goal of every consulting assignment is to provide the client with added value. Consultants' advice is – as previously mentioned – based upon a broad spectrum of services. They supply specific advice and special analyses for a specific problem; they act as sparring partner for management, and are active partners in the development process.

Traditional consultancy work consists of a study of the current situation, an analysis of the results, a report and a presentation to the company. In consultancy with added value, a consultant provides inspiration, and puts the results into perspective for management and staff by means of an active dialogue in which the consultant shows an understanding of both management's and the organisation's terms and conditions.

The successful consultant understands the interaction between these mechanisms and processes and can adapt the problem-solving process in cooperation with the client. This will ensure a strong focus on the client and an efficient utilisation of both the consultant's and the client's competences.

Challenges ahead – A consultant and a client perspective

There is nothing to suggest that the need for good advice will diminish in the future, nor are there any clear indications that the role of the consultant will be any less significant in the future – perhaps quite the opposite, if the complex reality of an organisation and the desire for flexibility in the composition of its resources are taken into consideration.

However, the general view that, if the consultancy industry is to continue to grow, there will be certain demands from both parties to ensure that benefits are gained from the partnership. Some of these demands or challenges should be emphasised in relation to consultants, clients and their interaction:

The challenges for consultants:
 1. A renewed concept of consulting
 2. Development of competences
 3. Value-based consulting

The reason for stressing these three points is the following: The *concept of consulting*, today, appears to have acquired a diversity which has made it rather obscure. Therefore, it seems as though there is a need for renewing the consulting concept and, perhaps in particular, the role of management consultants, which has been the focus of this chapter. In any case, greater clarity will make it easier for the client to preview the market (Greiner & Poulfelt, 2004).

In the future, the demands on consultants to develop their own competences will continue. In an age where knowledge quickly becomes outdated and clients often possess the same competencies, consultants are expected to be at the cutting edge. Therefore, developing competencies – such as professionalism, methodologies, and process – should be a high priority and, presumably, a higher priority than it has been in consulting companies.

The concept that a consultant should add value is nothing new. However, the concept of *value-based consulting* ought to be extended to include more emphasis on measuring the values created by this type of consulting, for both client and consultant. The question is: What types of learning and integration of knowledge actually take place in the various systems? Furthermore, value-based consulting can be extended to encompass the way in which consultants can and should be compensated in the future. And it is important to experiment with new compensation schemes, e.g. based on the value of the assignment for the client organisation rather than purely on time used.

The challenges for clients:
1. The optimal use of consultants
2. Return on investment
3. The professional client

Today, when assignments go awry, this is not always due to consultants that are not sufficiently qualified. It could also be the case that clients have not expressed themselves clearly or have not been sufficiently involved in the formulation of the assignment. Therefore, the moral must be that consultants should only be called in if there is a sensible and convincing reason for this. Thus, the client is required to consider – even more closely – whether assistance is required to solve the problem at hand: Should a consultant be called in or not? The *use of a consultant* requires the "right" assignment and the "right" situation. Therefore, timing is an important issue.

Good advice is expensive. Therefore, there should be greater focus on the added value gained by an organisation from a consulting project rather than the actual hourly or daily rates. This means that the *return on investment* is the benchmark – of course, with a touch of the business acumen that is an integral part of every business transaction. In addition, clients should require consultancies to provide a more precise idea of the benefits to be gained by the client organisation. This provides more transparency for the client and also legitimises the use of external resources, but it also means that the consulting organisation must be "on its toes" when creating proposals.

It seems evident that clients have become more skilled at using consultants. However, there is still great potential for improvement. Therefore, one must constantly be aware of the ways in which an organisation can improve decision-making, as well as selection and use of consultants – in order to optimise the benefits. One way of strengthening an organisation's qualifications in this area is to formulate a policy for the use of external consultants. Another way is to carry out a broader investigation of the consultancy industry before making a selection. In any case, it is surprising how little many users of consultants know about the industry and its competitors.

The challenges for the cooperation between consultant and client
   1. Achieved value
   2. Reflective collaboration
   3. Dual ethics

The involvement of external consultants still results in myths within many organisations. In many cases, greater openness and visibility can remedy this and ensure conditions more favourable for creating added value. The aim is to gain *recognition of the achieved value,* as this will also improve the chances of a successful implementation. A project's success is measured by its success of implementation – and not just by the good advice.

Every consulting assignment ought to contain moments of reflection on the progress of the project, and also be concluded with a mutual evaluation and *reflection* that will reinforce the learning process. Too many consultancy projects are weak in this area. In other words, the accumulation of experiences from consulting assignments is poor, which can have a major impact on the potential for learning – for both client and consultant.

Ethics is an important part of a consultant's profession and most consultants are quite aware of this. However, the point is that ethics is a joint concern for both consultant and client, and the client's ethical behaviour is just as important. The concept of *dual ethics* is, therefore, a crucial element for a successful collaboration. This is another area worthy of focus for consultants and their clients.

So, the bottom line is that consultants are useful when they create benefits, but a constructive and wholehearted effort is required by both parties. And "Thought consultancy" provides guidelines for the creation of value.

References

Abrahamson, E. (1996). Management Fashions. *The Academy of Management Review, Vol. 21, no. 1.*

Argyris, C. (2000). *Flawed Advice and the Management Trap.* Oxford: Oxford University Press.

Bauman, R.P., Jackson, P. & Lawrence, Joanne T. (1997). *From Promise to Performance.* Boston, Mass.: Harvard Business School Press.

Clark, T. (1995). *Managing Consultants. Consultancy as the Management of Impressions.* Buckingham: Open University Press.

Clark, Timothy & Robin Fincham (2002). *Critical consulting – New perspectives on the management advice industry.* Oxford: Blackwell Publishers.

Czerniawska, Fiona (2002). *Management Consultancy – What next?* London/Basingstoke: Palgrave Macmillan Press.

Czerniawska, Fiona (2002). *Value-based Consulting.* London/Basingstoke: Palgrave Macmillan Press.

The Danish Agency for Trade and Industry (1999). *Managementkonsulenter – kortlægning af en branche i vækst.* EFS Notat. København.

The Economist (1997). Trimming the fat – a survey of management consultancy. 22 March.

The Economist (2002). Consultant, heal thyself. 2 November.

Festinger, L. (1957). *Theory of Cognitive Dissonance.* Stanford: Stanford University Press.

Gluckler, Johannes & Armbruster, Thomas (2003): Bridging Uncertainty in Management Consulting: The Mechanisms of Trust and Networked Reputation. Berlin: *Organization Studies, Vol. 24, Iss. 2*, 269–285.

Greiner, L. & Poulfelt, F. (Eds.). (2004). *Handbook of Management Consulting. The Contemporary Consultant – Insights from World Experts.* Ohio: Thomson-South Western.

Kipping, M. & Engwall, L.(Ed.). (2002). *Management Consulting. Emergence and Dynamics of a Knowledge Industry.* Oxford: Oxford University Press.

Maister, D., Green, C.H. & Galford, R.M (2000). *The Trusted Advisor.* New York: Free Press.

McKenna, Christopher D. (2001). The World's Newest Profession: Management Consulting. *Enterprise & Society; Vol. 2, Iss. 4*, 673–684.

Mickletwait, J. & Wooldridge, A. (1996). The Witch Doctors. *Economist.*

O'Shea, J. & Madigan, C. (1997). *Dangerous Company – The Consulting Powerhouses and the Business They Save and Ruin.* London: NB Publishing.

Poulfelt, F. (1997). Ethics for Management Consultants. *Business Ethics – A European Review, Vol. 6, No. 2, April.*

Poulfelt, Flemming (2000). Konsulentrollens Anatomi. *Nordiske OrganisasjonsStudier 1/2000*, 25–48.

Poulfelt, F. & Payne, A. (1994). Management Consultants: Client and Consultant Perspectives. *Scandinavian Journal of Management, Vol 10, No 4:*421–436.

Rasiel, Ethan M. & Paul N. Friga (2002). *The McKinsey mind – Understanding and implementing the problem-solving tools and management techniques of the world's top strategic consulting firm.* New York: McGraw-Hill Education.

Schaffer R.H. (1997). *High-Impact Consulting.* Prentice Hall.

Schein, E. (1997). *Process Consultation II.* Reading, Mass.: Addison-Wesley.

Sheth, J. & Sobel, A. (2000). *Clients for Life.* New York: Simon & Schuster.

Thommen; Jean-Paul & Richter, Ansgar (Eds.). (2004). *Management Consulting Today.* Gabler.

Chapter 3

Experience with Scandinavian consultants

GÖRAN ROOS

"I think the consulting industry could improve immensely if consultants made an effort to improve management within their own companies, and not just in other companies."

Senior executive in a Scandinavian retail company

Introduction

In the past few years management consultancy has become a rather common phenomenon in most organisations. Most managers at higher levels have extensive experience in both hiring, and working, with management consultants (Pemer & Werr, 2005). Along with the increased use of consultants, there has also been an increase in the amount of critique concerning the rather limited results that consulting activities often provide. Quite often the promised results never materialise (de Caluwé & Stoppelburg, 2003), and the consultant's activities may even have harmful effects on some organisations (O'Shea & Madigan, 1997).

Some critics argue that managers like consultants because they can prove useful in the political battles within an organisation — the outcome of which may or may not be beneficial for profits, but is always beneficial for the top executives that hire the adviser (Jackall, 1988). Some have argued that there is a strong link between management consultancies and management fads. Fashionable ideas often trigger quick and superficial change initiatives that cost money and create disruption. As they are seldom considered thoroughly, these initiatives are rarely implemented properly, and are forsaken when a new wave of "more interesting" ideas and concepts catch managers' attention (Jackall, 1988; Pinault, 2000; Ramsay, 1996).

The purpose of this chapter is to illustrate the experiences that some Scandinavian senior managers have had with consultants and describe how they perceive the consulting industry. Six senior executives in Sweden,

Norway, Denmark, and Finland were asked to describe what they would consider to be good versus bad consultancy[1]. The interviews were based on a value hierarchy model that describes the value provided by consultants. The value hierarchy model (Pike & Roos, 2004) is based on an extensive literature review, and is shown in Figure 1.

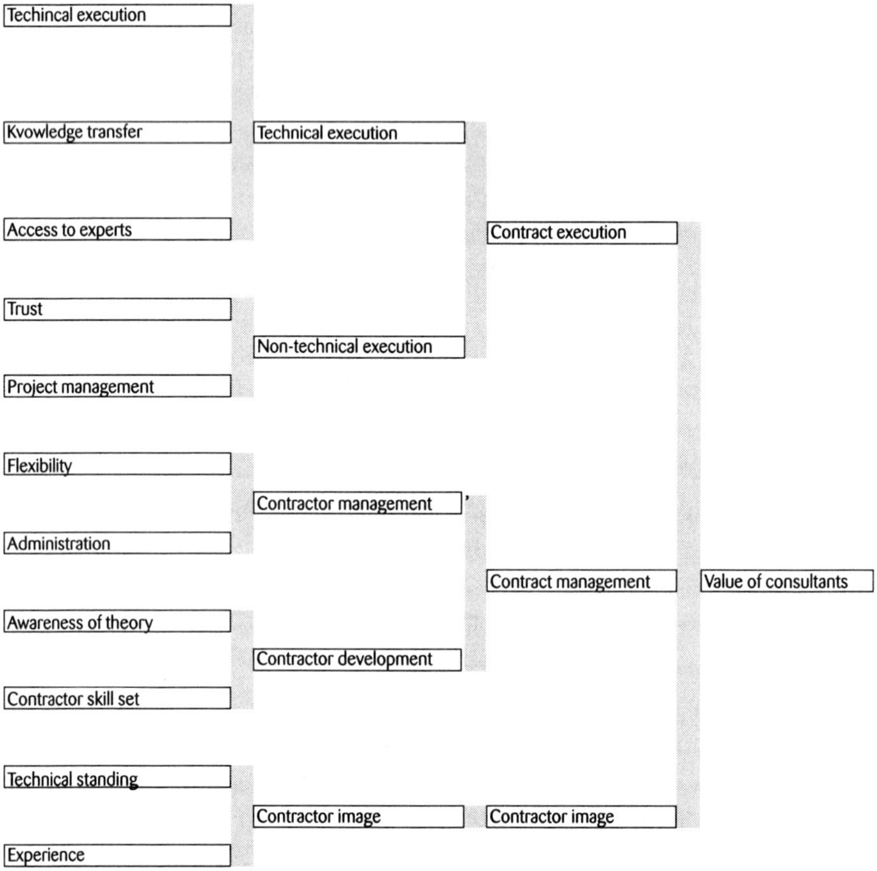

Figure 1 Value hierarchy structure (Pike & Roos, 2004)

Assuming that the convenience sample is representative, the interviews give us some insight into some key issues facing Scandinavian managers today: Why should you hire a consultant? How do you choose the right consultant? What consultancy firm is best suited?

---

[1] Due to confidentiality, please contact the author if further information about the interviewed executives is requested.

The main findings are summarised below, along with some relevant findings from the literature.

Flexible approach

"A good combination of theory, practice, and experience is the key to excellent consultancy."

Senior executive in a Scandinavian retail company

A good consultant understands the client's organisation, its industry, and the environment that the organisation operates within. Nevertheless, all this is not worth much unless it is combined with an innovative, creative, and flexible mindset.

According to some academics, consultants are limited by the models they use, and the concepts they push – that do not properly reflect reality or provide clients with valuable solutions (Alvesson & Svenningson, 2004). The larger companies are admired by many for their extensive knowledge base and structured methodology, but criticism reveals that their theoretical fundamentalism limits their creativity and even gets in the way of common sense. One of the interviewed executives expressed an example of this:

"Once we appointed a big international consulting company in order to develop a new concept for our department stores. The business model was upgraded and looked excellent but what they did not see was that this kind of model was not adaptable to our Nordic market."

Senior executive in a Scandinavian retail company

Consultants have to be able to see the big picture as well as the crucial details. They must have the ability to detect and take advantage of new and emerging trends, and adapt them effectively and structured to the right situations. A good consultant must have the capability to spot different opportunities, present different options, and be flexible in order to take opposition or ideas from management into account.

A recent survey by Metra Martech Ltd. (2001) shows that 38% of the companies they investigated, rated the size of the consultancy as an important factor in their selection process. Let us have a quick look at what the managers perceived to be the main differences between small and big consulting companies:

"Big firms have solid resources, extensive knowledge, and large networks. On the other hand they can be rigid, bureaucratic, and expensive. They also have a tendency to provide the same solution in every country without taking cultural differences into account. Small companies do not have the same resources and network but their advantage is that they are more personal and can focus more on narrow topics."
CEO of a Scandinavian retail company

"The small companies are a little more flexible and less costly, and they sometimes deliver more than they are expected to do. Conversely, flexibility could lead them to loose track of what we actually want to do. In addition, they may not have the necessary skills to run a project that goes beyond their, often quite narrow, area of expertise. The big companies will almost always be able to deal with complex and diverse matters."
Senior executive in a regional investment agency

It would seem quite evident that clients appreciate consultants that adopt a flexible approach. One of the main concerns voiced by the executives concerns the problem of consultants being too rigid and general in their approach. Could this problem possibly be solved by a closer cooperation with the management? In the following section we will take a closer look at the conditions under which the executives think it is appropriate to hire consultants, and how.

Providing partnership and guidance

"Sometimes you can't see the forest for the trees."

A company may have the best knowledge of their own organisation, but the consultants have broad experience with many different organisations, which provide them with a kind of benchmark and a wider spectrum of ideas for ways of doing things. Consulting companies are also usually focused on a specific area where they have a broad and thorough knowledge of the field.

"We usually take care of simple straightforward problems ourselves, nevertheless, in some cases where we feel we need more specific knowledge, we like to use consultants as discussion partners."
Former CEO of a Scandinavian research organisation

"We engage consultants when we want to have an external opinion on a project or when we feel the need for new ideas or honest critique of how things are being done."
Senior executive in a regional investment agency

Some authors stress that the "otherness" of consultants – the fact that consultants are outsiders to the client organisation and that therefore their knowledge, their methods, and their language differ from the client's – and this can be a considerable problem when interacting with the client – and may prevent consultants from being involved more immediately in the client's business. Nevertheless, their independent view is also considered one of their main strengths (Kubr, 1997).

It is therefore critical for client-consultant teams to overcome their interest differences in order to improve their communication, without the consultants loosing their "otherness" as external advisors and, consequently, their ability to foster change in practices, processes, and organisations (Nikolova & Devinney, 2004).

All managers interviewed emphasized the fact that they preferred the consultant to work more as a partner rather than being an external problem solver who is there just to get the job done and collect his invoice. As one executive stated:

"The consultant lost interest once the contract was settled. The company transferred responsibility to inexperienced colleagues within their organisation. We ended up solving the problems ourselves. The consultants were only a costly obstacle. The management of the company only contacted us to try to lock us into new commissions."
Former CEO of a Scandinavian research organisation

Clients prefer consultants to work as close partners, but there is always the risk that the consultant will gain access to important knowledge of the client organisation and its competitive advantage, and that this could be passed on to its competitors (Mastutik & Hill, 1998). Furthermore, the consultant-client relationship implied in the business partner situation increases the dependence of the client on the consultant, which, if left unbalanced, could have a negative effect on the client (Werr & Linnarsson, 2001).

"A bad consultant uses old frameworks and solutions to solve problems. A bad consultant thinks s/he has the best and single solution to a certain issue."
Senior executive in a Scandinavian retail company

"Bad consultancy is not being able keep within the set budget or time frame."
Senior executive in a regional investment agency

"A good consultant improves a company's ability to succeed on its own, that is, helping a company without making it dependent on future/continuous services."
Senior executive in the food supply industry

"Sometimes consultants do not reveal how they actually see the situation, they tend to adopt the clients' point of view in order to demonstrate unity. Although they must eventually adapt to the client's preferences in the end, this should not be done until the client has been given the whole picture and decided upon a preferred direction."
Former CEO of a Scandinavian research organisation

Milan Kubr (1997) identifies curiosity as a reason for hiring consultants. Managers may hire a consultant because s/he has the reputation of being someone who succeeds where others have failed. If you can afford the luxury of having a renowned expert give his or her view of your company's competitive situation – why not? According to the same author, insecurity is an even more common reason for hiring a consultant. Tough competition and growing criticism are just a couple of the situations where a confident and experienced consultant might provide relief to a stressed-out management. It can also be convenient to hire a consultant and thus be able to blame the consultant for any consequences that result from decisions taken, especially unpopular ones. Kubr also suggests learning as one of the most common reasons for employing a consultant. By solving a problem and transferring the skills for solving this type of problem to managers in the client company, the consultant's contribution is twofold (Kubr, 1997).

Trust and relationship building

There are no universal or standard criteria for choosing a consultant. However, the following eight criteria have helped many clients to select the right consultant according to Kubr (1997):

- Professional integrity
- Professional competence
- Relationship to the consultant
- Project design
- Ability to deliver
- Ability to mobilise additional resources
- Cost
- The reputation of the consultant

Nevertheless, living according to these criteria is easier said than done. Research suggests that having management consultants implies a great uncertainty for clients. This, i.e. legislation, professional standards, certification, and sanctions, is due to the fact that each of the formal standards, such as institutional barriers to entry, are minimal. The lack of quality control and formalized standards allows opportunistic behaviour and increases the likelihood that clients will run into suppliers that provide inferior service and, as such, represents a risk for the client. Furthermore, management consulting, like most other knowledge intensive business services, is performed after the contract has been signed, which transfers the risk of inferior quality or performance onto the client (Gluckler, 2003).

As a consequence of the above mentioned factors, clients appear to select consultants based on experienced-based trust and on network reputation. Research indicates that the network reputation is the key selection criteria when assignments are not awarded through direct trust relations (Gluckler, 2003).

As one of the Scandinavian executives stated:

"We use our network to ask about experiences people may have had with different consultants. After doing some own research we then end up with a short list consisting of three or four companies that we contact for discussion and presentation."
Senior executive in a regional investment agency

This finding is widely supported both historically and internationally. Dawns et al. (1992) and Page (1998) (in Gluckler, 2003) asked senior managers of client companies in Australia and New Zeeland to rate the most important criteria for selection of consultants, and the results are consistent with the answers suggested here. Furthermore, Clarke (1995) (in Gluckler, 2003) reviewed a number of empirical studies from the Anglo-American context and found that personal experience and recommendations within client networks were important.

The managers we talked to also emphasised the importance of the consultant's network:

"Some consulting companies are very open minded and willing to give access to their networks. Others will only provide access for an additional fee, which I find inappropriate as the consultant's network is a crucial part of what the consultant can deliver and should therefore be included in the package."
CEO of a technical research centre

Chemistry also seems to be an important factor when it comes to choosing a consultant, as one executive says:

"If I do not like the consultant that is presenting the idea to me, it will require a bit more effort to convince me to sign the firm on a project. We know we are going to work together for a long time so we need someone with whom we feel we can connect to on a personal level and trust."
Senior executive in a regional investment agency

The majority of the managers we have talked to prefer to use the same consultant over and over. You know how they perform and you know you work well together as a team – both crucial factors for a successful outcome. In addition, if you find a consultant you like, you save yourself the hassle of having to evaluate new candidates.

The consultant's initial presentation is obviously a crucial selling point for many consultancies. One of the interviewed executives praised the professional presentations but at the same time he expressed concern that a polished appearance may often conceal a lack of substance: "It makes the assessment even harder."

Recent research indicates that 88% of interviewed companies would use the same consultant again if they were to undertake a similar job. This also demonstrates that the companies using recommendations from external contacts are much more likely to be satisfied than those who do not (Metra Martech Ltd, 2001).

Inexperienced graduates showed to be an issue that concerned many of the managers, as another of the interviewed expressed it:

"Large consultancies will often parade their finest during the sell, but once the contract is signed, clients will often find themselves with inexperienced business school graduates working under little or no surveillance."
Senior executive in the food supply industry

Pemer and Werr (2005) divide buyers of consulting services into four different categories – the disappointed buyer, the trustful buyer, the strong buyer, and the instrumental buyer. This suggests that managers may have somewhat varying expectations of consultants and, as a result of this, approach them in different ways. Initially, the disappointed buyer has high hopes concerning performance and often ends up abandoning management consultants all together after repeated disappointment. The trustful buyer is more positive and often employs consultants to get a "second opinion" where the consultants contribute with ideas in an open and trustful relationship. The strong buyers tend to believe they possess at least as much knowledge and expertise as the consultants, and see them more as an "extra pair of hands". In order to ensure positive results, the strong buyer focuses on control when using consultants. The instrumental buyer is a combination of the trustful and the strong buyer, they expect consultants to deliver according to expectations. The authors also indicate that managers' views on consultants are not entirely personal, but emerge from experiences in an organisational context (Pemer & Werr, 2005). One manager, who probably falls into the category of disappointed buyer, declares:

"A negative result cannot only be blamed entirely on the consultant.
A disappointing outcome is often the result of poor communication prior to project commencement and, as such, initial meetings need to clarify issues like delivery goals and accessible resources."

The following example was partly due to poor communication which had lead to disappointing results:

"A couple of years ago a large consulting company was going to help us improve our project management. It was a long-term assignment, over a year or so, where they made a lot of interviews with people within the company and charged us a vast amount of money just to come up with a report that told us what we already knew."

Senior executive in the food supply industry

Another manager described an even worse experience:

"In some cases I haven't received any new ideas. Nothing great, nothing useless, no input at all, only invoices – of course! Some have even caused problems. We had one assignment where the hired consultant stirred up negative sentiments among employees. There was no understanding of business logics and no understanding of the current thinking within the company, or of humans in general! In the end I had to take responsibility for maintaining commitment and guiding the process in the right direction."

CEO of a technical research centre

Clients appreciate consultants that can be both objective and impartial. As a client you do not want to face someone that always agrees with you, but all the same, a professional that always gives his honest opinion, even if it differs from what you would like to hear, may be irritating. The challenge is to find a balance. Being impartial means not getting involved in the client organisation's internal politics. It also requires considerable self control so that the technical services are not tainted by emotions and prejudices (Kubr, 1997).

Conclusion

The consulting industry faces heavy critique from several directions, and this is reflected in the answers we got from the executives we interviewed.

There seems to be a structural mismatch between the way consultancies pitch and execute their services, and the expectations that customers have of consultancies in terms of service providing, as expressed in the interviews. There also seems to be a mismatch between the expectations of scientific rigour that clients have of consultants and the methodologies that consultancies actually employ.

A somewhat simplistic way of explaining this problem might be to suggest that the fact that, today, most managers have gone to the same business schools as the consultants, and this has removed the knowledge asymmetry that historically has given the consultant an advantage in terms of expertise when talking to the client. If you add this to an increased emphasis among many senior managers on keeping up to date with modern research-based findings, it quickly becomes clear that the consultant needs to work hard in order to maintain his or her information asymmetry through at least three routes:

- Keeping abreast of the academic research within his or her own area of expertise.
- Try to glean knowledge of business practices in the client firm on each assignment that might be generalised and subsequently transferred to new clients.
- Add to the existing body of research through empirical research.

We can safely say that not all consultants do this.

The implicit assumption of most assignments in consulting is that the client is buying a solution to a problem. It is thus quite obvious that the client expects to have access to the most knowledgeable consultants that the consultancy can provide, for the duration of the assignment, and not just during the sales pitch and final presentation phases of the assignment. This assumption runs contrary to the way most large firms are organised, especially in terms of reward systems. This is a constant source of friction between the consulting industry and its clients.

On top of this, each assignment will have some unique aspects that require customisation, and not standardisation. This in turn raises two issues. The first is, as mentioned above, that you require access to the experts who possess the ability to devise a customised solution. The second concerns the knowledge and expertise necessary to develop a methodologically sound and customised solution. It is safe to say that many solutions are not grounded in methodologically sound approaches. This can be illustrated with a simple question: How many of the solutions proposed to clients that involve measurement are developed in accordance with the axioms of measurement theory [a branch of applied mathematics], a requirement they must meet if they are to have any predictive validity whatsoever.

If we add to all this the paradox that there are currently no requirements needed in order to adorn the title "consultant", it is quite evident that the consulting industry is facing a few major challenges.

We believe that the consultant has many important roles to play in today's business world, but unless the consultant industry itself starts facing up to a number of its structural, organisational, process, knowledge, and attitude challenges, it risks becoming a bête noir in the board rooms of many organisations.

References

Aschford, M. (1998). *Con tricks. The shadowy world of management consultancy and how to make it work for you.* London: Simon & Schuster.

De Caluwé, L. & Stoppelenburg, A. (2003). The Quality of Management Consultancy at Central Government in the Netherlands. Paper presented at the Academy of Management Meeting 2003, Seattle.

Gluckler, J. (2003). Bridging uncertainty in management consulting: The mechanism of trust and networked reputation. University of Frankfurt, Department of Economic and Social Geography.

Jackall, R. (1988). *Moral Mazes.* Oxford: Oxford University Press.

Kubr, M. (1997). *How to select and use consultants: a clients guide (Management Development Series No 31).* Geneva: International Labour Office.

Lapsley I. & Oldfield, R. (2001). Transforming the public sector; management consultants as agents of change. *The European Accounting Review* 10:3, 523–543.

Metra Martech Ltd. 2001.

Nikolova, N. & Devinney, T. (2004). On Experts, Reflective Practitioners and Impression Managers: The Nature of Client-Consultant Interaction. *Australian Graduate School of Mangement.*

O'Shea, J. & Madigan, C. (1997). *Dangerous Company.* London: Nicholas Brealey Publishing.

Pemer, F. & Werr, A. (2005). Between exploitation and control – Client's conceptions of the consultant–client relationship. *SSE/EFI Working Paper Series in Business Administration No. 2005*: 4, Stockholm school of economics.

Pike, S. & Roos, G. (2004). Mathematics and Modern Business Measurement. *Journal of Intellectual Capital, Vol 5, No 2,* pp. 243–256.

Pinault, L. (2000). *Consulting Demons: Inside the Unscrupulous World of Global Corporate Consulting.* New York: Harper.

Ramsay, H. (1996). Managing sceptically: A critique of organizational fashion. In S. Clegg and F. Palmer (Eds.), *The Politics of Management Knowledge.* Sage: London.

Werr, A. & Linnarsson, H. (2001). Management Consulting for Client Learning? Clients' Perception on Learning in Management Consulting. *Fenix WP, 12, Version 2.*

INTRODUCTION TO PART II

Methodology as a source of competitiveness

STEINAR BJARTVEIT

Charlatans! Gurus! Autodidacts! God is known by many different names – and consultants by even more. But there are not many of the terms commonly used to describe consultants that are complimentary – or even friendly. The names given to consultants often question our professional and moral integrity. At the professional level this may concern the soundness of our knowledge base – or the manner in which we have acquired this knowledge. Questions on moral issues usually concern whether we are in fact providing what we claim to be providing. There has been some harsh criticism of the consultancy industry in recent years (Clark, 1995; Micklethwait & Wooldridge, 1996; O'Shea & Madigan, 1997; Toffler, 2003). At its worst, consulting resembles a charade, a modern version of *The Emperor's New Clothes*, where appearances matter more than substance or results. The buyers can't really make out the golden embroidery that is supposed to highlight the luscious silk, and they certainly don't understand how all this ingenuity could be stitched together using a tacking stitch, but all the other buyers seem ecstatic over the Imbalanced Scorecard and Business Crossover Revealing – so there must be something in it. There is a very real danger that we could be labeled the witch doctors of our time. If worse comes to worse, we can always admit the extent of our deception, and go on selling it to whomever is willing to pay the most … and at that price, it must be worth it.

Management consulting is a knowledge industry. What forms the basis for this knowledge? Modernism celebrated the triumph of empirical models over witchcraft, and the Enlightment taught us to appreciate verifiable facts over superstition. Science has become one of the cornerstones of modern civilization. We have got where we are today thanks to giants like Keppler, Bacon, and Galileo. Eppur si muove! The earth revolves around the sun – no matter how many papal bulls that claim the opposite or how many lay observations contradict this. We have actually come a long way from the days when man used to live in caves and whack animals with clubs, and each other, over the head. Scientific methodology is used to assess any claim of progress. It is no longer acceptable to suggest that evil demons have taken possession of the souls of those who are having an epileptic seizure. Nor can you brush off commentary that is critical of the existing order. And if you want to suggest that aura-massage is beneficial to leaders of state and improves their ability to make critical decisions – you'd better have the research to back this up. But do these scientific criteria apply to management consulting?

It is far too easy to brush off criticism and retort that consulting is not a scientific enterprise and that the client has neither the interest nor the funds to pay for such enterprise. But if the consulting industry is not scientific, what is it? Critics of consulting question the basis for our knowledge and the reliability of our methods. In the face of such criticism, extending the divide between science and practice is not the way to go. Rather than widen the gap, we should seek to close it and integrate science with practice. Proven knowledge will always form the basis for the consultant's practice. Theoretical models and empirical research are the source of our livelihood. Professional training and fresh insights provide us with a competitive edge. What else could the client possibly be interested in paying for? Unqualified guesswork and singular idiosyncrasies?

There are two areas of contention. The first concerns consultants' penchant for "pet" models. Large consultancies have recognized the benefits to standardizing their approaches and use a lot of resources teaching their consultants how to master these specific models. Some consultants may develop extensive knowledge of, and a fondness for, certain (more or less scientific) models. These models can easily become an element of the consultancy's brand image. And the consultant will invariably use these favorite models to approach every customer's problems. So how are these models developed? It is obvious that some of these models are firmly rooted in extensive and well-founded research. But it is equally obvious that some of these models do not have any scientific basis and that the lifecycle of these less than scientific models bears a striking resemblance to that of fashions: creation, climax, and fall (Abrahamson & Fairchild, 1999; Micklethwait & Wooldridge, 1996). The term *management fad* has emerged to describe all the different methodologies (preferably with three-letter acronyms) that have popped up: TQM, BPR, BSC, KPI … The turnaround time for some of these fads compares to that of the catwalk – and they last about as long as Pokemon or Digimon. Why do fashions fade from glory? In a rational world, we might assume that they were perhaps based on questionable assumptions – or that the fad became such an integrated part of your daily activities that it no longer required a special label or justification. Whatever the cause, it is dead to the world of fashion. Because the model's revenue potential will always be of greater concern than its empirical foundation or explanatory power. The market decides what is true. This would not create any problems if we were selling clothes, but when the product is knowledge …

Francis Bacon claimed that: "To understand nature we must consult nature and not the writings of Aristotle." It is bad news for the consulting industry when the validity of a model rests on its packaging or market value. Reality does not suddenly become self evident just because someone forces it into a two-by-two matrix and appeals to common sense. And the mere fact that the model is promoted by a renowned consultancy does not make it more reasonable. Man was once convinced that the earth stood still at the centre of the universe. The theory was simple, and backed by great authorities like Aristotle and Ptolemy. And everybody could see this for themselves: every day the sun moved across the sky and nobody got dizzy – which ruled out alternative explanations. There were some odd and inexplicable aberrations in the movements of the celestial bodies, but these were accounted for by a succession of ad hoc theories and a good deal of generosity. The earth stood still. And it did so while the believers fended off a growing number of counter arguments and empirical observations. For some people, the earth stood still right to the end of the 20th century – when the Vatican reopened the case against Galileo and exonerated him. The models that consultants use can not be granted immunity from scientific scrutiny. They cannot exist in a vacuum – completely detached from the reality they are supposed to explicate. A model can never be true in and of itself – it must be supported by substantive experience.

And this takes us to the second area of contention – because not everyone understands what it means for a model to be based on experience. There are those consultants that will unashamedly boast that the models they use are based on their own extensive experience – and not on the untested theories of some desk-jockey. They would have you believe that it is precisely this real-life experience that sets them apart from all those wide-eyed youngsters fresh out of business school, who, with their flashy suits and even flashier report cards, have never had first-hand experience of a customer. The consultant's claims are usually backed up by excellent references from isolated cases – that "prove" the efficacy of the consultant's analyses and interventions. At first glance, this evidence might seem convincing – past success should indicate future success. However, in reality, this evidence is anything but scientific. Despite the fact that this type of evidence rarely stands up to scrutiny, we often find ourselves being seduced by the consultant's eloquence. The reasoning behind this evidence is inherently flawed and rests on the same logical error that gives license to superstition and witchcraft. When we listen to these silver-haired orators claim with absolute certainty that based on their experience …, we would do well to remember that age alone does not assure wisdom, and that more often than not these claims are instances of inductive naivety (Chalmers, 1982). The process of inductive reasoning involves making inferences from isolated observations. It may sound simple, but inductive reasoning has one serious pitfall: even though all the arguments may be true – it does not necessarily follow that the conclusion will be! This is aptly illustrated by one of the prototypical examples from science philosophy: even though you may observe an endless procession of white swans following one after the other, it does not necessarily follow that the next swan will be white (there are in fact white swans). This demonstrates the problem with inductive reasoning – universal laws cannot be built upon isolated observations. Even though the evidence supports the conclusion, the conclusion does not follow logically from the evidence. If you live on the Riviera, you will expect to see the sun set every evening because that is what it always does. But if you live up north, close to the artic circle, you can witness the theory of the sun setting in the evening being disproved every year – it doesn't set during the summer, and even worse, it doesn't even rise during winter. Or, as Bertrand Russell pointed out: the inductivist turkey was blissfully convinced that the natural order of things was that he would be fed every morning at 9 a.m. – until Christmas Eve came along and his theory was voided.

The evidence of success provided by consultants is often disproved in much the same way. How could the efficacy of a particular approach or methodology possibly be verified from one isolated case – or even a number of cases? It could just as easily be a case of confirmation bias. How is it possible to transfer a recipe for success from one organization to another? There are also numerous examples of winning formulas being commandeered from one domain and dumped into another – as is the case when successful sports coaches try to pass on their secrets to business executives. Unless we adopt a methodological approach when acquiring knowledge and carrying out interventions, we will never know if it is the consultant's action that have led to success, or whether success is merely the result of a placebo effect – in which case it is not the intervention itself, but some other unidentified factor, such as expectations or focus of attention, that provides results. We have to be sure about these things.

Karl Popper (1959, 1963) is one of the most influential philosophers of science in our time. Popper suggests that all science starts with myths and the critique of myths, and that it is hypothetic-deductive reasoning that leads to progress in science. Our theories must either gain support or be rejected. There are too many theories that are allowed to exist in a protective vacuum – shielded from scientific scrutiny by circular reasoning and assumptions that cannot be verified. What does it take to reject a theoretical model? Any model must clearly state the conditions under which it can be falsified (which, paradoxically leads to the conclusion that you may not necessarily learn a lot from best practices, but you can learn a lot from worst practices!). Falsification is the hallmark of scientific progress – without falsification we cannot discern science from myth. Scientific method should not be the consultant's foe. Quite the contrary. A scientific approach ensures the quality of the knowledge that is in fact what consultants have to offer. This is what separates the best from the rest. Scientific method is a source of competitive advantage.

The following articles discuss different perspectives on this view. Carl Erik Grenness discusses the many allegations that management consulting is a form of pseudo-science. Andreas Werr explores the use of different management concepts in management consulting and discusses the different functions they perform. Finally, Mats Alvesson and Hugh Willmott adopt a more critical perspective, arguing that knowledge is not objective and neutral, and that knowledge creates truths that often form the basis for power.

What consultants should look for in this section:
- The consultant must be familiar with the limitations of the models s/he uses.
- The consultant should be careful about how s/he acquires knowledge, and wary of the difference between superstition and validated science.
- The consultant should be aware of the fact that extensive knowledge and detailed models may give the consultant the upper hand in discussion with the client – and this requires a degree of responsibility and conscientiousness.

What clients should look for in this section:
- The field of organizational theory is rife with different models based on current fads – one should be wary of conjecture, bullet-point epistemology, and "doing-what-everyone-else-is-doing".
- The consultant's model should have a firm base in theory and empirical research.
- The consultant should have extensive knowledge of and be well-versed in the models s/he uses, but at the same time s/he should maintain a critical eye to the methods s/he uses.

References

Abrahamson, E. & Fairchild, G. (1999). Management fashion: Lifecycles, triggers and collective learning processes. *Academy of Management Review, Vol.* 44:708–740.

Chalmers, A.F. (1982). *What is this thing called science?* 2nd ed. Milton Keynes: Open University Press.

Clark, T. (1995). *Managing consultants. Consultancy as the management of impressions.* Buckingham, Philadelphia: Open University Press.

Micklethwait, J. and Wooldridge, A. (1996). *The witch doctors. What the management gurus are saying, why it matters and how to make sense of it.* London: Heinemann.

O'Shea, J. and Madigan, C. (1997). *Dangerous company. The consulting powerhouses and the businesses they save and ruin.* London: Nicholas Brealey Publishing.

Popper, K.R. (1959). *The logic of scientific discovery.* London: Routledge Classics.

Popper, K.R. (1963). *Conjectures and refutations: The growth of scientific knowledge.* London: Routledge Classics.

Toffler, B. L. (2003). *Final accounting. Ambition, greed, and the fall of Arthur Andersen.* New York: Broadway Books.

Chapter 4

Consultants: A critical perspective

CARL ERIK GRENNESS

What are consultants?

Historical background and typology of consultants

The term "consultant" is derived from "consul" – the leader of a "consilium", and translates roughly into "council leader". However, in the context of dealing with specific problems that the organization faces, the consultant is commonly assigned a role that is perceived as being "above" the organization's leader, not literally – but in the sense of "meta" or "para". The consultant becomes an external qualification for what lies inside the organization and is the responsibility of the leader. As such, although the consultant is an outsider in terms of responsibility, s/he exerts a direct influence on affairs that lie within the organization.

Historically there have been many different models seeking to describe the function (in terms of profession or role in society) of the consultant in the *client – consultant* relationship. There is some overlap between these definitions, but many of them are relevant to the current role of the consultant:

1. The Guru – the religious and politically visionary leader. Much has been written about how consultants are ascribed guru status, and worshiped by their "believers".
2. The Priest – the religious communicator and interpreter. It is not uncommon for consultants to have a theological background. However, there are other sciences, such as psychology, that can also be conveyed as religious truths. The content is believed without being subjected to scientific scrutiny.
3. The Shaman – the healer. Consultants offer a variety of different services, from increasing employee motivation to resolving inter-office conflict, helping to reduce or overcome stress, and even facilitating per-

sonal growth (especially for leaders). An increasing number of consultants come from a background in psychology or psychiatry.
4 The Scribe – the wordsmith among illiterates. This description is particularly appropriate in fields that require specific knowledge or skills, such as law, accounting, and auditing. The scribe is an expert in bureaucratic lingo (and other obscure technical jargon).
5 The Oracle – the one that speaks the magic words that solve complex and difficult situations. The consultant might help to clarify issues pertaining to complicated decisions. It is always the responsibility of the decision-maker to interpret and act on the advice, just like it was for those who listened to the Oracle at Delphi. Philosophers (those familiar with Socrates "know thy self"-thinking) are gaining popularity as consultants.
6 The Wise Man – the narrator and the cultural steward. This is a new profession among consultants that may be drawn from the humanities.
7 The Master – the most competent one. It is more common for the master to serve as mentor – or coach, rather than play an active role. The increased use of the term coach – drawn form the world of sports, has led to an increase in the recruitment of former athletes and team coaches to positions as consultants.
8 The Researcher – the one that stimulates innovation and creates ingenious solutions. Even though this type of consultant is commonly portrayed in the management literature, the researcher has had some difficulties being accepted as a consultant, as research is often linked with having a long-term perspective and being full of complexity and uncertainty. All the same, the phrase: "research shows us that …" serves as a mantra in many organizations.
9 The Technician – the engineer or bricoleur, who masters the cutting edge of technology and can repair or assist should the need arise. This type of consultant is common in the IT sector.

Although consultants prefer to describe these functions using more businesslike terms, these historical definitions remain appropriate and they aptly describe clients' needs in terms of different kinds of expertise, and the increasing degree of specialization among consultants.

The nature and causes of growth in the consulting sector

During the period from 1985–1992 growth in the consulting sector was 200%. At the same time, growth in the industrial sector was a mere 6% (Clark, 1995). Even though this growth rate may have plateaued, there is no reason to assume that the difference between growth rates for consultancies and growth rates in the industrial sector has diminished. The basis for the tremendous growth in consulting lies with business leaders and their lack of confidence in their own leadership skills, which as been exacerbated by the pace of radical change in the last few decades. This insecurity has been kindled by the many articles and books written by consultants, with academic backgrounds, and read by leaders – who share the same academic background as many of the consultants.

Consultants are hired by leaders that cannot cope with the challenges of radical change that their companies face. Some of the issues that leaders must deal with are:

1. Knowledge, business models, and procedures based on past experience no longer fit the bill and seem inadequate to meet new requirements and challenges. This is indeed the central theme for most of the management literature.
2. There is increasing pressure for organizations to learn – and to abandon procedures that are taken for granted. In general terms, companies are encouraged to get rid of their existing culture, which is often described as lacking in customer- and/or market orientation.
3. Leaders find themselves confronted with staggering, and often contradictory, demands, as evident from job descriptions, in the expectations of stakeholders, in the media, and in management literature.
4. Leadership is becoming more and more of a personal burden to leaders.

In addition, consultants are hired because many of the issues that organizations must deal with, are seen as being "prototypical" for situations in which consultants are required. Such as:

1. Implementing new organizational structures, especially network organizations and flat organizations.
2. Implementing new concepts that provide legitimacy and bravado in the market (JIT, TQM).
3. New demands on leadership (from the traditional businesslike manage-

ment style to more people-oriented leadership, and especially transformational leadership).
4. Demand for more variation in job tasks and increased work sharing, while the information needed for integration across organizational boundaries is scarce.
5. Specialization within market segments and the need to retain core competencies – which in turn leads to outsourcing of peripheral tasks.
6. The need for training in new areas of technology where the company does not have the relevant knowledge.
7. Inbred helplessness due to insufficient development of new skills.
8. Large personnel reductions.
9. When the use of external expertise may validate processes or provide legitimacy for leadership in such a way that employees experience difficult processes as being fair and just.
10. To avoid costly and unnecessary confrontations in situations where this might occur.

One of the main concerns related to these issues is that consultants, and their academic corps, are the driving force in a never-ending cycle, where all these demands are presented as being essential, and of course require the expertise of consultants. Even for the key figures within a company it can at times be difficult to distinguish between cause and effect when it comes to change processes that prototypically require the assistance of consultants. The consultancy sector would seem to generate the problems – for which they then offer their expertise to resolve.

Do we need consultants?
Even though many companies routinely hire consultants to assist in matters of strategic importance, there is a discernible scepticism regarding the wisdom of this expenditure. Headlines like this one are not uncommon: "Successful change process conducted without consultants". There is a consensus that the best thing for the organization is to sort out its problems using its own competencies. Consultants may be unnecessary and costly, and may even contribute to the breakdown of change processes, if key responsibilities and competency is taken away from leaders and awarded to external consultants.

In his book, Jacques (1996), takes a close look at the knowledge base that consultants base their profession on and suggests that the MBA education, business schools in general, management literature, and the consultancy sector are all products of American enterprise, that are being exported around the world with no thought to their suitability. What is happening is that an ideologically repressive understanding of what organizations are, what they strive for, who their employees are and what values they hold, is being forced upon the rest of the world as common sense, and this is actually thwarting radical change within many organizations. At the same time some of the consultancy sector's most prominent figures (Peters, Kanter, and Drucker) are writing "manifests for revolution" within organizations – with much the same content. Argyris, who has himself developed a school of thought in consulting, claims that this form of "double talk" is quite common in organizations, that it is fashioned by management, and that it prevents insight into the need for, as well as the ability to, implement radical change. Argyris has not directed this criticism towards the consultancy sector – despite the fact that a large number of consultants have been recruited from leadership positions.

Double talk and *decoupling* pervade organizations. This is due to the fact that organizations carry out a multitude of tasks in society, and there is a need to distinguish between instrumental tasks (providing goods and/or services) and symbolic tasks (legitimize the organization's role and value to society). Sometimes there can be a huge discrepancy between what is said, and what is actually done – for example during a crisis when the environment surrounding the organization (especially the media) focuses heavily on how the crisis is handled. Leadership's ability to decouple (what is said from what is actually being done) can determine the future of the organization as well as the future career of its leaders. Consultants seem to thrive in this duplicity, and this phenomenon can sometimes make it difficult to see what function consultants provide to the company.

Selection criteria for choosing among consultants

The services of consultants are on offer in a market, and, as is the case with many other markets, it is hard to select the best product on offer. The abundance and variety of competency and the plethora of services on offer make it difficult to fathom. There are also a few principle issues involved when selecting a consultancy.

First, the investment, in time and money, when using consultants is high and almost always irreversible. Research in decision theory shows that these conditions can easily lead to self-fulfilling prophecies and post-rationalization, which makes it hard for people to admit that an investment decision was erroneous. There is a confirmation bias in effect, as no one (especially not leaders) likes to admit fault.

Second, there is no such thing as quality assurance when hiring consultants – there are no standards requirements that need to be met (e.g. academic degrees) when starting a consultancy. There are standards for many professions – engineers, economists, lawyers, psychologists, that are often linked to their academic background, but there are no such requirements for consultants, which makes the title consultant rather unclear. It is still a free market with no form of certification required, although some parties are trying to rectify this. It is somewhat of a paradox that even as international requirements for certification of quality control in production and services are being implemented, there exists no such requirement for those that provide the competency to implement quality control.

Third, consultants provide a form of service – and as is the case for most services, they are difficult, if not impossible to evaluate. In general, services are characterized by:

a) intangibility – consultants cannot provide evidence of quality of the services in advance – making it very difficult for the customer to evaluate quality up front.
b) the end result depends on the interaction between buyer and seller, and thus the responsibility for a poor result may well rest with the client, and not the consultant.
c) there is a large degree of heterogeneity and discretion in the service sector
d) it is often difficult to replicate or adhere to a piece of advice once it has been given.

The upshot of all this is that evaluation and selection of consultants is often determined by the relationship, or chemistry, that forms between the buyer and the seller. If the consultant uses tried and tested "scripts" for making a sale, the customer will usually respond enthusiastically.

The consultant's reputation will often have a strong influence on the customers perception of competence and on their faith in the consultant. Clark (1995) has empirical data that support this finding. Previous experience with a consultant and the consultant's reputation are the key determinants for choosing among consultants. You will often find that a new leader has a favourite consultant in tow when s/he takes over responsibility for a new organization.

That fact that it is difficult to judge the efficacy of the services provided by consultants leads to reduced learning. The model that would seem to most accurately describe this type of process is Argyris' model of first and second order correction or learning. Whereas the leader's strategic decisions are continuously measured against substantive feedback and thus subject to rational control, the consultant operates at the level of what Argyris has termed "guiding values", in effect parameters that cannot be measured and will not be evident until much later. Under these conditions, learning and correction becomes difficult.

Since it is difficult to make an accurate estimate of the value of knowledge as a product (you can never really be sure you have all the pertinent information), the value of this knowledge is often tied to its price in the market. In this kind of system, the seller who sets a steep price on his product is perceived as providing a product that is a cut above those who set a lower price on their wares. Quality is thus determined by price, not the other way round; because it is difficult to assess the quality of a consultant's expertise. As a result of this, organizations are prone to buy expensive and often over-simplified reports form consultants, rather than study easily obtainable academic articles that deal with the same topic. When evaluating consultants' performance (leadership development and training is a good example of this) these evaluations are often based on the subjective opinions of the participants, and not on any tangible results.

Consulting and science
Consulting as pseudoscience
Consultants are often regarded as professionals because so many of them hail from an academic background. While professions often base their legitimacy on scientific research within their field, there are huge differences between the way scientists create and manage knowledge – and the way practitioners use this knowledge. Surprisingly, studies have shown that in reality there are many professions where practitioners have little or no knowledge of the research-based knowledge within their field. Even in the medical profession it is common to find that a specific treatment has a

weak link to "evidence-based treatment". The main reason for this is that academic institutions provide what is primarily seen as knowledge without context – whereas application of this knowledge usually requires contextual and process-based know-how. Professions base their skills on 1) practical experience, 2) rules and regulations that are passed down, and 3) a professional code of ethics – and not on scientific research.

The difference between academic knowledge and practical know-how raises the question of which of these two, consultants base their profession on. There is a very real danger that they will disseminate what is called "pseudo-science" (from the Greek word for "false"). We should take a closer look at what separates science from pseudo-science.

Radner & Radner (1982) have examined some well-known forms of pseudo-science (e.g. astrology), and have arrived at the following description:

1. Pseudo-sciences are anachronistic – that is, they use dated knowledge as a basis for their science, and deliberately disregard the fact that scientific progress requires that existing knowledge must be updated – and even sometimes discarded.
2. Those who believe in pseudo-sciences are often preoccupied with what remains mystical and are less interested in solutions that solve known problems, but more open to hearing about new ones.
3. Knowledge is very similar in character to myths (that is, historical beliefs that are passed down).
4. Evidence often comes in the form of single cases – and no thought is given to the statistical probability of these phenomena.
5. Knowledge is often formulated in such a vague and general manner that falsification (using empirical evidence) is impossible.
6. The relationships between events is usually based on coincidental, and often qualitative, similarities gained from many different fields, whereas the process of exploring variations, based on quantitative methodology (the basis of scientific arguments), is entirely absent.
7. Explanations for phenomena consist of scenarios describing possible relationships, but there is no mention of causal relationships.
8. The motive for conducting research is exegetic – that is, attempting to confirm what is already believed (at least by authorities within the field) to be true, and not the systematic agnosticism that characterizes scientific reasoning.

9 One final characteristic is that proponents of pseudo-science refuse to revise and update their knowledge, even when their claims are refuted by scientific research.

It is obvious that many of the books written by consultant gurus bear the distinct markings of pseudo-science, and this is further evidenced by the allegations that the major theories of consultancy are mere fads. It has been suggested that a new management fad has seen the light of day every year since the 1950s, and that there is now a plethora of fads (Huczynski, 1993). *One minute leadership* and *In Search of Excellence* are prototypical examples of these management fads. It is actually somewhat disturbing to realize that many of the books promoting these management fads are written by academic researchers, which just goes to show that pseudo-science even exists within academia.

Academic knowledge versus practical know-how

There are a number of significant differences between the type of knowledge essential to the researcher and the knowledge that characterizes the professional consultant:

1 Academic research is guided by methodology – not phenomena. Practitioners often find that academic knowledge does not take the reality of their day-to-day challenges into account. Academics are concerned with applying theory, whereas practitioners want relevant theory that they can use in practice. These two interests are often at odds. Practical theories are scarce in scientific knowledge, and this is in part due to the fact that theoretical researchers lack practical insight. Theoreticians regard their objects of study as just that – objects. Conversely, consultants view their phenomena as subjects, as associates working on the same project. This has lead to the development of what has been called action research. Many consultants are comfortable with the philosophy of action research.
2 Academics prefer to explore conditional variables, whereas practitioners are more concerned with processes and change. The explanation for this is that it is exceedingly difficult to measure change without using exacting methods. This requires studying the phenomenon over a long period of time (longitudinal studies) – and getting very uncertain

results. As a result of this, academics tended to eschew this type of research.

3 Practitioners are partial to data that supports common sense views, while academics usually prefer contra-intuitive data; data that actually contests what most commonly believe to be true. This is an unfortunate characteristic in the approach consultants have toward cutting-edge research. Since most research does not support popular beliefs, it is rejected as inapplicable. We would expect that, especially in connection with work on change processes, the use of contra-intuitive data might help to solve the conflicts that tend to arise as a natural consequence of human resistance to change.

4 A final example of the difference in knowledge used by academics versus practitioners, concerns the fact that the practitioner will draw on knowledge from multiple fields where knowledge of context is of more importance than detailed knowledge within any specific area. Conversely, researchers will often have a narrow focus – not just to a single field, but even within that field, and this fragmented knowledge becomes irrelevant for practical purposes. Practical solutions often involve multidisciplinary cooperation where knowledge of context is crucial. By taking the comprehensive view of the practitioner into account, theoretical and professional integration might be achieved.

5 In conclusion, it could be suggested that while academic knowledge is based on theory, methodology, and precise data, practical knowledge is based on instrumental values. If we place value-driven and theory-driven research at each end of a continuum, we might be so bold as to suggest that our confidence in, and our benefit of, knowledge, is at its optimum where values and academic criteria converge. When conclusions are too heavily founded in values, they forgo their basis in objective research. Conversely, research that doesn't take any practical considerations into account, is of little consequence outside the academic community.

The language of consultants

Consultants have played a major part in the development of what has come to be known as "bullet-point epistemology": the message is presented on a computer screen or projected on to a screen in the form of bullet points. Arguments are reduced to one-word expressions, often in the form of slogans; words are animated and even written vertically. To differentiate the message from that of a book, the page is rotated 90 degrees so that the orientation is horizontal. This form of communication has become a necessary prerequisite at all seminars and meetings, and has spread from the business world to academia. Even doctoral disputes feature this type of communication where onlookers become more attuned to reading arguments than listening to them. Erik Henningsen (as referred by Nickelsen, 2004) has studied this form of communication from an anthropological perspective.

In consulting, message content is very simplistic, and therefore it can flow freely between companies and even between cultures. Since these messages are simple and easy to convey, they can also be quickly transformed – which is entirely in keeping with the predominant "use and lose"-mentality. New terms quickly become fads, such as "coaching", and in Norway it is a definite pre if the words retain their English form. Many of these terms are already known from other contexts (from sports in the case of coach), and are thus perceived as well-known, obvious, and legitimate insights. At the same time these terms carry just the right amount of mystical aura so as not to be entirely obvious to clients. In fact, consultants are often asked to explain the theoretical and practical meaning of these terms. The confirmation bias is present in the mindset of both leaders and consultants. As a result of this, consultants become the interpreters and communicators of knowledge and ideologies concerning economic and organizational change processes in business. Consultants often link these terms to critical events that leaders feel compelled to take part in to keep abreast of the field, for example leadership- or teambuilding seminars.

In actual fact, many consultants function as distributors of new technology and other types of analytical systems (e.g. accounting). The type of consultant we are most concerned with here is big on "soft" issues: motivation, conflict, knowledge, culture, creativity, and values – aspects of organizations that are not easy to quantify or represent in precise terms. That is why it is so important for consultants to cast themselves in the role of academics (disseminators of the latest and greatest research in the field), while steering clear of the pitfalls of traditional academic language. This is why bullet-point language is so important.

The bullet-point form gives the knowledge an aura of precision, science, and traditional logic. Bullet points dissect and compress knowledge in such a way that insights become singular truths or information bites. Rows of names and words become more important than reasoning, which can seem liberating when set up against the systematic incertitude, reservations, and complexities of academic knowledge. Knowledge becomes accessible and seems almost self-evident. Truths can be isolated and are presented as part of the same reality, tacitly joined together by the implicit conjunction ("and"). Any questions concerning the fact that terminology is conveniently vague and taken from different logical and ontological levels are ignored. Since each word derives its meaning as a single word, the method of communication is characterized more by invoking truths than describing or analyzing. These magical terms are perceived as being wonderfully substantial and closely linked to practical reality. And if these magical words should fail, this is of course not due to the fact that the analysis is wrong or that reality is more complex than assumed, but merely that the wrong magical word was chosen.

The common sense of consultants and organizational theorists

Jacques (1996) has mapped consultants' relationship to common sense. Common sense is at the core of every MBA school theory. MBA, business schools, managerial publishing, and consulting – are all exported from the US. Jacques describes the common sense element in consultants' perception of reality according to this formula:

1 "There are organizations …" Organizations are legally defined entities, but it is not immediately evident who owns an organization from a psychological perspective, or who the stakeholders are. Consultants overlook the fact that organizations are the result of a complex social construction characterized by reifying, categorical mistakes, and mystification.
2 "… that need to develop innovative solutions …" The majority of what is presented as new, is just the same old wisdom dressed up in a new catchphrase (old wine in new bottles). Creativity and flexibility are often the greatest challenges in change processes, but more often than not this is presented as a problem to be solved by convergent (the opposite of creative), effective thinking.
3 "… for managing their employees …" But how do you tell the leaders and employees apart? Are not leaders also employees – who also need

to be managed? All in all, it is not entirely clear who is actually (as opposed to nominally) running the organization. There is a tendency to underestimate employees' ability to govern their own activities.
4 "... in an international setting ..." Internationalization is often held up as something new, but has in fact existed for centuries. Modern economic history has been heavily influenced by the discovery of America in 1496, and the colonial empires that were established all over the world. By the end of the 19th century, the US had gained significant international influence, and had the fastest growth rate in production in the world.
5 "... with the goal of increased efficiency and productivity ..." The importance of values other than efficiency and productivity are overlooked. What of values such as flexibility, creativity, and socially responsible behaviour? What about building long-term relationships? A number of researchers have found that the relentless pressure to increase efficiency may be counterproductive in the long run.
6 "... and competition." The term is erroneously taken to mean compete *against* each other as opposed to compete *together*. The fact that cooperation and trust are just as important as competition for the modern organization, and may be even more so in the future, is completely overlooked. And the increasing importance of ethics, relationships, and altruism is disregarded.

To reduce the dependency of common sense on dated knowledge, leaders, consultants, and academics must learn how to apply the principles of philosophy; that is, they need to become more critical and *reflective practitioners* (Donald Schon's term for theoretical practitioners and practical theoreticians). They need to ask themselves some fundamental questions about what we really mean by organizations and employees; what purpose and meaning do organizations have in society; what rights, responsibilities, and values do the members of the organization need; and what constitutes power and the execution of power within these organizations?

Consultants lack this ability for critical reflection because they are preoccupied with confirming their own suppositions (hypotheses), and because their livelihood depends on their ability to provide tenable "solutions". As a result, they are unaware of the importance of falsification for learning. The notion of learning from mistakes is a casualty in most organizations. Under the leadership of consultants, organizations often fall prey to the perils of confirmation bias, keeping up appearances, self-fulfilling prophecies, idolizing, and unfounded optimism.

Consultants and actionism

Leaders will often find themselves forced into actionism, by consultants and by management literature – first they establish the problem, then they offer you the solution. From a scientific perspective, actionism is like solving puzzles (ref. Gareth Morgan's description of science as solving puzzles) with no master plan or paradigm. As a result you are blind to the overall structures or contexts that provide meaning at lower levels – as Chris Argyris outlines in his model of higher order learning.

An actionistic approach can hamper:
- refection – the ability to step back and get the whole picture
- thinking for the long term (as opposed to appeasing short-term interests)
- self-control (as opposed to impulsive action)
- understanding context and impacting constraints
- identification of underlying causes for problems
- evaluation – the ability to learn from the past
- productive dialogue between people with opposing views
- learning from one's own mistakes
- development of new theoretical tools (used to meet challenges)

Everyone agrees that now is the time for radical change (management authors such as Peters, Kanter, and Drucker use the word revolution as though it were a litany), but seems to overlook the fact that new problems arise during periods of transition and that conventional thinking becomes the main obstacle. All learning leads to conservatism in terms of forgetting what you already know. This applies to scientific knowledge (ref. Kuhn's conception of paradigms) and, above all, it applies to the practical knowledge that consultants bring to market.

We need some new concepts, a new language, new methodologies, fresh empirical data, and some new theories (maybe even a new epistemology), but much of what has been presented as cutting-edge knowledge in the consulting sector these past decades is in actual fact conventional wisdom from the 50s and the 60s. TQM is based on W. Edwards Deming's theory of statistical quality control. Deming, who was an engineer with a background in Taylor's Scientific Management, developed his concept prior to the Second World War. Peter Senge's (1990) book – *The Fifth Discipline* is based on theoretical models that were developed during the 1960s and is essentially just a practical application of Karl Weick's *The Social Psychology of Organizing* from 1969. It could also be suggested that some of the best thinking from the 1960s has yet to be employed – e.g. McGregor's theory X versus theory Y (which is, by the way, widely misunderstood).

One of the main issues concerning the practical knowledge that consultants apply, is that is inherently backward-looking – to what has previously achieved results in other organizations. This is not limited to the practical know-how of the "bricoleur", but also concerns the science-based experience of the "ingenieur." There is a dearth of knowledge based on: 1) going beyond boundaries, the future, creativity; 2) system-wide thinking, big picture thinking (or holistic thinking); 3) social- (and thus) emotional intelligence.

Herriot & Pemberson (1995) identify three types of knowledge. The first type is what we commonly think of as *how*. This is equivalent to practical expertise and know-how – and is typically rooted in the past. The second type is what Herriot and Pemberson call knowledge *of* (that) – this is the equivalent of traditional theory-based knowledge. The third type of knowledge, what they call "learning beyond" is the most important for learning organizations. *Beyond* knowledge means the ability to imagine what can be. This type of knowledge is crucial for innovation, but it is usually disguised in the form "visions" that are delivered from on high by consultants and leaders in an attempt to win over their hearts rather than appeal to their common sense. This knowledge has to be created by those most suited to anticipate what the future will bring within their respective fields, and must be made available at all levels throughout the organization. In the past history perspective, organizations are typically represented as machines, as organisms in the modern perspective, and as network models in the future vision of organizations. A prerequisite for developing this kind of knowledge is a greater emphasis on diversity, team work, and development programs for all key employees.

A critical review of the type of knowledge that consultants represent is that it: 1) applies inappropriate methods; 2) uses simplistic models; 3) is often outdated; 4) is based on experience and without theoretical support; and 5) is dominated by gurus. The consequence of all this is that consultancy has a frail link to scientific knowledge and is in actual fact a social practice founded on a pseudo-scientific perspective, that, and this is a paradox, represents something that is radically new.

Consultants' competence

What is competence?

Knowledge is often taken to be synonymous with competence. However, these terms should be kept apart. While "knowledge" is a neutral term that suggests what we know of a specific topic, "competence" should be used to describe knowledge that is actually being applied. Competence is subject to evaluation according to certain standards – that vary depending on the topic, the time, and the place. Competence is a measure of the ability to perform in a specific context, and as such the criteria for measuring competence are restricted to this context. Thus, learning is a prerequisite for competence, and competence is a result of learning.

Based on these definitions of "knowledge" and "competence" we could justify the weak scientific foundation for consultants' activities by arguing that their main contribution is the competence they provide in the form of improved competitiveness. In a similar vein, Livingston (1971) suggests that you cannot predict how leaders will perform their executive duties based on their education, grades, or number of degrees. Academic prowess is simply not an appropriate measure of leadership potential. A formal education does not prepare one for the complexity involved in learning leadership. The ones that make it to the top have developed skills that are not taught in leadership programs – and which may even be difficult to learn within the context of a regular job. The same might be said of consultants' competencies, and perhaps we should take a closer look at these competencies that consultants claim to possess.

There are many different types of competencies. The literature on leader development illustrates the fact that not only is there a tremendous amount of research in this field, but there are also distinct similarities between the competencies we expect leaders to possess and the competencies we expect from consultants. Some lists of leadership competencies contain 3-4 items, while other may cite upwards of 20 qualities and skills that leaders are expected to possess, depending on how the researcher decides to group the different skills. Docherty and Nyhan (1997) cites four general classes of competency: a) *knowledge and intellectual* skills, e.g. problem-solving skills; b) *perceptual and motor skills*, related to dexterity; c) *social skills* – the ability to communicate and cooperate, and; d) more general attitudes such as responsibility, commitment, loyalty, and personal traits such as confidence and trustworthiness. It has also been suggested that other competencies, such as e) strategic competence; f) ethical and moral virtues, and; g) business-specific qualities like entrepreneurial spirit, should be considered prerequisite leadership qualities.

There are a number of researchers that use the science philosopher Polanyis's term "tacit knowledge" to explicate what they consider an important aspect of the practitioner's competence. Tacit knowledge is subjective, difficult to substantiate, and closely tied to the individual's personal experiences. Splender (1996) outlined what he considered to be the nature and strategic importance of tacit knowledge, and suggests that it is not entirely subjective. To a certain extent it is ingrained in the common practices and the physical context in which it is evident. As such, the study of tacit knowledge must not be limited to the practices of individuals, but must also take into account the possibility that knowledge exists at a social level and may be an integral part of procedures and physical surroundings. Consultants are often portrayed as masters of tacit knowledge, but the problem with this is that tacit knowledge is founded on previous experience and not easy to update.

Critique of consultants' knowledge

Textbooks on organizational psychology tend to adopt an instrumental approach to what constitutes relevant knowledge. As long as you can identify the problems the organization faces, you will always find some knowledge on how to identify and deal with these problems. Czander (1993) has criticized consultants for so readily adopting this view of the organization, claiming that it treats organizations (and thus the people within these organizations) as rational systems guided by causes that are readily apparent. Their methods of intervention involve experimental manipulation of variables, and as a result they focus almost entirely on extrinsic factors that can be manipulated.

Consultants consider themselves to be the *external experts* that possess the *technology* needed to solve the organization's problems. But in doing so they overlook: 1) the importance of cognitive factors (not easily manipulated); 2) the impact of factors that no one is consciously aware of; 3) the systemic complexity of organizations; 4) the stochastic (happenstance) nature of events within the organization, and; 5) the significance of the consultant being in the organization and interacting with the organization. Most studies of organizational efficiency fail to identify causal relationships, as both causal factors and resultant effects can be perceptual and cognitive social constructions. In actual fact, the consultant is not an *external expert* (outside the system as a true experimenter would be) that can use technological know-how/competency to manipulate isolated elements within the system in order to solve the systems problems.

According to Czanders, consultants often violate the requirements of professional behavior as they frequently operate without a firm theoretical and philosophical valuation base, and rarely engage in the required self-reflection that is vital when one engages in research, where results are generalized and applied. The extensive amount of research on job satisfaction as a determinant for performance illustrates this point: despite numerous studies employing different conditions, no relationship has been proven.

The models that consultants employ, such as the universal claim that organizations will perform better if everybody is working towards a common goal, are generally unfounded. March & Sutton (1997) criticize what they consider to be an overly simplistic view of organizations, and argue that the goals of organizations cannot be expressed as though they are singular and internally consistent. But despite this, it is common to hear consultants claim that it is possible.

Both researchers and consultants attempt to explain variations in performance or efficiency by using organizational behavior as an explanatory variable. However, this type of explanation overlooks the fact that analyzing performance at an aggregate level implies using a social construction of organizational efficiency.

Performance is generally considered to be a dependent variable, influenced by independent precursors such as style of leadership, teamwork, etc. However, performance could just as easily be an independent variable. Trying to influence organizational efficiency is difficult because the causal relationships between factors are complex. The common method of approach is to analyze *historical data*, and this is rarely carried out within an experimental framework. There are three sticky issues involved in this type of approach:

1 The measured variance between different factors influencing organizational influence is reduced due to the fact that organizations tend to imitate successful behavior (i.e. best practices, and new fads like TQM, JIT etc.). Consultants are themselves one of the main driving forces of this cycle. The mere fact that organizations tend to adopt the same methods over time makes it difficult to identify discriminating factors. Findings are often coincidental – but they're implemented if the behavior seems to bear success.

2 It is common to use simplistic models to portray a reality that involves complex feedback loops. Historical performance impacts future performance, which in turn leads to self-fulfilling prophecies (to wit, the effect of performance on satisfaction, but not vice versa). A good performance score can create a positive outlook and lead to positive self-attribution. But this will in turn lead to a reduction variety-seeking behavior and in creativity, which in turn may result in a future downturn (witness the negative effect of success). This type of destructive cycle is usually referred to as a competence trap – of which consultants are a major driving force. There are is also large difficulties with the measures of (short-term) efficiency and (long-term) adaptivity.

3 It is difficult to isolate contributing factors when empirical data is based on recollection. Factors that are not observed directly are not observed over time – this applies to both narrative- and classical statistical methods of analysis. This leads to a retrospective bias where knowledge of performance distorts the recollection of all other pertinent information. The business world is rife with tales of what leads to good performance and what results in poor performance. The process of recollection can easily become one of reconstruction, where memory of actual events is interspersed with conventional wisdom. Studies have shown that students that are provided with (misleading) information that overstates the performance of the group they belong to will rate the level of cohesion and communication higher (which can thus be interpreted as independent factors influencing response) than students who receive information that suggests the group performed poorly. Old tales, and the personal interests of key informants, such as leaders, produce "data". This has been shown to be the case in studies where leaders receive positive ratings based on how they measure up against "images" of good leadership – despite the fact that they would rate poorly on common

measures of effective leadership. Consultants are often the proponents of such self-fulfilling images.

Consultants struggle with the challenge of trying to be both academic researcher and practicing professional to the client. There is ample opportunity for these two roles to conflict and for communication to become ambiguous. The same individual may assume the role of champion of organizational efficiency (consultant) and of preacher (academic) of the integrity of science. There is a very real danger that one does not "walk the talk" (one does not actually do what one suggests one will do). Despite the fact that the consultant may not be a researcher, "scientific evidence" is proffered in support of the consultant's models and suggested interventions. This type of "evidence" is usually more concerned with perpetuating key social norms than with providing a sound basis for making decisions. There is a fundamental conflict between what is assumed to be true – and what can actually be supported by evidence; between the practitioners magic and the researcher's rationality; between passive observation and active participation; between the virtue of being pure and the evils of appeasement. As such, one should be careful about proposing sweeping changes and broad generalizations based on elegant, but unsupported, mathematical models, rather than on firm empirical conclusions.

We need to reflect on ambivalence, dilemmas and risks, and between, speaking up and remaining silent. Scholarly virtue is more of a struggle than an achievement. Knowledge is a process; a dance; a passage rather than an arrival.

Consulting, impression management, and guru-leadership

To a certain degree, consulting consists of propagating the latest management fad. Some researchers have suggested that one new management fad emerges every year, and since most of these fads are kept alive by consultancies, there is a plethora of organizational perspectives to choose from. This growth has been paralleled by the growth in the number of business school programs, and in the development of organizational psychology as a major field of research (through publications) and study. At the same time, Human Resources Management (HRM) has grown from being an operative discipline to a topic of study in business schools.

One important aspect of fads is their impact on self-image and impression management. People are generally concerned with the way others perceive them, and as a result of this, they try to manage the impressions others form of them. Impression management happens at three different levels: 1) General impression management through structures or via third party; 2) Direct influence on the opinion of others through social interaction; 3) cognitive influence of personal self-image. Consultants generally operate at all three levels.

Researchers that have studied the Guru ritual, describe it as a neatly scripted process consisting of the following elements:

1 Intense process, here and now
2 Far-reaching and irreversible actions
3 High risk – even for bystanders
4 Initiation rituals, that may involve status change
5 The locale is used organically and specifically
6 Everything that happens is determined by the performer
7 The audience become a medium for the performance
8 The duration is entirely dependent on the performer
9 High levels of energy, excitement, suspense
10 The experience appeals to emotion
11 Elements of surprises, puzzles, mystery, and paradox

Impression management involves a dynamic and recursive process that consists of interactions between conscious and unconscious processes, and involves monitoring and even trying to control behavior. As such the consultant/client relationship can be somewhat fluid in character. Czander (1993) suggests that this relationship is distinguished by internal resistance and division: Good or bad characteristics are continuously projected onto the consultant. The consultant is idolized to some degree – as if in the hope that this person will provide savior. For their part, consultants are characterized by the fact that they often employ the defensive tactics of intellectualization and rationalization, and; as a result of this, consultants find it difficult to acknowledge their own limitations. One of the primary responsibilities for experts is to stay within their area of expertise. However, in the case of consulting, both client and expert would seem to undermine this, and in the end learning is hampered for both consultant and client.

Consulting and professional code of ethics

Organizations can be viewed as instruments for achieving specific targets, and the organization's competence as its ability to perform the tasks necessary for achieving success. This competence is not just the sum of the individual employees' competencies, but also comprises resources, such as technological, organizational know-how, procedures, and culture. Cooperation is a prerequisite for achieving shared goals, and cooperation is often heavily influenced by ethical guidelines. Ethical competence thus becomes a key element of organizational competence, or, (as Bourdieu would say) organizational capital.

Ethical competency is critical, not just for the organization as a whole, or for the individuals that make up the organization, but also for anyone involved in developing competencies within the organization. As such, the ability to impart ethical competency is a prime asset for consultants, and this requires that they have this competence themselves. The best way to provide ethical competence is by establishing a code of ethics, and we will take a closer look at what this type of codex usually contains.

Professional competence is a fundamental requirement in the code of ethics for most professions. It is not enough that practitioners exhibit keen ethical awareness and have a grasp of ethics. They also need to possess the required professional competence, and must continually develop this competence. A key aspect of competence involves knowing and recognizing the limitations of one's own competence, and this extends to the methodologies one employs as well as the constraints imposed by the environment in which one is operating. A study of the tests that consultants routinely employ in selection procedures showed that less than 20% of these tests met the fundamental requirements for scientific research in terms of reliability and validity. The clients for this type service are rarely informed of these limitations; limitations that in fact mean that these "objective tests" are no more scientific than reading tealeaves. This is a prototypical example of the kind of "pseudo-science" and lack of ethical competence that characterizes consultants. Similar criticisms can be leveled at other areas of consultants' self-acclaimed competencies.

A further requirement for a professional code of ethics is respect for the fundamental rights of the individual with regards to dignity and integrity, and concerns issues such as confidentiality, informed consent, client privilege, limitations of the service to be provided, and the individual's right to make informed choices. To date, no studies have examined all the possible consequences of consultants having breached these ethical requirements, but it is an unavoidable fact that consultants are employed by senior management and tend to side with management if and when conflict arises.

A third requirement in the code of ethics is that consultants assume responsibility for their actions, avoid misconduct, deal with ethical dilemmas, ensure continuity in the services provided, and acknowledge that their responsibility extends to everyone in the organization. In this sense the consultant's role as an "outsider" complicates the issue, as it suggests that the consultant is not directly responsible for goings-on within the client organization. However, consultants should feel responsible for everyone within the organization, and not just for the people that employed them. The issue of being responsible for the whole client organization is problematic for many of the professions that provide services that may affect people's lives.

A fourth requirement is that consultants respect their own integrity, as well as that of their clients. Integrity involves being honest, truthful, fair, and forthright in all professional activities. And in particular this means avoiding conflicting roles, as can be the case when there is uncertainty as to whether the consultant is present in the capacity of a practitioner or as a friend or confidant of the principal. Most professions require a strict separation of roles in order to avoid conflicts between professional duties and private life. In other words, consultants should avoid clients with whom they may have close and personal relationships to.

There are a few implicit requirements, such as the professional being responsible for his or her own personal development, and a sense of responsibility towards one's own profession and to society.

Tobias (1990) suggests that we adopt a clinical perspective of consultancy as an ethical profession. Making jobs more human is one of the greatest challenges facing organizations. Professional ethics could thus be said to involve: 1) caring for people and, 2) being realistic when dealing with others. The main objective of the consultant should be to help leaders and employees deal with psychological realities in such a way that they are able to take care of the individuals within the organization. At present, it is difficult to see that consultants adhere to the requirements of a professional code of conduct.

References

Berger, P. & Luckman, T. (1967). *The Social Construction of Reality*. New York: Penguin.

Clark, T. (1995). *Managing Consultants. Consultancy as the Management of Impressions*. Buckingham: Open University Press.

Conyne, R.K. & O'Neil, J.M. (1992). *Organizational Consultation. A Casebook*. Newbury Park: Sage.

Czander, W.M. (1993). *The Psychodynamics of Work and Organizations*. New York: Guilford.

Docherty, P. & Nyhan, B. (1997). *Human Competence and Business Development*. Springer Verlag.

Ebeltoft, A. (1993). *Konsulenten og forskeren i endringsaktive roller*. Rapport 4/93. Oslo: Arbeidsforskningsinstituttet.

Hardy, C. (Ed.). (1994). *Strategic Action*. London: Sage.

Haslebo, G. & Nielsen, K.S. (1997). *Konsultation i organisationer – hvordan mennesker skaber ny mening*. København: Dansk Psykologisk Forlag.

Heriot, P. & Pemberson, C. (1995). *Competitive Advantage through Diversity*. London: Sage.

Heron, J. (1990). *Helping the Client*. London: Sage.

Heron, J. (1992). *Feeling and Personhood*. London: Sage.

Huczynski, A.A. (1993). *Management gurus. What makes them and how to become one*. London: Routledge.

Jacques, R. (1996). *Manufacturing the Employee. Management Knowledge from the 19th to the 21st Centuries*. London: Sage.

Leary, M.R. & Kowalski, R.M. (1990). Impression Management: A Literature Review and Two-Component Model. *Psychological Bulletin 1990, Vol. 107*, No.1, 34–47.

Livingston, J. S. (1971). Myth of the well-educated manager. *Harvard Business Review*, January-February, 79–89.

March J. G. & Sutton, R.I. (1997). Organizational Performance as a Dependent Variable. *Organization Science, Vol. 8*. No. 6, 698–706.

Meyer, J.L. (1996). Coaching and Counselling in Organizational Psychology. In M.J. Schabracq, J.A.M. Winnubst & C.L. Cooper (Eds.), *Handbook of Work and Health Psychology*. Chichester: Wiley.

Nickelsen, T. (2004). Når verden tenker i kulepunkter. *Apollon* nr. 1.

Radner, D. & Radner, M. (1982). *Science and Unreason*. Belmont, C: Wadsworth.

Sackett, P.R., Burris, L.R. & Ryan, A.M. (1989). Coaching and Practice Effects in Personnel Selection. In C.L. Copper & I. Robertson (Eds.), *International Review of Industrial and Organizational Psychology 1989*. Chichester: Wiley.

Scientific American (1997). Science versus Antiscience. *Scientific American*, January.

Shrabanek, P. & McCormick, J. (1990). *Follies and Fallacies in Medicine*. Buffalo, New York: Prometheus Books.

Sperry, L. (1996). *Corporate Therapy and Consulting*. New York: Brunner/Mazel.

Standarder for Norsk psykologisk embedseksamen. 13.06.1990.

Tidsskrift for Organiasjonspsykologi Vol. 8, nr. 1, 2000.

Tobias, L.L. (1990). *Psychological Consulting to Management*. New York: Brunner/Mazel.

von Krogh, G. & Roos, G. (1996). *Managing Knowledge. Perspectives on Cooperation and Competition*. London: Sage.

Chapter 5

The roles of popular management concepts in management consulting

ANDREAS WERR

Introduction

Popular management concepts – often described as management fads or fashions – have proliferated rapidly in the past two decades. In 2001, the average manager applied 11,4 different management tools (Rigby, 2001a). Total Quality Management, Just in Time, Time Based Management, Business Process Reengineering, Knowledge Management, etc are examples of management concepts that spread throughout organizations all over the world as remedies to all the different challenges that organizations face, one after the other. Management concepts, each following bell shaped popularity curves, have followed each other. Each new concept has been positioned as being very different from the last one, and thus has encouraged organizations to initiate yet another large scale change initiative. However the presence of any real differences between each concept might be questioned (see e.g. Cole, 1994 for a comparison of TQM and BPR).

The rapid development of popular management concepts has been paralleled by an explosive growth in the management consulting industry, a link that some would claim to be more than just a coincidence. Management consultants have been heavily involved in both the creation and proliferation of popular management concepts (Abrahamson, 1996; Suddaby & Greenwood, 2001) and it has been argued that the increasing supply of management concepts has been driven by management consultants' growth strategies rather than by organizations' needs for solutions. While management concepts may provide the solutions to managers' existing problems, it has also been argued that they contribute to the creation of new problems. New ways of understanding and talking about organizations and their management create dysfunctionalities which may not have been apparent previously (Bloomfield & Best, 1992; Czarniawska, 1988).

Regardless of whether management concepts provide solutions or create new problems, they do create a need for management consultants. As argued by Berglund & Werr (2000), management concepts provide desirable and ambitious visions, without actually spelling out in detail how to achieve these. Thus, the need for management consultants and other claimed experts of the concepts is created (see e.g. Hatchuel & Weil, 1995). Based on claims of extensive experience, and of "having done it before", experts promise their clients that they will achieve the, often highly ambitious, goals promised by the concepts. It has thus been argued that the alliance between management consultants and management concepts is one mainly driven by, and beneficial to the management consulting industry (Kieser, 1998), and that the development of management concepts is driven by marketing efforts rather than any real advances in knowledge (Abrahamson, 1996; Furusten, 1995).

Management consultants, and the management concepts they promote, have thus been met with increasing scepticism and come under criticism from a variety of sources. A common theme in the criticism from both scholars and practitioners has been that management concepts are old wine in new bottles, 'mere fashion', and panaceas that deal more with what is politically correct than with actual improvements in organizational practice. The popularity of 'non-practical' books – that explain how and why popular management ideas don't really work (e.g. Blomberg, 1998), the success of Dilbert – a comic star that mocks with what has generally become known as 'Corporate Bullshit', the numerous articles in business media that explicitly deal with what's in and what's out, and the critique against the "standardized solutions" delivered by management consultants (O'Shea & Madigan, 1997; Pringle, 1998; Sartain, 1998) all bear witness to the fact that academics are not alone in questioning the nature and efficacy of management concepts and their promoted management consultants.

Management consultants are often aware of the level of scepticism towards their profession and may have serious doubts about popular management concepts themselves (cf. Brulin, 1997). They have even created an acronym to describe the lack of enthusiasm shown by members of client organizations for popular management concepts: The BOHICA Syndrome (Bend Over, Here It Comes Again) – so describing organizations' resistance to yet another change program based on a new management concept.

The literature has explored the phenomenon of popular management concepts and their links to management consultants from two rather different perspectives (Røvik, 1998). From a tools perspective, the concepts are viewed as representing knowledge directly applicable by managers (or consultants) in their efforts to improve organizations. From a symbolic perspective, popular management concepts are viewed as symbols of rationality and progress designed to boost the legitimacy of their users. While both these perspectives provide some insight into the manner in which popular management concepts are applied by management consultants, they are rather incomplete. In this chapter we will use findings from empirical studies of management consultants, to create a more nuanced understanding of the interaction between management consultants and popular management concepts. We propose that popular management concepts, through their manifestation in detailed methods and as tools in consultancies, are more than just simple tools or legitimating symbols. In fact we suggest that these concepts may represent a form of *language* that aids consultants in their problem-solving activities, in their communication with the client, and in the global management of knowledge.

This chapter is structured as follows: In the next section, the concept of "popular management" will be elaborated by using a conceptualization that consists of three aspects – a management philosophy, a technical substrate, and a simplified organizational scheme. This is followed by a review of the literature and its treatment of management concepts in management consulting. Two views are identified – management concepts as tools and management concepts as legitimizing symbols. Next, we investigate the production and use of popular management concepts in management consultancies. Three central uses of management concepts are identified – in consultants' problem-solving activities, in consultants' communication with clients, and in internal knowledge sharing within consultancies. We conclude this chapter with a discussion of the proposal that management concepts should be viewed as a form of language.

A conceptualization of popular management concepts

It is possible to gauge the popularity of a particular management concept by determining the popularity of its label. Like all fashions, management concepts follow a pattern of growth and decline (c.f. Abrahamson, 1996), and this pattern will emerge in the number of citations in literature databases or in managers' use of the concept's label (more often than not this will be a three-letter acronym such as TQM; BPR; etc.) (Rigby, 2001b). However, popular management concepts are more than just a label. For the purpose of this chapter a more fine-grained understanding is needed. Based on Hatchuel & Weil (1995), management concepts will be understood as being composed of three different elements – a management philosophy, a technical substrate, and a simplified organizational scheme.

The central element in every planned change process is the vision of the future state – which is the aim of the change process. This vision is provided by the *management philosophy*, which defines the elements of the organization to be changed as well as the desired direction of this change. The management philosophy helps to determine the current state of the organization, what problems are inherent in the organization, and how these problems might be solved. As such, the management philosophy provides meaning and purpose to the more operational elements of the management concept, i.e. procedures and tools, view of organizational actors, etc.

Even with the knowledge of what to change and why, the question of how still remains. This knowledge can be subdivided into knowledge of procedures, tools, a language (a media of communication in the change process), and a description of central actors, all aimed at accomplishing the goals as defined by the management philosophy. The *technical substrate* describes the activities of the change process as well as the prerequisites for, and results of these activities. The technical substrate also includes specific tools that will aid in solving problems that may arise in connection with the different activities. Finally, the *simplified organizational scheme* specifies the different roles in the change process, i.e. who does what and who is responsible.

Two perspectives on popular management concepts

Our current understanding of popular management concepts and their role in management consulting may be divided into two perspectives that suggest rather different views (Røvik, 1998). From a tools perspective, they are viewed as representations of knowledge to be directly applied in consultants' (or managers') efforts to improve organizations. However, in the symbolic perspective, concepts form the basis of their users' legitimacy. These two perspectives will be briefly reviewed as a basis for the empirical investigations following.

Management concepts as tools for change

The *tools perspective* is based on the view of organizations as rational entities that constantly improve the efficiency of their operations in order to secure their survival. In line with a rational-instrumental stream in organization theory, pioneered by authors such as Taylor (1911) with his concept of scientific management, concepts are seen as tools to be applied by managers in order to improve efficiency and effectiveness in operations. This view is implicit in most of the current popular management literature that prescribes its solutions as tested and proven road-maps to organizational success (Furusten, 1995; Huczynski, 1993). The more popular a concept is, the more efficient it is assumed to be. Consequently, the decline in popularity of a concept is viewed as a reflection of decreased efficiency – either because the nature of the problems that need to be solved have changed or because new, more efficient concepts have emerged.

Viewing management concepts as tools of change suggests that managers select them as the result of a rational search process. Managers are continually on the lookout for more efficient concepts to solve their problems, and once they find a promising concept, they implement it as thoroughly as possible. Broad and consistent implementation is seen as increasing the chance of success.

In the perspective of management concepts as tools, management consultants play multiple roles. They design the concepts – bringing together substantial experience from organizations all over the world. Management consultants' exposure to many different types of organizations is viewed as a prerequisite for creating good management knowledge (c.f. Sarvary, 1999). Consultants may also aid managers in selecting the most appropriate management concept and help them adapt the concept to local conditions, as this is often viewed as a critical success factor. The extensive experience that management consultants derive from having worked with a specific management concept in numerous different settings, and thus the knowledge of what works when and where, are central reasons for using management consultants in conjunction with the adoption of popular management concepts (Kubr, 2002).

Management concepts as legitimacy creating symbols

The *symbolic perspective* on popular management concepts and their role in management consulting is anchored in a neo-institutional view of organizations. This perspective regards organizations as being embedded in an institutional environment that confronts organizations with norms and ideas of how efficient organizations are structured and run. In order to survive this perspective contends, organizations need not only be efficient but must also reflect institutional values and norms (Meyer & Rowan, 1991). As the organizational norms are under constant change, organizations are similarly under constant pressure to adapt to the new "rationalized myths" of efficient management in their environment (ibid.).

Popular management concepts are manifestations of such rationalized myths of how organizations should be run. Thus, organizations primarily adopt popular management concepts for their symbolic value – concepts that convey rationality, progress and modernity – in order to gain legitimacy, support, and resources from their environment (DiMaggio & Powell, 1991). The adoption of a certain management concept gains symbolic value as it illustrates the organization's commitment to the latest management knowledge. As argued by Meyer & Rowan (1991) symbolic acts of this kind provide organizations with legitimacy, which may be as important for survival as efficiency.

From the symbolic perspective, the popularity of management concepts is thus explained by the modern and progressive air that they provide. This also explains why concepts are continuously evolving. No concept can be "modern" for ever, but the evolution of concepts is built into the institutionalized idea of constant progress (Meyer, 1994). The longevity of management concepts is thus only loosely coupled to their efficiency in improving operations within organizations. Further, it is not necessarily the norm that management concepts are implemented in a broad and consistent manner. From a neo-institutional perspective organizations are viewed as loosely coupled systems in which different parts of the organization could well adopt different management concepts in order to reflect the norms of different constituencies.

Given the strong symbolic rather than operational value of management concepts, their use is mainly discussed in relation to the needs of high level managers and the specific challenges they face. Huczynski (1993), exploring the success of management gurus, argues that management concepts are accepted because they deal with many of the predictability, control, social, and personal needs that today's managers perceive as their major challenges. In the author's own words (Huczynski, 1993, p. 171) – "the nature of organizational life places responsibility on managers to *perform,* and *achieve* in a context where often they neither understand how their actions produce results, nor are able to influence the most volatile element in the organization – other people". The popular concepts contribute both to making the world understandable and to legitimizing the role of the leader, which in turn make them almost irresistible to managers. Popular management concepts provide problem definitions as well as problem solutions, something which managers find attractive because it means that these concepts provide both simplifications of the less ordered reality as well as a point of departure for corrective action (Røvik, 1998).

In a similar vein, management consultants and their use of management concepts are also closely linked to providing legitimacy, to the organization, the manager, and to the managerial role itself. It is often claimed that a central role for management consultants is to legitimize the actions of management and to signal that a certain problem is being taken seriously and dealt with in accordance with the latest in management knowledge (i.e. popular management concepts). But management consultants, as pointed out by e.g. Clark & Salaman, (1996), also play an important role in supporting and maintaining the managerial identity, with popular management concepts being an important tool for creating a simplified illustration of the organization in which managers operate (c.f. Furusten, 1995; Huczynski, 1993).

Popular management concepts in consulting practice

Following this review of the two prevailing perspectives on popular management concepts and their role in management consulting, we will now turn to an exploration of management concepts as practised by management consulting organizations. This section is mainly based on a number of empirical studies on the use of management concepts and their manifestations in detailed methods and tools in management consulting organizations (see Werr, 1999 for details). The empirical focus of the studies was the so called "big five"-consulting firms with backgrounds in auditing services and a focus on operational efficiency/process reengineering projects (e.g. Ernst & Young (now Cap Gemini) and Accenture). However, some interviews in addition also covered the classic strategy consultancies (e.g. McKinsey, Boston Consulting Group). Data was gathered concerning the organizations' design and use of detailed methods and tools, and observations were carried out in a business process reengineering project concerned with the use of the detailed BPR methodology. Interviews were also carried out with representatives of the client organization in the BPR project in order to ascertain their opinion and evaluation of the method. Before we take a closer look at the actual use of management concepts within the observed consultancies, we will look into the development of these concepts. This investigation is primarily based on studies carried out by others.

The production of management concepts in consultancies

As a rule, the large management consulting organizations are highly involved in the development of popular management concepts and the detailed procedures and tools necessary to employ them (the technical substrate in terms of the outlined framework). An illustrative example is the case of Business Process Reengineering, a very popular concept in the mid 90's. Two books, both written by consultants of large consultancies, were instrumental in popularizing the concept – Michael Hammer's (CSC Index) *Reengineering the Corporation* (1993) and Thomas Davenport's (Ernst & Young) *Process Innovation* (1993).

For management consulting organizations, the development and adherence to management concepts may be viewed as a way to spotlight and legitimate the knowledge base of management consultants (as argued by the symbolic perspective), but in addition it is also as a way for consultancies to develop new or improved practices that they can offer to their clients. Global management consultancies may employ hundreds of people dedicated to the development and maintenance of their consulting methodologies (Chard, 1997), and provide their consultants with time and resources necessary to leverage their own and colleagues' experiences in new or improved concepts or methods (see e.g. Peters, 1992).

Czerniawska (2004) identifies four strategies for what she calls "thought leadership", that consultancies may adopt in relation to popular management ideas. *Initiator* firms are the ones that generate a continuous stream of new management concepts covering a large variety of different applications, but rarely develop them to any great extent. The large, general service consultancies are examples of this strategy. Initiator firms will typically be the birthplace of new popular management concepts. *Developer* firms focus more narrowly on a limited number of topics and develop more in-depth material and applications for these. Specialist consultancies in the HR area are examples of this strategy. While these firms may not initiate new general concepts, they typically focus on the application of these concepts in specific areas – such as HR – and develop the technical substrate in terms of detailed methods and tools. *Asset manager* firms apply a focused strategy similar to that of developer firms, but will focus on a specific sector and develop or adapt rather detailed concepts for that sector. Finally, *niche specialist* firms focus on a particular sector and the specific needs of organizations in that sector. In this type of organization less priority is given to documenting and managing knowledge and descriptions of the detailed methods and tools they use. Concept development in the latter two types of organizations will typically involve adaptation of popular management concepts rather than the development of new ones.

While this framework provides some insights into different ways in which consultancies may relate to popular management concepts, it reveals little of the internal processes through which consultancies develop, or adapt to, popular management concepts. Heusinkveld & Benders (2002) identify two approaches through which consultancies incorporate and develop their management concepts – a professional driven approach and a corporate driven approach. The *professional driven approach* arises from the entrepreneurial endeavours and "professional hobbies" of individual consultants. New concepts or trends may be identified by individual consultants, who start developing more specific offerings within the field. They may attract the attention of colleagues with similar interests and form informal networks in order to further develop the ideas. These ideas give rise to new services that are offered to clients, and consequently the technical substrate is defined through direct interaction with the client. The development of methods and tools is thus incremental and intimately linked to working with clients.

The *corporate driven approach* is more centralized, in that the choice of concepts to develop and engage in, is determined by management. Once a concept has been selected, a team of experts from within the consulting organization is assigned to develop the concept, including the managerial philosophy, the simplified organizational scheme, and especially the technical substrate. The development project is provided with a budget, and the goal is to create a detailed method for roll-out throughout the entire organization. Previous experience and existing tools may be incorporated into the new method, but overall it is a desktop design, which may be further refined as the organization gains experience from working with it (c.f. Werr, 1999). Once completed, the new concept is to be shared throughout the organization. This is supported by extensive documentation, either printed or in electronic media, as well as by training programs. All consultants working with specific types of projects are expected to adhere to the new methodology.

The use of management concepts in consultancies

Following this brief investigation into the development of management concepts, we will now turn to the use of these concepts in the operational activities of management consultants. The organizations studied here may be characterized as initiator or developer firms, and methods were developed primarily from a corporate driven approach. We will describe three main roles for management concepts in the work of management consultants: aiding individual consultants in their problem-solving activities, supporting communication with the client, and enabling knowledge sharing within the consulting organization.

Management concepts as problem-solving support

The view underlying most management concepts is in line with the tools perspective – that is that they may function as guides for the consultants (or managers) in their problem-solving. This was illustrated by the large investments that the consultancies in our studies made towards the development of very detailed procedures and tools for carrying out different kinds of projects. These methods detailed more than 100 steps to be followed in a specific kind of project. Each activity was further supported by checklists, role-definitions, document templates, etc.

In the course of their daily activities, management consultants find themselves involved in both complex and ambiguous situations (Sturdy, 1997). They are hired to solve the problems that managers in the client organization were unable to solve. The business problem to be solved in this type of situation can either be linked to functional knowledge, e.g. how to carry out an accurate process mapping, or to more interpersonal aspects, e.g. the failure of specific managers to communicate with each other due to political conflicts. Quite often, consultants are faced with aspects of both kinds of problem. Such situations are very challenging and stressful for management consultants as they have been specifically hired for their ability to deal with these problems. Managers expect them to possess the necessary expertise and skills to deal with the situation, regardless of its complexity. Consultants showing uncertainty or doubt concerning the problem and its solution are in trouble (Clark & Salaman, 1996). Management concepts, that have a detailed technical substrate, may provide support to consultants when they are dealing with their own anxiety.

Several of the consultants that were interviewed described their management concepts as a method of reducing uncertainty, and as a way of making sure that they would not overlook anything important. Concepts were seen as an overall check list of activities to be carried out, that had to be adapted to each specific case. The check-list function of a concept was generally of more importance to junior consultants. However, even more senior consultants mentioned the need to refresh their memories by revisiting the concept:

"The methodology is a checklist, which makes it easier to remember what to do in different phases of the process". *senior consultant*

"Before beginning a new phase in the project, I check the methodology – just to make sure that I do not forget anything". *senior consultant*

"If I need help, or don't understand something, I can consult the methodology …" *junior consultant*

However, the use of the concept as an aid for the individual consultant dealing with a specific client related problem was not mentioned as often as might be expected, especially when considering the concept from the tools perspective. With the exceptions of those cited above, all the consultants that were interviewed agreed that the concepts provided had limited value in guiding their actions. Following a specific concept in every detail was not only viewed as difficult, but even as being detrimental to the success of a project:

"Methods work like recipes – the first time you follow them, then you improvise." *senior consultant*

"The method is for us mainly a reference object, but you can't put the method in the hands of an inexperienced consultant, and thereby achieve a successful project. But it is a way of making the consultant more professional and learning faster than without anything. But one should not become a slave of the method." *senior consultant*

This indicates that management concepts play a limited role as direct guides for the actions of consultants, although it does not mean that consultants' activities are entirely disconnected from the content of concepts, methods and tools. Consultants described methods as being "at their fingertips" and "in the back of their heads" rather than detailed guides for actions.

"The method and the structure is at your fingertips."

"We do not follow methods rigidly … they are ingrained in your mind."

"As a consultant, I think it is extremely important to have methods in the back of your head – to lean on."

A closer investigation into the activities and methodologies of consultants revealed that even though the methods were not applied in detail, they did influence to a large extent the consultants' definition of a client's problem, the proposed solutions, and the approach to the consulting project (see Werr, 1999).

Management concepts as communication support

A central issue in management consultants' relations with their clients is that of creating an image of the services to be delivered (Clark, 1995). This image is important both for the selling process – in order to give the buyer an idea of what s/he is buying, as well as in the ongoing project work in order to give the organizational members an idea of what they are doing and why and how this is related to both past and upcoming activities, and the sense that they are progressing towards a predetermined goal. A senior consultant in a multinational consulting organization described his use of their rather detailed concept in the following way:

"The concept is very important in our work. Its major role is as a support of communication when selling projects and during project execution. In the sales phase a well tested and detailed concept gives an impression of competence that creates trust. Also in ongoing projects, the concept as a map of the process is very important. The concept's description of the consulting process in a number of sequential steps is used to communicate the design of the project."

The management concepts are thus an important resource to the consultants in their efforts to communicate the content of their services. A description of the different phases of the consulting process, and the more detailed content in each phase was an important part of sales presentations. But, as indicated by the senior consultant's statement above, it was not only the overall description of the concept, but also its physical manifestation in the form of a couple of thick binders detailing different activities, providing checklists, templates, etc. that was important. The latter provided an impression of "competence, which creates trust". This view is confirmed by a client in a large consulting project:

"The method is very important to create confidence in the consultant. I would have had large difficulties working with someone who couldn't present a well tested and accepted approach they were to follow."

project group member

However, the concept was not only used in the sales phase but also as a way to present the consultants' service as a sequence of activities. The consultants would start each project group meeting by relating the specific meeting to the overall sequence of activities prescribed by the applied concept. Thus, a sense of progress towards a specific goal was imbued in the participants. This feeling was especially important in the organization that was studied, which, like many other organizations, has experienced numerous change initiatives that were never completed. In this context, the concept and its detailed technical substrate was an important symbol of the consultants' expertise, experience, and commitment, and this helped to motivate people in the client organization despite their previous negative experiences (see also Rogberg & Werr, 2000).

Management concepts as knowledge sharing support

The challenge of communicating the complex and immaterial nature of consulting services is not limited to the consultant-client interface, but also applies to the internal communication within consulting organizations. As argued above, management consultants, at least from a tools perspective, are perceived as experts that possess superior knowledge within specific fields – often packaged in the form of management concepts. As knowledge creation in management consulting is to a large extent linked to experiences made in the day to day work with clients (Sarvary, 1999; Werr, 1999), it is important that the knowledge gained from these experiences is gathered and distributed throughout the organization in such a way that consultants may draw not only on their own experience, but also on that of the entire consulting organization.

Consultants often described the management concepts shared by the consulting organization as an important vehicle for internal communication. They provided both a general framework for designing and executing projects, and a set of concepts – a common language – to communicate these issues to others. In one of the consultancies that were studied, consultants described how the internal exchange of knowledge gained from experience – at both formal meetings and in the more informal hallway meetings – was facilitated by the existence of a common management concept, with its frameworks and activities. When someone mentioned the "visioning seminar" everybody knew what that person was talking about. In another consultancy the concepts' role in facilitating communication between senior and junior consultants was emphasized:

"In order to reduce the non value-adding dialogue between junior and senior consultant, they can communicate through the method. "We are going to work with these issues now. You can start preparing the interview schedules that support these activities. Then we can have a look at them." By using the method you can avoid explaining everything from the beginning each time. The method is to a large extent about supporting internal communication."

In addition to being conducive for direct communication between consultants, the existence of a shared management concept also facilitated the exchange of more explicit knowledge elements, such as documents from previous projects (e.g. project proposals, project plans, process maps, etc). Documents such as these were an important source of knowledge for the individual consultants, especially in the large, multinational consulting organizations. The structures and notions provided by the shared management concept made it possible for consultants all over the world to understand and use each others' documents (Werr & Stjernberg, 2003).

Beyond tools and symbols – management concepts as language

Current approaches to the roles of management concepts in management consulting have viewed these as either efficient tools to be employed by efficiency seeking change agents or as legitimacy creating symbols aimed at creating a need for consulting services. However, the investigation into the roles of management concepts in the practice of management consulting enables us to paint a richer image. These investigations show a rather close and complex relationship between management concepts and management consulting involving concepts both as tools *and* as symbols.

The two different views of management concepts that we have reviewed – tools or symbols, are often presented as being incommensurable, but our investigation indicates that these two perspectives on popular management concepts may not only co-exist, but might even support each other. For example, the role of management concepts as symbols of the consultants' competence relies on the existence of a detailed methodology outlining activities, tools, and templates that the client can appreciate as evidence of expertise. Similarly, the concept's symbolic value, as evidence of well tested knowledge, made it efficient as a tool for providing a point of departure for the consultants' actions.

Against the background of the interdependent rather than conflicting nature of the tools and symbolic perspectives of management concepts, a third view of management concepts, transcending the "tools" and "symbols" views, will be presented – that of management concepts as a form of language. In the consultants' problem-solving activities, communication between client and consultants, and internal knowledge-sharing, the two perspectives on management concepts that we have discussed, share some common denominators. In each context the concept aided understanding and communication of complex issues, both internally and externally. This is a central function of language as described by e.g. Berger & Luckmann (1966, p. 173):

"… language objectifies the world, transforming the panta rhei of experience into a cohesive order. In the establishment of order, language realizes a world, in the double sense of apprehending and producing it."

Such a view of popular management concepts acknowledges the symbolic role they play in creating specific images of reality, and also acknowledges the tools oriented perspective in which the concepts actually help to bring about envisioned reality. As argued above, even when management concepts were not followed in detail, they were influential in guiding the perceptions and actions of their users.

But it is not only due to the role of concepts in creating and communicating images of reality that it is meaningful to talk about them in terms of being a language, but also because of their ability to create images that are shared and collectively understood. Berger & Luckmann (1966, p. 53) further argue, that:

"Language also typifies experience, allowing me to subsume them under broad categories in terms of which they have meaning not only to me but also to my fellowmen."

This communicative function of management concepts was especially evident in the management concepts' support of communication between consultant and client and between consultants within the consulting organization. In the latter case, the concepts were instrumental in accumulating collective knowledge, based on the experience of all consultants within large consultancies, providing an important "raison d'étre" for global management consultancies (Bäcklund & Werr, 2004; Werr, Stjernberg & Docherty, 1997)

While the notion of "popular management concepts" implies a constant change in concepts, the notion of language implies some stability. Language is deeply intertwined with identity and the skilful application of language is a rather intuitive act, learned from extensive experience (Berger & Luckmann, 1966). This characteristic was clearly observed in relation to popular management concepts in consultancies – where a majority of consultants described their management concepts as "ingrained", "at their fingertips", or "in the back of their head". However, this view of management concepts as factors of stability would seem to be at odds with the rapid succession of management concepts within the business world, but a closer look at the content of different management concepts indicates that these are more similar than claimed by the accompanying rhetoric.

Our conceptualization of popular management concepts as "language" may have several implications, for both researchers and practitioners. For researchers these findings would seem to indicate the need for a more open-ended and empirically-based investigation into the use of management concepts. Further research needs to be conducted on the relationship between the content and form of different "concept languages", and the practice of these by consultants. How do different levels of detail in the technical substrate affect the practice of consultants? Are there differences between the "concept languages" of different kinds of consultancies'? How does this affect their practice and so forth?

For consultants, these findings may give cause to revisit their concepts and to reflect upon the roles they play in specific contexts. Our conceptualization of management concepts as "language" also indicates that these concepts have limits in terms of providing a detailed guide for consultants' actions. Rather it highlights the roles of concepts in providing a framework for making sense of the effect an action has on reality, and for enabling communication. This conceptualization may suggest the need for a new way of handling popular management concepts both in terms of their development (Who is involved? How often are they changed? How are they communicated? Etc.) and their form (What is the level of detail? What is the focus – the management philosophy, the technical substrate, or the simplified organizational scheme, etc?). While the answers to these questions will differ for different organizations and for different situations, the aim of this chapter has been to provide some insights that may inform future discussion on these issues.

References

Abrahamson, E. (1996). Technical and aesthetic fashion. In B. Czarniawska, & G. Sevon (Eds.), *Translating Organizational Change* (pp. 117–137). Berlin: Walter de Gruyter.

Bäcklund, J., & Werr, A. (2004). The Social Construction of Global Management Consulting. A Study of Consultancy Web Presentations. In A. Buono (Ed.), *Creative Consulting: Innovative Perspectives on Management Consulting*, pp. 27–50, Vol. 4. Greenwich: Information Age Publishing.

Berger, P., & Luckmann, T. (1966). *The Social Construction of Reality*. London: Penguin Books.

Berglund, J., & Werr, A. (2000). The Invincible Character of Management Consulting Rhetorics. *Organization*, 7(4): 633–655.

Blomberg, J. (1998). *Myter om projekt*. Stockholm: Nerenius & Santerus.

Bloomfield, B. P., & Best, A. (1992). Management consultants: systems development, power and the translation of problems. *The Sociological Review*, 40(3): 533–560.

Brulin, G. (1997). Företagsledningskonsulternas kunskapsbas. In Å. Sandberg (Ed.), *Ledning för alla? Om perspektivbrytningar i företagsledning* (pp. 291–313). Stockholm: SNS Förlag.

Chard, M. (1997). Knowledge Management at Ernst and Young. Stanford: Graduate School of Business, Stanford University.

Clark, T. (1995). *Managing Consultants*. Buckingham: Open University Press.

Clark, T., & Salaman, G. (1996). Telling Tales: Management Consultancy as the Art of Story Telling. In D. Grant, & C. Oswick (Eds.), *Metaphor and Organizations* (pp. 167–184). London: Sage.

Cole, R. E. (1994). Reengineering the Corporation: A Review Essay. University of California at Berkley, Center for Research in Management.

Czarniawska, B. (1988). *To coin a phrase: on organizational talk, organizational control and management consulting*. Stockholm: The Economic Research Institute.

Czerniawska, F. (2004). *The Consulting Industry: Thought leader or thought follower?* Paper presented at the 2nd International Conference on Management Consulting, Lausanne.

Davenport, T. H. (1993). *Process Innovation – Reengineering Work through Infor-*

mation Technology. Boston: Harvard Business School Press; Ernst & Young, Center for Information Technology and Strategy.

DiMaggio, P. J., & Powell, W. W. (1991). The Iron Cage Revisited: Institutional Isomorphism and Collective Rationality in Organizational Fields. In W. W. Powell, & P. J. DiMaggio (Eds.), *The New Institutionalism in Organizational Analysis* (pp. 63–82). Chicago & London: The University of Chicago Press.

Furusten, S. (1995). *The Managerial Discourse – a study of the creation and diffusion of popular management knowledge.* Uppsala: Department of Business Studies, Uppsala University.

Hammer, M., & Champy, J. (1993). *Reengineering the Corporation: A Manifesto for Business Revolution.* New York: Harper Collins Publishers.

Hatchuel, A., & Weil, B. (1995). *Experts in Organizations – A Knowledge-Based Perspective on Organizational Change.* Berlin: Walter de Gruyter.

Heusinkveld, S., & Benders, J. (2002). Between Professional Dedication and Corporate Desing – Exploring Forms of New Concept Development in Consultancies. *International Studies of Management and Organization,* 32(4): 104–122.

Huczynski, A. (1993). *Management Gurus.* London: Routledge.

Kieser, A. (1998). Unternehmensberater – Händler in Problemen, Praktiken und Sinn. In H. Glaser, E. F. Schröder, & A. v. Werder (Eds.), *Organisation im Wandel der Märkte* (pp. 191–226). Wiesbaden: Dr. Th. Gabler Verlag.

Kubr, M. (2002). *Management Consulting – a guide to the profession* (4th edition Ed.). Geneva: International Labour Office.

Meyer, J. W. (1994). Rationalized Environments. In W. Scott, & J. W. Meyer (Eds.), *Institutional environments and organizations* (pp. 28–54). Thousand Oaks, CA: Sage.

Meyer, J. W., & Rowan, B. (1991). Institutionalized Organizations: Formal Structure as Myth and Ceremony. In W. W. Powell, & P. J. DiMaggio (Eds.), *The New Institutionalism in Organizational Analysis* (pp. 41–62). Chicago: The University of Chicago Press.

O'Shea, J., & Madigan, C. (1997). *Dangerous Company.* London: Nicholas Brealey Publishing.

Peters, T. (1992). *Liberation Management.* New York: Alfred A. Knopf.

Pringle, E. G. (1998). Do Proprietary Tools Lead to Cookie Cutter Consulting? *Journal of Management Consulting,* 10(1): 3–7.

Rigby, D. (2001a). Management Tools and Techniques: A Survey. *California Management Review*, 43(2): 2139–2160.

Rigby, D. (2001b). Putting tools to the test: senior executives rate 25 top management tools. *Strategy and Leadership*, 29(3): 4–12.

Rogberg, M., & Werr, A. (2000). Om acceptansen av populära managementmodeller – en studie av införandet av BPR. *Nordiska Organisationsstudier*, 2(1): 107–128.

Røvik, K. A. (1998). *Moderne organisasjoner – Trender i organisationstenkningen ved tusenårsskiftet*. Bergen: Fagbokforlaget.

Sartain, L. (1998). Why and How Southwest Airlines Uses Consultants. *Journal of Management Consulting*, 10(2): 12–17.

Sarvary, M. (1999). Knowledge management and competition in the consulting industry. *California Management Review*, 41(2): 95–107.

Sturdy, A. (1997). The Consultancy Process – an Insecure Business. *Journal of Management Studies*, 34(3): 389–413.

Suddaby, R., & Greenwood, R. (2001). Colonizing knowledge: Commodification as a dynamic of jurisdictional expansion in professional service firms. *Human Relations*, 54(7): 933–953.

Taylor, F. W. (1911). *The Principles of Scientific Management*. New York: Harper & Brothers.

Werr, A. (1999). *The Language of Change – the roles of methods in the work of management consultants*. PhD Thesis, Stockholm School of Economics, Stockholm.

Werr, A., & Stjernberg, T. (2003). Exploring Management Consulting Firms as Knowledge Systems. *Organization Studies*, 24(6): 881–908.

Werr, A., Stjernberg, T., & Docherty, P. (1997). The Functions of Methods of Change in Management Consulting. *Journal of Organizational Change Management,* 10 (4): 288–307.

Chapter 6

The power of science and the science of power

MATS ALVESSON AND HUGH WILLMOTT

Introduction by Mats Alvesson

It is not uncommon to view knowledge in positive terms. Knowledge is frequently seen as a functional resource that contributes to positive outcomes. Professions such as consultancy are often regarded as knowledge-based, either using their knowledge and/or contributing with knowledge as an output. Higher education, on-the-job-training, experience, and interactions between professionals are considered to be key elements of a consultant's background. This is what characterizes a consultant's work – the use of knowledge in combination with qualified judgement and creativity. Quite often, the result consists of knowledge: a report consisting of a description and analysis of a spesific phenomenon: situation-analysis of an industry, the characteristics and perceptions of customers, sources of inefficiencies in an organization, etc.

Knowledge is often thought of in academic terms. Sound knowledge is a result of science or is at least somehow dominated by science and its representatives. Schools and universities are considered to be the institutions that provide profound knowledge.

Consultants frequently rely, more or less explicitly, on knowledge associated with science. Management and organizational consultants tend to regard the social sciences as a mixed blessing – they provide some status and is seen as more respectable than many other forms of knowledge, but at the same time, they are abstract, theoretical, and do not offer clear direction or tangible results.

There is much uncertainty, conflict, and doubt in many of the contemporary fields of social sciences. It is difficult for anyone to claim that they possess or can use objective and reliable knowledge in an unproblematic way. Knowledge is increasingly viewed as partial, biased, and often influenced by values and interests. While there has been a lot of debate around the social sciences and their ties to values and special interests over the years, from Weber and onwards, certain trends and developments have underscored the depth and importance of these ties. One element of great importance to this book is the paradigm debate. Theories and forms of knowledge are not just reflections of reality, but are heavily influenced by the worldview from which they emerge. It is not so much the world itself that informs outcomes of knowledge projects – whether academic research or consultancy assignements – as it is the assumptions on which this world view is based. Burrell & Morgan (1979) emphasize the significance of ontology (the nature of the world), epistemology (the character of the knowledge that we can develop), human nature (do individuals exist as autonomous beings, are they contingent upon social processes, or are they constituted by various discourses?), and the nature of society (a gigantic family, a huge market, a jungle, a madhouse?).

It is one thing to acknowledge that knowledge, and efforts to use knowledge, are related to, and even infused with values and interests. It is another thing altogether to bring this insight into reflective knowledge development, whether as researcher, consultant, or any form of professional. When approaching an organization as a school, we are not open and neutral. Do we assume that this is a system for developing knowledge, a socialization agency, or a regulatory institution for keeping adolescents away from the streets? Does the school system reflect a 'knowledge society', demanding a lot of education and qualification? Or is the contemporary school about producing a specific kind of people, well prepared for the mix of paid labour, adaptivity, and the desire for fun and entertainment, that perhaps characterizes today's society? Or is the current school reflective of postindustrial society, where machines and rationalizations have radically reduced the number of jobs or need/possibilities for employment and where the challenge is to keep as many as possible busy?

Most proponents of knowledge – in one form or another – emphasize knowledge as innocent, neutral, or positive. But knowledge is not always that harmless. As Foucault said, the problem with knowledge is not whether it reveals or distorts the truth, the problem is that it creates the truth. We used knowledge of strategy to create companies based on ideas of portfolios and conglomerates in the 70's, and on the theory of concentrating on core competence and outsourcing in the 90's. This knowledge leads to different realities being formed. Ideas on leadership encourage managers that used to focus on administration and supervision to try 'coaching' and communicate visions – but according to our research many managers have great problems complying with the current norm of 'leadership'. The current interest in 'emotional intelligence' fits with what some people refer to as the narcissistic culture and the therapeutic society and an increasing preoccupation with one's self, and one's emotions, and the cult of intimacy in the workplace. This could be the outcome of the rapid expansion of professions and knowledge forms concerned with engineering and optimizing the self – the execution of power thus invades, and may even overwhelm – the inner lifes of people.

The fact that science and knowledge can never be separated from the social context in which it was created – and the values and interests that characterize their context, and that science and knowledge can be used for different purposes, has often been the subject of debate. It is, however, important to emphasize that science and knowledge 'in themselves' tend to fuse with and embody interests, values and power effects. The following chapter attempts to illustrate this point through a discussion of Weber's view on science and values and of the more radical position taken by Critical Theory.

The power of science and the science of power
by Mats Alvesson and Hugh Willmott

The development of modern Western societies has been dominated by two principal powers, capitalism and science, both of which have been supported and promoted by patriarchal values and priorities. A critical basis for analysing the former was established by Marx whose reflections upon the historical potency of scientific thinking were restricted to an appreciation of its role in industrializing the labour process, and thereby securing the subsumption of labour under pressures for accumulation. Comparatively overlooked by Marx was the revolutionary but *equivocal* role of scientific thinking in debunking conventional wisdoms and identifying as normative all political and ethical claims that could not be empirically proven. The equivocality of science was addressed more directly by Weber and has been a central focus for Critical Theory. This chapter explores the relationship between knowledge, values, and power. At its centre are the questions of what counts as science and what are the limits of its authority. Why are we concerned with such questions? Not only because, in modern societies, science is the dominant source of legitimate knowledge but also because science tends to encourage the view that objective, value-free knowledge is attainable. The latter view is questionable and potentially dangerous.

The idea of value-free knowledge is questionable because it deflects attention from how, in practice, what counts as 'scientific knowledge' is the product of value judgement (e.g. about ontology and epistemology) that are conditioned by the specific, historical, and cultural contexts of their production. Whatever grand claims science may make, its knowledge remains a contingent product of the particular values that give it meaning and direction. For this reason, it makes little sense to counterpose 'science' to 'ideology', as if it were possible to generate impartial, non-ideologist knowledge about an independently given world. Instead, the term ideology is more appropriately applied to whatever knowledge is revealed to be partial when inflated claims to be neutral, acontextual, 'scientific', etc. are debunked. Social science has often given a spurious credibility to managerial expertise, and thereby provides a seemingly authoritative justification for the exercise of particular kinds of management control. It is this that makes the idea of value-free scientific knowledge potentially dangerous, especially when the aura of science is used, more or less consciously, to inhibit or suppress debate about the desirability of ends as well as the rationality of means. We develop this argument in the reminder of this chapter.

We begin by considering the view that social science is, or should be, value-free. We do this for two principal reasons. First, because the idea of value-freedom continues to exert an appeal that is as seductive as it is perilous – and not least among management academics who, since the appearance of Frederick Taylor's *Principles of Scientific Management* (1911), have sought to revise his ideas rather than contest their scientific aspirations. Second, we contend that an appreciation of the principled advocacy of value-free science, though ultimately mistaken, is helpful in illuminating key issues and problems that bedevil claims to be able to produce objective knowledge.

We then draw upon the influential paradigm framework developed by Burrell and Morgan (1979) to illustrate the claim that different value-commitments, analysed in terms of contrasting combinations of assumptions about science and society, are productive of different forms of knowledge. We commend the heuristic value of Burrell and Morgan's framework for mapping and clarifying differences of approach to the study of social and organizational phenomena. However, while we accept the heuristic value of their framework, we reject Burrell and Morgan's claim that paradigms are mutually exclusive (Willmott, 1990, 1993). In preference, we commend Habermas' theory of cognitive interests on the grounds that the production of different kinds of knowledge is formulated in relation to 'human interests' rather than their allegiance to particular sets of ideas about science and society, and support his related plea for their mutual advancement.

The limits of science and the challenge to technocracy

The belief that science, including management science, can produce objective knowledge assumes that it is possible, ultimately, to remove all 'subjective bias'. When armed with what are believed to be the objective facts, there is then the prospect of organizing and managing people in Taylor's (1911) advocacy of Scientific Management is perhaps the most celebrated example of such thinking. That Taylor dubbed his philosophy 'scientific' was no accident; he fervently believed that he had identified practice from established methods of management.[1] Technocratic disciples of Taylor, the most recent of whom are the advocates of Business Process and refine his project — often by incorporating more sophisticated theories of coherence of the technocratic impulse to perfect the scientific control of human productivity.

It is precisely the use — and/or abuse — of scientific thinking to promote and legitimize all kinds of divisive and destructive social technologies that

---

[1] Whereas established management practice relied upon the vagaries of custom and practice, Taylor's scientific principles claimed to articulate the rational specification of managerial and worker behaviour. Taylor took it for granted that everyone has a broadly equal stake in productive activity — managers and workers as well as shareholders — and would therefore each accept the rationality of his principles of organization. Quite apart from the resistance of shopfloor workers who resented the loss of control over the pace and variety of their work, Taylor failed to grasp that managers — the experts — would not be unequivocally unenthusiastic about the additional burden of responsibility that his system placed upon them. Although the realization of this technocratic vision was found to be flawed by its unrealistic assumptions, Taylor's ideas did much to cement the ideal of managerial prerogative and control. Subsequent revisions of management theory have rejected his principles without abandoning his technocratic vision.

Weber (1948, 1949) sought to confront and resist. Even so, Weber's attitude toward science is deeply ambivalent. On the one hand, he identifies science as a powerful, positive force for dispelling myths and prejudices: it strips away preconceptions to reveal unvarnished facts.[2] By drawing upon scientific findings, Weber argues, modern individuals can become less deluded about themselves and their world. They can also better identify how their commitment to particular values might be more effectively fulfilled. In these respects, science is understood to make a potent contribution to the development of individual clarity and responsibility. On the other hand, Weber is deeply disquieted by the disenchanting effects of science upon established traditions and moral values. Where the limits of scientific authority are not adequately appreciated, he cautions, its debunking power can be destructive of institutions and practices that, despite being scientifically indefensible, are nonetheless highly fulfilling and meaningful for those who participate in them.

In short, Weber sees both the enlightening and the destructive aspects of scientific knowledge and is therefore concerned that its limits be fully appreciated and respected. This concern is addressed in his insistence upon sharply distinguishing between (a) the production of facts by science and (b) the making of value-judgements about the merits of social institutions. Science, Weber contends, simply presents the facts; it cannot require the individual to accept these facts or to comply with their demands if these contradict the ultimate values to which the individual is committed. Questions of how to arbitrate between several different conflicting ends, for example, are deemed to be 'entirely matters of choice and compromise. There is no (rational or empirical) scientific procedure of any kind whatsoever which can provide us with a decision here' (Weber, 1949, p. 67). In short, fundamental to Weber's position is the claim that there is no scientific way of adjudication between competing norms of behaviour. Views about life 'can never be the products of increasing empirical knowledge' (ibid.: 576; see also Weber, 1948, p. 143).

---

[2] Underpinning Weber's understanding of the role of science in modern society is his existential view that the social world is essentially meaningless and devoid of ethical content. Since the world is ethically irrational, whatever meanings (or ethics) are ascribed to the world are endowed entirely by the, more or less intentional, commitment of human beings to particular values and projects. This understanding emphasizes the responsibility of human beings for the interpretations and choices that are made – a responsibility that cannot be shuffled off onto an allegedly absolute authority, whether this takes the form of, for example, the Bible of science.

Weber's conception of science aspires to accommodate and strengthen the process of self-formation whereby individuals wrestle with the claims of competing values (see Willmott, 1993). He does not want science to weaken or terminate the self-formation process by suggesting that there are authoritative, scientific answers to the fundamental human dilemmas of value-commitment. For Weber, it is *value-rational* to acknowledge the *scientific* indefensibility of a particular belief or practice but, nonetheless, to be *personally* fully committed to it. For Weber, the danger is that scientific knowledge is (mis)understood and applied in ways that impede or mystify the process of self-formation – for example, by suggesting that only one way of organizing work is 'scientific' and, by implication, that alternatives must be rejected. Though seductive, this kind of reasoning is unacceptable because, from a Weberian standpoint, human action that is worthy of the name (i.e. is not simply reactive, impulsive, or driven by immediate material self-interest without reference to ultimate values that provide life with meaning) involves an exercise of judgement that cannot legitimately be replaced by scientific authority. While science can inform us about the likely implications of making a particular choice, it cannot remove from individuals the responsibility for choosing between competing ultimate values.

Weber's conception of the nature and limits of value-free science is of critical importance because it directly challenges the use and/or abuse of science to support or legitimate particular values or projects and, in principle, undercuts modern technocratic decision making in which allusions and appeals are routinely made to the scientific authority of experts. For example, it directly challenges the coherence of the claim made by the champions of Business Process Reengineering (BPR) that BPR is value-free insofar as it 'begins with no assumptions and no givens' (Hammer and Champy, 1993, p. 33). Commenting upon the common misconception that an accumulation of facts can resolve choices between values, Weber observes that

> "If the notion that (value-) standpoints can be derived from the 'facts themselves' continually recurs, it is due to the naive self-deception of the specialist who is unaware that it is due to the evaluative ideas with which he unconsciously approaches his (sic) subject matter, that he has selected from an absolute infinity a tiny portion with the study of which he *concerns* himself." (Weber, 1949, p. 82)

We might, for example, think of the manager who, looking at a set of accounts, declares that 'the facts speak for themselves' when seeking to justify the need for additional investment or when making a case for compulsory redundancies. Or we might think of the politician or management consultant who declares that leaders' intent upon making changes that lack widespread support 'often have no choice in how they deal with those attempting to impede their efforts' (Hammer, 1994, p. 47). From a Weberian standpoint such claims are bogus because, no matter how many facts are accumulated about a particular subject (e.g. management), they will be insufficient in themselves to adjudicate between different value-standpoints – for example the standpoint of those who are resistant to its appeals. The denial of choice is an exercise of power, not of rationality. Or, to put this in a way that anticipates the critique of Weber's arguments from the perspective of Critical Theory (see below), the facts only speak for themselves – as 'truth' – when relations of power ensure that their basis in a value-standpoint is unacknowledge and/or undetected.

An evaluation of the Weberian vision

Anxious that the idea of science would be enlisted by all kinds of cranks and demagogues to justify and champion their personal convictions (both Hitler and Hammer come to mind ... See Bauman, 1989), Weber sought to make a sharp division between values and facts, arguing that facts could *inform* the process of making value-judgements but could not legitimately *prove* or *justify* value-judgements since this would necessarily involve a leap of faith (Weber, 1949, p. 55). For Weber, Scientific Method (in the singular) can determine the facts; but any amount of facts cannot, in themselves, disprove a value-judgement.

The idea that management can be made scientific – extolled in the notion of 'management science' and most famously promoted in Taylor's (1911) *Principles of Scientific Management* – clearly illustrates Weber's anxieties that the jargon of science could be used, in a specious way, to 'prove' the objective superiority of particular evaluative ideas. The separation of facts and values, Weber believed, or at least hoped, would allow science to progress unhindered by value-judgements. And, at the same time, it would procure a space for individuals to develop their own political and ethical views without being tyrannized by the seemingly compelling authority of scientific facts. What sense are we to make of Weber's ideas about the possibility of value-free knowledge? Can they withstand critical scrutiny?

Weber accepts that the choice and constitution of the topic of scientific investigation is 'coloured by our value-conditioned interest' (Weber, 1949, p. 76). But *he does not admit* that the commitment of science to objectivity is necessarily refracted through diverse sets of value-commitments – a social and political process that produces *different forms* of scientific knowledge. Where his argument founders is in its failure to recognize and accept that *different value standpoints promote their own distinctive conception of science*. Weber does accept that the production of facts about specific topics always depends upon a pre-existing dominant value-standpoint, but he does not reflect critically upon this insight (cf. Habermas, 1988, p. 16). Weber notes how the evaluative ideas with which the scientist approaches the subject matter enables him or her to select 'from an absolute infinity a tiny portion with the study of which he (sic) *concerns* himself' (Weber, 1948, p. 82, emphasis added), *but* he spares science from this thesis. In other words, the particular value-standpoint of science cannot be problematized within the scientific realm. In effect, this means that the scientist *qua* scientist is in no position to challenge the relevance or desirability of the agenda set by the dominant value-standpoint. The scientist simply takes up for investigation whatever 'portion of existing concrete reality (that) is coloured by our value-conditioned interest' (Weber, op. cit.).

Positively, Weber's advocacy of the value-free principle is to be welcomed insofar as it helps counter the irrational, modernist tendency to justify and realize particular value-commitments by exploiting the (seemingly incontrovertible) authority of science. By informing each individual's pursuit of valued ends, science (as contrasted with dogma and ideology) is understood to make an important, and perhaps the most important, contribution to the development of a more rational society. However, in Weber's formulation, the contribution of science is necessarily limited as it is excluded from the sphere in which choices are made between ultimate values. In this sphere, Weber contends, moral philosophy may be of assistance in identifying and debating the rights and wrongs of different ultimate values. But, reason and science can play no direct part in determining the choice of values. Why not? Because choices between competing values involve a leap of faith, a leap that is fundamentally non-rational.

This disturbing conclusion has been questioned by critical thinkers who have argued that the claimed separation between 'science' and 'morality' or between 'is' and 'ought' is itself unconvincing, except as a rhetorical gambit, because it fails to acknowledge that the scientist engages the reader or audience in a process of persuasion, and not mere demonstration. As Giddens (1989, pp. 291–2) has observed, 'I do not see how it would be possible to maintain the division between "is" and "ought" presumed by Weber ... Whenever we look at any actual debates concerning social issues and related observations, we find *networks of factual and evaluative judgements, organised through argumentation*' (emphasis added). Critical thinking questions the Weberian claim that the realms of science (facts) and values (judgements) are, in reality, ever separate or separable; and argues that to make this assumption is to be seduced and duped by an illusion of 'pure theory' which assumes the possibility of generating knowledge that is untainted by the practical embeddedness of theory in worldly ways of thinking about knowledge.[3]

Critical Theory (CT) shares Weber's concerns insofar as it seeks to mobilize the debunking capacity of science while avoiding the use/abuse of science to justify political and ethical claims. But, in contrast to Weber, CT situates the impulse of science firmly in the Enlightenment tradition. That is to say, it retains a belief in the possibility of applying reason to *dissolve,* and not just to expose, forms of irrationality – ignorance, superstition, dogmatism, etc. Whereas the Weberian response to potential abuses of science is to insist upon the strict separation of facts and values. Critical Theory argues that facts are invariably imbedded in particular value-standpoints; and that, ultimately, the adequacy of scientific claims should be judged in terms of their contribution to the (dynamic) project of Enlightenment, and not in terms of their (static) reflection of social realities.

What, then, is the position on science developed within the tradition of Critical Theory? It is difficult to generalize. Nonetheless, we can say that instead of regarding reason as something that is found in pure form in the work of science, CT argues that the practical realization of this ideal, to

---

[3] Critical Theory contends that science becomes ideological when its roots in the suffering of being and the preconditions of communication are forgotten. Pure theory, Habermas (1972, pp. 314–5) argues, 'wanting to derive everything from itself, succumbs to unacknowledged external conditions and becomes ideological. Only when philosophy discovers in the dialectical course of history the traces of violence that deform repeated attempts at dialogue and recurrently close off the path to unconstrained communication does it further the process whose suspension it otherwise legitimated: mankind's evolution toward *Mundigkeit*. *Mundigkeit* can be loosely translated as autonomy and responsibility in the conduct of life.'

which science aspires, is conditional upon transforming the social relations in which it is produced. From the standpoint of Critical Theory, a fundamental, emancipatory impulse of critical is not to create or refine scientific knowledge of the world but, rather, to challenge and transform relationships that are productive of socially unnecessary suffering. CT directly contests the equation of reason with bourgeois science, as endorsed and defended by Weber.

In sum, Weber's understanding of science assumes the possibility of the value-free scientist standing outside of, or above, the society in which s/he works. For Weber, a key question is how the value and limitations of scientific knowledge can best be appreciated and recognized by those individuals (necessarily an élite) who have the opportunity to reflect upon its findings in order to frame and inform their choices. In contrast, CT focuses upon the political conditions of knowledge generation and dissemination. Its focus is not the deliberations of the individual decision maker but the structures of communication that impede or promote the very opportunity and facility to engage in such deliberations.

The social production of sciences

We have noted that any appreciation of how power relations operate to define the methods of science, and not just its agendas, is marginalized in Weber's understanding of science. His doctrine of value-freedom also excludes any rational basis for mounting a challenge to the determination of topics (and scientific procedures) by dominant values. Indeed, a perverse consequence of the Weberian doctrine of value-freedom – dubbed by Gouldner (1973, p. 63) a 'salvational myth' – has been its succouring of an ideology of scientism that represents particular knowledge-claims produced by Scientific Method as indisputably authoritative. Instead of leaving a space for critical reflection, as Weber intended, scientism ineluctably acts to devalue and frustrate processes of clarification and the development of responsibility. As science is equated with value-free knowledge, all other forms of knowledge are obliged either to defer to scientistic discourse by striving to comply with its terms, or to become marginalized as unscientific. As Habermas wryly observes, when 'science attains a monopoly in the guidance of rational action, then all competing claims to a scientific orientation for action must be rejected' (Habermas, 1974, p. 264).

In contrast, Critical Theory starts from the understanding that whatever is deemed to be objective knowledge, whether by scientists or lay persons, is conditioned by power relations in which competing ideas, methods and findings are developed and sanctioned as authoritative forms of knowledge. CT urges that human reason be mobilized to interrogate and challenge the rationality of this knowledge, and not merely to investigate or to perfect its generation. In other words, *contra* Weber, CT directly presupposes and champions the possibility of a critical science that addresses and strives to promote the *rationality of ends* as well as the rationality of means. The Weberian conception of science is preoccupied with the refinement of 'methodology' for discovering the 'truth' about some portion of 'reality'. CT, in contrast, is concerned to show how representations of Reality and Truth are conditioned and coloured by the social relations through which truth claims are articulated and accepted. Only by transforming these relations, CT argues, is it possible to develop less partial or dogmatic representations of their reality – a shift in understanding that can itself create important conditions for social change.

As we noted above, the Weberian doctrine of value-free knowledge is an example of what Habermas (1972) terms 'the illusion of pure theory' – the belief that perfect, historical, disembodied knowledge can be produced by imperfect, historical, embodied (human) beings. When caught within this illusion, it is assumed that (scientific) knowledge can be separated from the politics that impel its production. For CT, in contrast, a belief in the idea that 'facts' can be separated from values and interests is symptomatic of a forgetfulness of the connection between the production of knowledge and the practical, human problems – of self-consciousness and self-determination – that arise out of the 'cultural break with nature' (ibid.: 312) and which cannot be suspended even when involved in science. We now elaborate this understanding.

Three types of science

The production of scientific knowledge, Habermas (1972) argues, is rooted in the distinctive relationship of human beings to nature. In an effort to come to terms with the openness of this relationship – that is, the cultural break with nature – three basic knowledges are stimulated, each of which is susceptible to more rigorous, scientific development. First, the relationship to nature provokes a cognitive interest in gaining greater *pre-*

diction and control over unruly natural and social forces. Guided by this cognitive interest, diverse kinds of technologies have been developed in attempts to calculate and master the behaviour of humans as well as the elements of the natural world. This type of science, which Habermas characterizes as 'empirical-analytic', is not confined to the natural sciences but penetrates the social sciences, including the field of management and organization studies. It is manifest, for example, in the studies that have sought to identify the contingencies that are deemed to render employee productivity and consumer behaviour more predictable and controllable.

The second type of knowledge arises from the efforts of human beings to *understand and communicate with each other*. The purpose of such communication, Habermas contends, is not simply to improve our capacity to predict and control the natural and social worlds. Developing a fuller understanding of the lifeworlds of other people, he maintains, can be a meaningful and fulfilling project in itself. The cognitive interest that prompts the development of this kind of knowledge is not prediction or manipulation, but a concern to enhance mutual understanding. In the guises of the *historical-hermeneutic sciences,* this knowledge-constitutive interest seeks, for example, to enrich our appreciation of what organizational work means to people, thereby improving our ability to comprehend their world and enabling us to communicate more easily with them. In the field of management, the mobilization of this interest goes beyond the identification of variables that condition human behaviour (e.g. employee productivity); treated as producers or customers, irrespective of what instrumental uses such knowledge may have.

The appreciation and understanding of other's social worlds can be illuminating and even enlightening. But it can also leave unexamined and unchallenged the historical and political forces that condition these worlds, and the content and process of understanding their reality. An attentiveness to the relationship between the exercise of power and the construction and representation of reality is the province of *critically reflective* knowledge, the production of which, Habermas argues, is motivated by an *emancipatory interest*. The distinguishing feature of this interest resides in a concern to expose forms of domination and exploitation – such as, for example, the connection between experiences of frustration and suffering and the existence of patriarchal practices and institutions – that can, in principle, be transformed. In the form of *critical science,* knowledge is generated that discloses such connections by *reconstructing* the processes whereby 'relations of dependence' become 'ideologically frozen' (Habermas, 1972, p. 310). While having an affinity with historical-hermeneutic science, the focus of critical science is upon the role of power in institutionalizing and sustaining needless forms of oppression, confusion, and suffering. When this concern to expose forms of domination goes beyond a purely abstract, academic orientation, it takes the form of *critique*.

The pros and cons of the historical-hermeneutic and critical sciences has been debated by Habermas and Gadamer and, in the field of organization and management studies by Van Maanen and Deetz (Putnam et al., 1993, pp. 221–35). Taking the side of critical science against that of the ethnographers' concern to provide a persuasive account of the field of study, Deetz has observed:

> "The quality of research from a critical theory standpoint is not based on the ability to tell a good tale but on the ability to participate in a human struggle – a struggle that is not always vicious or visible but a struggle that is always present. Research should be part of a larger human struggle rooted in the right to participate in the construction of meanings that affect our lives." (ibid.: 227)

Critical science is concerned to understand how the practices and institutions of management are developed and legitimized within relations of power and domination (e.g. capitalism, patriarchy) that, potentially, are capable of transformation. Conventional approaches to the generation of knowledge about management assume that established relations of power and authority are prefiguratively rational, though as yet imperfectly so. Their mission is to produce more accurate knowledge of the reality of management so that a more efficient and effective allocation of resources can be achieved. Critical analysis subjects the rationality of such understandings and objectives to close scrutiny, arguing that the espoused rationality of conventional management theory and practice takes for granted the prevailing structure of power relations and is preoccupied with preserving the status quo, to the detriment of advancing a more rational society in which socially unnecessary forms of domination are addressed and progressively eliminated. This look can be read as a modest contribution to this project. To the extent that critical analysis provides insights that provoke or facilitate emancipatory personal and social change, it also contributes to critique.

The unfolding of critical thinking about management and organization

In recent years, there has been a growing scepticism on the relevance and value of empirical-analytical forms of science (see above) for addressing and solving the problems of modern society. This weakening of confidence is evident in the more progressive texts and commentaries on management and organization (see chapter 1 in Alvesson, M. & Willott, H., 1996). Less is heard about 'management/organization science'; more is heard about 'management/organization studies'. Less is heard about the authority of hard facts; more is heard about the persuasive power of symbols and metaphors. In this process, established analyses and prescriptions have not been displaced. But they have been complemented and somewhat unsettled by alternative perspectives. Agendas of theory and practice developed by practitioners and advocates of functionalist theory (see below) have been challenged by agendas drawn from the broader terrains of social and political theory, including the intellectual traditions of phenomenology and Marxism[4] – a development that has clearly alarmed those who would prefer to establish (*trans.*: impose) a greater degree of consensus about how to make sense of management and organization (e.g. Pfeffer, 1993).

Burrell and Morgan's pathfinding *Sociological Paradigms and Organisational Analysis* (1979) (hereafter *Paradigms*), has been particularly influential in articulating and fuelling emergent doubts about the exhaustiveness of established approaches. In addition to its impact in the broad area of organization studies, this book has inspired a series of calls for a broadening of agendas in the specialisms of marketing (Arndt, 1985), accounting (Hopper and Powell, 1985), operational research (Jackson, 1982), etc. At the heart of *Paradigms* is the idea (introduced earlier), that differing value-

---

[4] Clearly, there have always been criticisms from outside the sphere of management – for example, from trade unionists and from radicals of both the Left and the Right. Those on the Left have viewed management as agents of capital whose oppressive function is to keep workers in their place. From the Right, management is criticized for building self-serving bureaucratic empires that harbour inefficiency, impede competitiveness and dampen individual initiative.

commitments, demarcated in terms of their assumptions about society and social science, result in different forms of (organizational) analysis. We now briefly outline Burrell and Morgan's four paradigms of social scientific analysis before using their framework to locate the distinctive contours and contribution of CT in relation to a number of other, closely related approaches. To do this, we suspend our doubts about Burrell and Morgan's rigid division of social and organizational knowledge into four mutually exclusive paradigms (Willmott, 1990, 1993) as we commend its heuristic value. The coherence of the framework is an issue to which we return when we compare and contrast Burrell and Morgan's (1979) conceptualization with Habermas' (1982) theory of cognitive interests, as briefly outlined above.

Competing assumptions about science and society

Burrell and Morgan (1979) draw upon diverse traditions of social and organizational analysis to identify four fundamentally different lenses, or paradigms, through which social and organizational realities can be interpreted. The four paradigms are differentiated by assumptions that are made about social science and society (see Figure 2.1). Of most direct relevance for the present discussion, Burrell and Morgan contend that each paradigm has a legitimate claim to be accepted as science. Contesting the view that only one (value-free) approach can be 'truly' scientific, they argue that both 'subjectivist' and 'objectivist' philosophies of science are coherent in their own terms. Similarly, 'consensus' and 'conflict' theories of society are understood to be as valid as each other. By perming philosophies of science with theories of society, the four distinctive paradigms of analysis are drawn up.

Subjectivist v. Objectivist Philosophies of Science Objectivist philosophies assume the existence of a reality 'out there' that can be faithfully captured or mirrored by the application of scientific methods. The reality of the social world is assumed to be similar to, if not precisely the same as, the natural world. It is believed that social phenomena can be observed and measured using equivalent methods. Typically, the favoured methodology involves the careful construction of 'objective' instruments (e.g. questionnaires) that are designed to provide comparative information about the variables that are believed to make up the social world – such as the attitudes of employees or the type and variety of roles or functions performed by managers.

Subjectivist philosophies of science, in contrast, assume that social phenomena are fundamentally different from natural phenomena and therefore cannot be mirrored or captured by so-called objective instruments. Unlike the constituent elements of nature, whose properties remain constant for all practical purposes, the social world is understood, from a subjectivist standpoint, to be continuously constructed, reproduced and transformed through intersubjective processes of communication. Only by being attentive to the meanings through which reality is rendered 'objectively' real to its members, this philosophy of science contends, can an adequate appreciation of the social world be developed. Typically, the methodology favoured by 'subjectivist' researchers requires a close involvement with those who are being researched in order to discover how the meaning of concepts – such as 'centralization' or 'prerogative' – are actually formulated and interpreted by different members of an organization, and how this meaning is negotiated and changed over time.

Regulation v. Radical Change Theories of Society The vertical dimension of the Burrell and Morgan matrix divides theories of regulation from theories of radical change. Theories of regulation assume that modern societies and their organizations are characterized more by order than by conflict. Evidence of order in organizations and society is interpreted as reflective of a fundamental equilibrium and consensus among their members. Conversely, disorder is interpreted as a temporary and necessary means of re-establishing equilibrium. Consensus is assumed or taken at face value, and attention is concentrated upon the issue of how cohesiveness and functional adaptation is accomplished and sustained. Since social order is deemed to be the outcome of an unconstrained accord between the constituent elements of organizations and society, attention is focused upon how existing mechanisms for preserving social order can be strengthened – for example, by developing mechanisms that enable dynamic equilibrium in organizations and society to be sustained.

Theories of radical change, in contrast, assume that social relations are conditioned more by contradictory pressures for transformation than by forces of continuity and integration. Evidence of consensus is associated with forms of social domination that impose or instill order and consensus through direct repression or through a repressive form of tolerance in which dissenting voices are at once accommodated and marginalized. The appearance of order and stability is then connected with, for example, processes of mass subordination to the individualizing disciplines of market relations (e.g. economic dependence) and/or insidious kinds of socialization (e.g. technocratic indoctrination through education and the mass media). Needless to say, the 'same' phenomenon, such as corporate culture, can be a topic within each tradition, but their representation of its value and effects is very different (see Alvesson, 1991).

From this radical change perspective on people and organizations, to which CT makes a key contribution (see below), the reproduction (and transformation) of prevailing institutions and routines is understood to depend upon, and be potentially blown apart by, the contradictory effects of deep-seated, institutionalized inequalities and injustices. What may traditionally appear to be natural or inevitable forms of authority (e.g. patriarchy) and sources of meaning (e.g. chauvinism) can become problematical and untenable; and the effort to restore their authority is as likely to accelerate their decline and demise as to dampen the politico-economic pressures that support them. When diverse sources of tension combine, and prove resistant to suppression or accommodation, major expressions of revolt and radical change can occur – such as the widespread revolt amongst students and workers in Western Europe in 1968 and the 'liberation' of Central Europe during the latter half of 1989.[5]

Four paradigms for analysing management

So far we have identified two contrasting conceptions of social science and two divergent ways of making sense of society. By combining subjective/objective philosophies of science and regulation/radical change theories of society, four paradigms of analysis are identified. We briefly outline

---

[5] The example of Eastern Europe serves to illustrate how the contradictions of state socialism can be contained through military oppression, routine surveillance and corruption as well as less transparent processes of indoctrination and mystification. The crushing of urban oppositional elements in China in 1989 and in Russia during 1995 and 1996 has illustrated how the use of violence by the state can be sustained and brutally exercised in the face of resistance. The coercive use of the army as well as the police during the Miners' Strike in the UK revealed the iron fist beneath the velvet glove of a modern 'democratic' state. The example of Eastern Europe also indicates how, as the coercive grin of totalitarianism is loosened, other forces can emerge to fill the vacuum. In the absence of a well-organized working class, the breakdown of order presents an opportunity for various reactionary ideologies and criminal practices to assert themselves, often with former communist *apparatchiks* remaining in key positions.

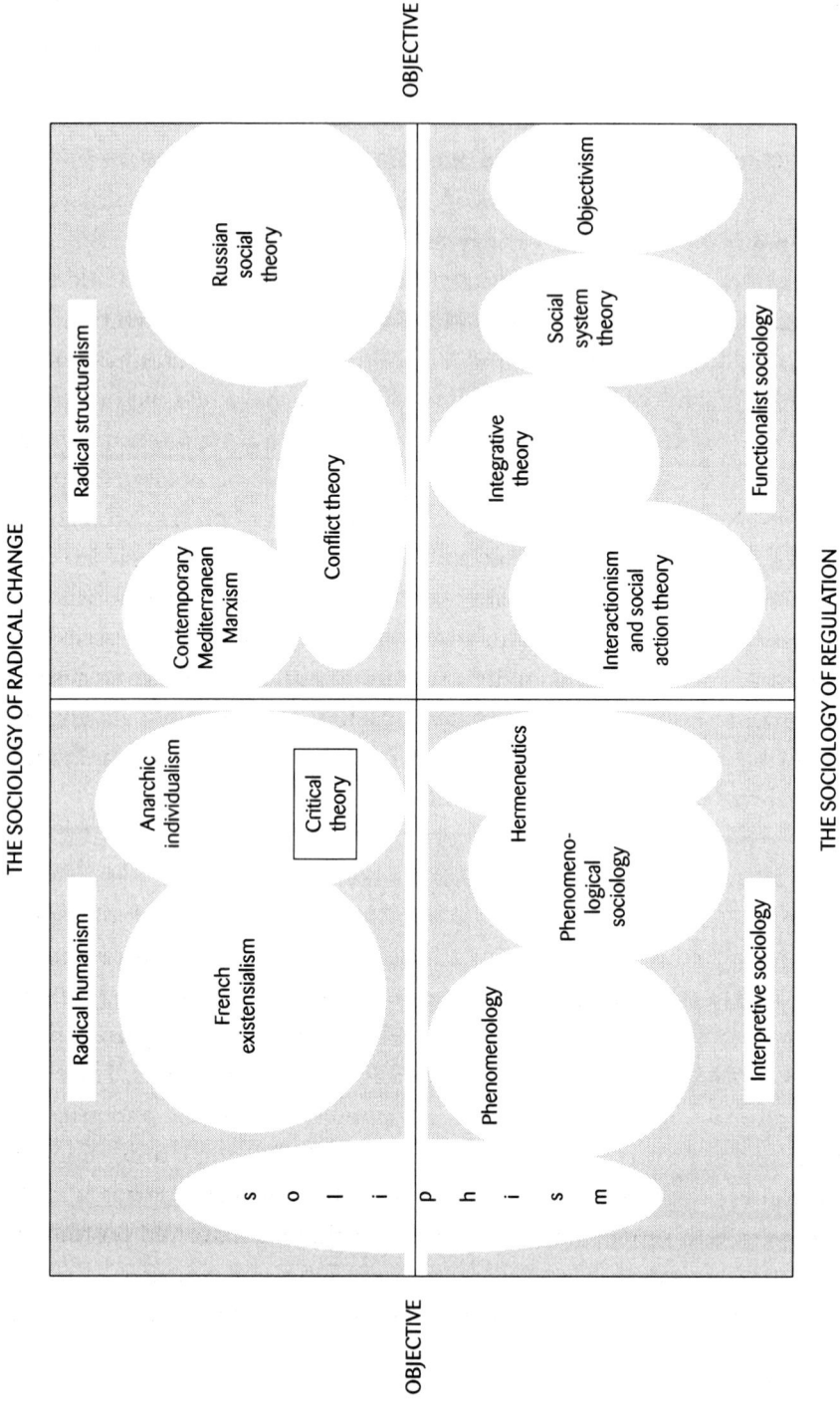

Figure 2.1 *The four sociological paradigms (Burrell and Morgan, 1979, p. 29)*

the two 'regulation' paradigms – functionalism and interpretivism – before paying more detailed attention to the radical structuralist and radical humanist paradigms.

The functionalist and interpretivist paradigms

The *functionalist paradigm* combines an objectivist philosophy of science with a regulation theory of society. Burrell and Morgan identify this as the dominant paradigm in social science and comment that it tends to be 'highly pragmatic in orientation … problem-oriented in approach … [and] … firmly committed to a philosophy of social engineering as a basis of social change' (1979, p. 26). We echoed this view when we noted how knowledge based upon assumptions of this kind has dominated management textbooks and is deeply engrained in the teaching of management in business schools. It is probably fair to say that much of the knowledge production and dissemination undertaken within this paradigm pays little attention to Weber's concerns about the use/abuse of science: much of its authority is derived from an unacknowledged reliance upon established common-sense values and understandings about what counts as respectable and responsible scientific activity. Below we will note its affinities with Habermas' conception of empirical-analytic sciences that are guided by a technical interest in production and control.

The *interpretive paradigm* is concerned to understand how people use symbols (e.g. words, gestures) to render their world 'objectively real'. Conceiving of organizational realities as 'little more than a network of assumptions and intersubjectively shared meanings' (ibid.: 29–31), this realities as comprising hard, measurable elements or contingencies. In the 1970s, the interpretive paradigm was viewed as highly esoteric, being sparsely populated by 'weirdo' phenomenologists and ethnomethodologists. Their concerns resonate most deeply with the interest in mutual understanding articulated by historical-hermeneutic science. Following a disillusionment with the capacity of 'hard', functionalist analysis to get to grips with the complexity and slipperiness of allegedly postbureaucratic and postmodern forms of organizational work, new watered-down and managerialized versions of interpretivism have been steadily seeping into management textbooks and the writings of management gurus.

The continuity of functionalist and interpretivist analysis lies in their shared reliance upon a regulation theory of society. This is most clearly evident in the interpretivist inclination to abstract its examination of processes of intersubjective meaning construction from any consideration of the relations of power and domination through which meanings are socially generated and legitimized (see quotation from Deetz, 1994, p. 51). To acknowledge and analyse these relations, it is necessary to flip from the paradigms of regulation to the paradigms of radical change.

The radical structuralist paradigm

The *radical structuralist paradigm* is distinguished by its combination of an objectivist philosophy of social science with a radical change theory of society. Organizational behaviour is understood to be conditioned, if not determined, by structures of domination – such as the institutionalized exploitation of labour within the capitalist mode of production. Fundamental to the radical structuralist paradigm is the understanding that what individuals think and do is conditioned more by the operation of structural forces than by their own consciousness or intentionality. As Burrell and Morgan (1979, p. 378) put it, 'the system as a whole retains an undiminished elementality – that is, men [sic] may seek to understand it but, like the wind or tides, it remains beyond their control'. In this regard, radical structuralism shares with functionalism an objectivist philosophy of science. Where it departs from functionalism is in its assumption that, latent within established structures, there are fundamental contradictions which render the reproduction of domination highly unstable. These contradictions are understood to account for the existence of more or less overtly coercive or insidious institutions (e.g. secret police, compulsory state education, mass media) that ensure continuity of social order. The structural contradictions, it is claimed, also explain the presence of recurrent conflicts and tensions in organizations and society – contradictions which contain within them a potential for radical change that is released whenever the structures are no longer able to regulate this instability.

When considering the development and prospects of capitalism, radical structuralists identify a basic contradiction between the organization of work within factories and offices (socialized production of goods and services) and the appropriation by capitalists of the surpluses produced by employees' labour (private accumulation of wealth) – a contradiction that, when not effectively massaged by the welfare state or checked by monetarist policies that bring high unemployment, erupts as industrial conflict and public disorder. Efforts to contain such contradictions in one area (e.g. increase unemployment to reduce wage demands) are understood to generate increased tensions in related spheres (e.g. fiscal crisis resulting from the fall in taxation revenues and added expenditure on benefits). To secure the appearance of order, reactionary and repressive measures (e.g. reduction in civil liberties, greater powers given to judiciary and police, etc.) are applied. Their effect is to re-establish order in the short term but at the risk of further undermining the legitimacy of the capitalist state. From a radical structuralist standpoint, then, the roots of social and environmental problems and disorder – as manifested in ecological crisis, widespread psychological distress, degraded work conditions, poor housing, juvenile delinquency, drug abuse, etc. – lie in the structures of capitalism. These problems may be moderated through reform. But they can be fully resolved only through a radical and revolutionary transformation of the capitalist system – a transformation which is propelled principally by systemic contradictions rather than by the efforts of people, either individually or collectively, to hasten its (inevitable) arrival.

Within the field of management and organization studies, Braverman's (1974) *Labor and Monopoly Capital* has been a major source of inspiration for the development of radical structuralist analyses of management and organization. Reviving and updating Marxian labour process analysis, Braverman directly challenges the claims of conventional accounts of work organization and employee consciousness, arguing that findings of studies concerned with job satisfaction, for example, take no account of how worker expectations are conditioned by wider structural factors. The finding that most workers report that they are 'satisfied' with their jobs, radical structuralists contend, tells us more about how employee expectations have been shaped to cope with (deskilled) work than about their degraded experience of employment (see Salaman, 1981; Sievers, 1986).

Subsequent radical structuralist analysis has challenged Braverman's tendency to equate the exercise of management control with the degradation and deskilling of work. *Contra* Braverman, it has been argued that managers will seek to deploy whatever strategies of control they find effective in improving profitability – including strategies that involve upskilling and expanding the sphere of employee autonomy, albeit within narrow limits (Friedman, 1977; Knights and Willmott, 1990). From a radical structuralist perspective, such moves are interpreted not as a process of 'humanizing work' or even of lowering the barriers between managers and managed, although this may conceivably be their, largely unintended, effect. Rather, they are interpreted either as a means of securing and/or extending management control – for example, by 'involving' workers more directly in their productive activity – or as a pragmatic, expedient move intended to reduce the costs of direct surveillance through the development of more sophisticated systems of self-discipline.

The radical humanist paradigm

Finally, in the *radical humanist paradigm,* a subjectivist philosophy of science is combined with a radical change theory of society. In common with radical structuralism, the radical humanist paradigm understands social order to be a product of coercion, rather than consent. But its focus is upon contradictions within consciousness rather than contradictions with the structures of (capitalist) society:

> "One of the most basic notions underlying the whole of this paradigm is that the consciousness of man (sic) is dominated by the ideological superstructures with which he interacts, and that these drive a cognitive wedge between himself and his true consciousness ... The major concern for theorists approaching the human predicament in these terms is with release from the constraints which existing social arrangements place upon human development." (Burrell and Morgan, 1979, p. 32, emphasis omitted)

Critical Theory has probably been the most influential of the several approaches located by Burrell and Morgan in the radical humanist paradigm. Bracketed together with the work of other neo-Marxist traditions, such as those associated with Lukacs (1971) and Gramsci (1971), Critical Theory is positioned 'in the least subjectivist region of the radical humanist paradigm' (Burrell and Morgan, 1979, p. 283),[6] and is therefore adjacent

---

[6] In this respect, Critical Theory is distanced from other elements of the radical humanist paradigm – such as the traditions of anarchism (e.g. Stirner, 1907) and existentialism (Cooper, 1990) which disregard the historical and material conditions of action. While these philosophies are directly concerned with issues of human freedom, their marginalization of the importance of the historical embeddedness of human existence leads them to become fixated upon what one Critical Theorist has characterized as the self-absorbed jargon of authenticity (Adorno, 1973).

to the radical structuralist paradigm. But, in contrast to the unmediated materialism of the radical structuralist paradigm, Critical Theory takes greater account of *the role of ideas* in the formation and reproduction of consciousness and society. For the radical humanist, the potential for radical change resides in the contradictions between, on the one side, the demands upon consciousness made by dominant (e.g. patriarchal) structures and, on the other side, the capacity of human beings to be creative and self-determining in ways that are fundamentally antagonistic to the reproduction of the status quo.

As the young Marx (1976) argued, the otherwise progressive, modernizing forces of capitalism are understood, from a radical humanist perspective, to exert the contradictory effect of alienating people from each other, from nature and from themselves. Communities are torn apart; industrial work is socially divisive; market relations transform people into commodities; people have limited opportunities for creative and spiritual growth. Through critiques of this kind, radical humanism makes its appeal to *every person* who is *oppressed within, and alienated from, modern institutions,* and not just those who are identified as members of the proletariat. The mission of radical humanist analysis is, first, to raise awareness of how 'normality' is oppressive; and, then, to facilitate the creative and self-determining liberation of individuals from the 'psychic prison' in which they/we are deemed to be incarcerated. Virtually everyone, radical humanists believe, is a victim of systemic oppression – oppression that is so taken for granted that it is routinely viewed as 'life'. But they also believe that, when subjected to critical reflection, such experience can spur and inspire critical reflection upon, and opposition to, forces of domination.

Within the paradigm of radical humanism, CT is best viewed as a key, constructive resource for advancing ideas and practices that share a commitment to the construction of a more rational society. Instead of focusing mainly, it not exclusively, upon the struggle between capital and labour over the control of the labour process and the distribution of surpluses, CT has consistently stressed the more Weberian view that the keys to understanding human interaction, including management and organization, are the meanings and ideologies through which institutions are organized and changed. For example, censuring Braverman (1974) for failing to appreciate the ideological importance of Taylorism as a mode of technocratic thinking (i.e. thinking that presents managers as impartial experts whose rule is legitimized by the possession of knowledge that would increase efficiency – see Stark, 1980), Burawoy, himself a leading exponent of labour process analysis, has drawn upon CT, noting that: 'Habermas and Marcuse [leading Critical Theorists] argue that under advanced capitalism political problems are no longer masked by the "natural" working of the market but are projected as problems of science and technology. ... The pursuit of "efficiency" became the basis of a new ideology, a new form of domination' (1985, p. 42).

While CT certainly shares Weber's attentiveness to the role of ideas in society and their potentially mesmerizing effects upon populations, it is also important, as we stressed earlier, to appreciate its distance from the Weberian standpoint on the role of social science in relation to the understanding and critique of dominant ideas and values. Weber was more influenced by the ascetic and élitist tendencies of Nietzsche than by the worldly and democratic impulses of Marx. He was resigned to a process of rationalization from which only those with exceptional moral fibre would be spared. Critical Theorists, in contrast, have kept alive the Enlightenment idea that critical reason can be mobilized to transform society, and not just to enhance the clarity and responsibility or bolster the authority of an élite. For example, if technology is to enrich rather than impoverish human experience (cf. Marcuse, 1964), it is argued that its development and use must be placed under more democratic forms of control. To this end, the values of alternative and intermediate technologies are to be commended because, quite apart from their ecological benefits, they are seen to present decentralized means of empowering local communities to develop their own solutions and shape their own fate. Whereas a Weberian standpoint favours technocratic control by a knowledgeable élite, CT stresses the value of self-determination in which material and social technologies are developed and deployed in ways that are reflective and supportive of democratic decision making. But, equally, CT distances itself from a conception of Marxism in which scientific analysis is equated with the identification and analysis of contradictions within structures that, eventually, will produce a largely predestined process of revolutionary transformation. CT is less sanguine about the inevitability of radical emancipatory change. A socially progressive outcome of the breakdown of prevailing structures is by no means assumed. Any substantial and sustained reduction in socially unnecessary suffering is understood to be conditional upon the development and dissemination of critical science (practical rationality). By advancing and applying critical science, CT seeks to realize ends that are more *practically rational,* in the sense that they are more congruent with the expansion of autonomy and responsibility. From this perspective, the attainment of practical rationality, in contrast with the refinement of technical or instrumental rationality, is at once a condition and a consequence of the open, democratic determination of ends.

Incommensurable paradigms and complementary types of science

Burrell and Morgan's (1979) identification of four paradigms of scientific analysis has been influential in opening up the field of organization and management studies to diverse traditions of social theory. By paying attention to the diversity of ideas about science and society, it has provided a basis for questioning the dominance of functionalist thinking in defining what counts (and what does not count) as 'scientific knowledge' of management and organizations. However, from a CT standpoint, there are also significant difficulties with Burrell and Morgan's contention that the four paradigms are incommensurable as this effectively protects each of them, including the functionalist paradigm, from external critique. In Burrell and Morgan's framework, a tendency within social science towards dualistic forms of analysis (e.g. individual v. society; action v. structure, etc.) is cast into a metaphysical principle. As a consequence, the possibility and coherence of studies that seek to synthesize 'subjective' and 'objective' approaches is denied (Willmott, 1990, 1993; Deetz, 1994).

Consider the case of CT. Earlier we noted that Burrell and Morgan place CT in the subjectivist realm of the philosophy of social science. However, if we examine Habermas' *Legitimation Crisis* (1975a), for example, we find that this study is no less concerned with the so-called objective structures of society than are key texts of radical structuralism, even though, as its title indicates, *Legitimation Crisis* is also attentive to issues of ideology and individual motivation that are credited to the radical humanist paradigm. In fact, and revealingly, Burrell and Morgan (1979, p. 294) acknowledge, in passing, that their framework struggles to accommodate the interparadigmatic quality of CT. Later, they are once again compelled to acknowledge that despite Habermas' attentiveness to the role of language (which marks him as a 'subjectivist' in Burrell and Morgan's eyes), he is 'at pains to stress that the theory of communicative competence must be linked to the fundamental assumptions of historical materialism if it is to be adequate and effective'; and that 'the materialist and idealist strands within Habermas's work are always yoked in a relationship of great tension, and his theoretical orientation aims at their reconciliation' (ibid.: 296). Having saddled themselves with a dualistic framework, Burrell and Morgan are forced to pigeon-hole CT somewhere. They slot it into the radical humanist paradigm, presumably on the grounds that CT is less deterministic and economistic than structuralist Marxism and, perhaps, on the more expedient grounds that, without it, the radical humanist box would be embarrassingly bereft of content.

At this point it is appropriate to return briefly to the theory of knowledge constitutive interests developed by Habermas for identifying and differentiating between types of scientific knowledge. As we noted earlier, this theory understands the production of different kinds of knowledge to be sparked by the problems and opportunities that accompany humankind's cultural break from nature – a break that signifies the release of human beings from the compulsion of instinctual drives. In contrast to Burrell and Morgan, who connect generation of knowledge with mutually incompatible sets of *ideas* about science and society, Habermas connects the production of knowledge to the materially grounded arousal of cognitive *interests*.[7] The challenge to social scientists, including students of management and organizations, posed by Habermas is not simply to extend their analyses beyond the confines of the functionalist paradigm. Rather, the challenge is to render the connection between the generation of knowledge and the realization of human interest more visible (through processes reconstruction and critical self-reflection); and thereby to promote the removal of practices and institutions that frustrate and distort processes of emancipation.

In sum, from a Critical Theoretic perspective, the Burrell and Morgan framework is flawed by its limited grasp of the connection between science/knowledge and politics/human interests. Most tellingly, Burrell and

---

[7] As we discuss in Chapter 3 in Alvesson, M. & Willmott, H., 1996, this initial formulation, which focuses upon the *consciousness* of individuals, was subsequently revised but not abandoned by Habermas when he located the emancipatory impulse in *language*.

Morgan are unreflective about how their representation of the contours of organizational analysis in a two-by-two matrix is itself value-laden or interest-guided. In Weberian fashion, their framework is presented as if it were a reflection of the terrain of organizational analysis. It thus exemplifies 'the illusion of pure theory' (see above) – albeit one whose topic is texts rather than the practices that these texts seek to report. In contrast, CT is more self-conscious about the presence and worth of values and politics in shaping particular forms of knowledge. Instead of appearing to stand outside the process of knowledge production, Habermas' theory of cognitive interests is self-consciously located, as an exemplar of critical science, *within* the terrain that it strives to elucidate and transform.

And feminism?

Setting aside for a moment the conceptual difficulties with *Paradigms*, there are also some major substantive omissions in its discussion of structural inequality and radical change. In particular, any recognition of patriarchy and feminist theory is conspicuous by its absence – a dereliction that is only partially excusable by its (late 1970s) date of preparation.[8] However, it is also relevant to acknowledge the failure of Critical Theorists to engage with feminist theory and to appreciate its significance as a social movement. That all leading Critical Theorists have been men is perhaps not unrelated to this omission. The neglect is particularly conspicuous in Habermas' case[9] because he has demonstrated such a willingness to debate with and draw upon so many other varieties of social theory. We return to feminism in Chapter 3, where its critique of Critical Theory is briefly reviewed, and also in Chapter 5 where we make passing reference to feminist organization theory. Here we briefly outline some central strands of anti-patriarchal thinking.

Feminists argue that the very structures of modern society are phallocentric and patriarchal; and that change is necessary if women (and men) are to be emancipated from male domination. *Liberal feminism* tends to share the basic assumptions of functionalism as it concentrates on promoting a narrow set of equal opportunity issues, such as the careers of female

---

[8] Subsequently, this has been partially corrected by the contribution of Gibson Burrell to the study of gender and especially sexuality in organizations (e.g. Hearn et al., 1989).
[9] The women's movement merits only a single paragraph in *The Theory of Communicative Action*, vol. 2, p. 393 (Habermas, 1987).

managers. The concerns of *radical feminists* go well beyond the demands of liberal feminists for equal opportunity (e.g. the demand that women must be able to compete without prejudice for positions presently occupied by men and must be enabled to do so by the provision of policies and services, such as child care, that allegedly make this possible). In isolation from other more radical demands, such as the equal valuing of the unpaid work in the home that many women presently do, the winning of equal opportunities does little more than legitimize dominant institutions by making them appear ungendered (Collinson et al., 1990). Since it is principally men who have defined and colonized what is acceptably 'feminine', radical feminists seek to change the institutions within and through which their sense of self-identity is constituted.

These concerns echo and support radical humanist thinking insofar as they are critical of the neglect of 'non-economic' forces in radical structuralist analysis. However, a key issue for radical feminists is the limited and marginalized critique of patriarchal structures of domination in both 'humanist' and 'structuralist' variants of radicalism (Walby, 1986). Without necessarily denying the importance of politico-economic forces and contradictions in the organization of modern societies, radical feminists highlight and question the genderedness of modern institutions. In particular, their critiques have drawn attention to how, in these work organizations, men have occupied positions of social and economic advantage, in terms of status, wealth and influence, relative to women, and have therefore been able to shape and solidify (patriarchal) forms of institutional development. The challenge of radical feminism is very far-reaching: it encompasses all manifestations of gendered practices, and not just the right of access to positions which embody patriarchal values. This includes apparently impersonal and neutral terrain, such as nature (Merchant, 1980), science (Harding, 1986) and the market (Hartsock, 1984).

Perhaps the most extreme – or most pure – form of radical resistance to patriarchy, which ostensibly amounts to a total rejection, is *separatist feminism* in which women undertake to create their own institutions by excluding participation by men on the grounds that their involvement renders social relationship violent, subordinating and demeaning. Partly as a reaction to what may be regarded as the excesses of separatist feminism (which effectively disregard or deny any active role or responsibility of women in reproducing patriarchal forms of domination), *radical postfemi-*

nism has sought to retrieve and re-value aspects of femininity (e.g. motherhood) that other varieties of radical feminism have tended to deny or reject as symptomatic of female subordination (see, for example, Freely, 1995). Radical postfeminists are concerned about the unintended, self-defeating consequences of feminisms that impede, rather than facilitate, communication with other groups who are potentially supportive of the feminist goal of dissolving patriarchal institutions (see Gore, 1992). For example, postfeminists more readily place a positive value upon the sensuality and nurturing quality of femininity, though these qualities are also seen to be distorted and exploited within patriarchal societies. In some versions, such qualities are identified with a universalistic conception of 'the feminine' (e.g. Marshall, 1993), albeit one to which both sexes have some degree of access. In other versions, what counts as 'feminine' or 'feminine values' has no essence but, instead, is understood to be historically and culturally contingent (Flax, 1990b). The latter position opens a space for addressing issues of gender relations in a way that subverts the, perhaps perverse, tendency to regard (and marginalize) 'feminism' as an exclusively women's issue (Flax, 1990a). Arguably, this stance, which challenges the dualism of masculine/feminine issues, is also more consonant with the Habermasian understanding that different types of knowledge are potentially complementary rather than irremediably incommensurable.

Within the field of management and organization, the feminist voice has been slow in being heard, probably because management theory and practice has been so long dominated by men and by discourses that privilege the trappings of masculinity (Hearn et al., 1989; Calas and Smircich, 1991). An early feminist contribution to critical organizational analysis was made by Ferguson (1984) who argues, *contra* Weber, that processes of rationalization can be resisted, and that the rise of feminism presents a potent challenge to bureaucratic values and practices. Others (e.g. Pringle, 1988; Collinson et al., 1990) have built upon and revised this foundation by showing how patterns of dominance and subordination are reproduced within work organizations. However, reference to radical feminist work has been conspicuously absent from critical textbooks and readers on organizations (e.g. Thompson and McHugh, 1995; Clegg, 1990; Alvesson and Willmott, 1992). To our knowledge, a broad and thorough feminist analysis and critique of the gendering of management theory and practice, including its inhibition or manipulation of emotionality (Mumby and

Putnam, 1992; Jaggar and Bordo, 1989), has yet to be undertaken and, indeed, is well overdue.

Summary and conclusion

In this chapter we have considered the central role played by knowledge in society: it informs and justifies how we act. Whenever knowledge is, for all practical purposes, accepted as truth – when, for example, it is taken for granted that managers make decisions or that married women go to work for pin money – some forms of action are facilitated as others are impeded. In this sense, knowledge is powerful especially when it is represented and understood as neutral and authoritative (i.e. scientific). Because knowledge is a potent medium of domination, it is necessarily a focal topic of critical analysis.

In the first part of the chapter, we deployed Weber's discussion of the role of science to challenge the claims of technocracy. Here the logic of Weber's advocacy of the value of reason in guiding human affairs was not denied. But, it was argued, the idea of one, authoritative value-free science effectively devalues and suppresses alternative knowledges and conceptions of science. Burrell and Morgan's paradigms framework was introduced to illustrate the diversity of scientific analysis. It was shown to have heuristic value in highlighting the existence of different value-based approaches to the production of scientific knowledge about organizations and management. This framework also enabled us to locate CT in the wider terrain of social scientific enquiry and provided a heuristic device for comparing and contrasting other varieties of 'radical' analysis – notably labour process theory and feminist theory. However, it was also criticized *inter alia* for encouraging the dualistic idea (of 'pure theory') that scientists can stand outside of their object of study – whether this object is the world of management and organizations or the texts that present accounts of this world. Burrell and Morgan's book usefully exposes the powerful grip of 'functionalist science' upon management and organization studies and, by relativizing its claims in relation to the other paradigms, opens a space for more radical types of inquiry. However, it simultaneously disregards the central issue of how choices are made between different kinds (or paradigms) of analysis and, relatedly, the ways in which such choices are rooted in what Habermas terms knowledge-constitutive human interests.

So, while Burrell and Morgan's framework has been helpful in opening up management and organizational studies to 'radical' analysis, it demands either a full commitment to functionalist analysis or the total rejection of it. In contrast, Habermas' formulation of three cognitive interests permits, and indeed actively encourages, the development of the empirical-analytic sciences, including functionalist analysis, *within* a broader critical vision of science as a potentially emancipatory force. In short, CT complements an appreciation of the power of science with a reflexive understanding of the science of power.

From the standpoint of Critical Theory, the central problem in making sense of social reality, including the theory and practice of management, is *not* how to rid *the* scientific method of normative bias. Such an 'objectivist' ambition cannot be fulfilled, CT argues, because facts cannot be separated from values. Nor does CT advocate, in 'subjectivist' fashion, the abandonment of epistemological questions. Instead, as Habermas has argued, different types of science are understood to be embedded in different kinds of human interests. For CT, the central issue is *what kinds* of normative bias should inform the production of knowledge. CT contends that the identification and pursuit of means and ends can be more or less rational, depending upon the openness and symmetry of the power relations through which decisions about ends are reached. Accordingly, the development of less distorted forms of knowledge is conditional upon the removal of institutional and psychological obstacles, such as patriarchy and egoism, that currently impede greater openness and symmetry.

References

Adorno, T. (1973). *The Jargon of Authenticity*. London: Routledge.

Alvesson, M. (1991). Organizational Symbolism and Ideology. *Journal of Management Studies, 28, 3*: 207–25.

Alvesson, M. & Willmott, H. (Eds.). (1992). *Critical Management Studies*. London: Sage.

Alvesson, M. & Willmott, H. (1996). *Making Sense of Management: A Critical Introduction*. London: Sage.

Arndt, J. (1985). On Making Marketing Science more Scientific: The Role of Observations, Paradigms, Metaphors, and Puzzle Solving. *Journal of Marketing, 49:* 11–23.

Bauman, Z. (1989). *Modernity and the Holocaust*. Cambridge: Polity.

Braverman, H. (1974). *Labor and Monopoly Capital*. New York: Monthly Review Press.

Burrell, G. & Morgan, G. (1979). *Sociological Paradigms and Organisational Analysis*. London: Heinemann.

Calas, M. & Smircich, L. (1991). Voicing Seduction to Silence Leadership. *Organization Studies, 12, 4*: 567–602.

Clegg, S. (1990). *Modern Organizations: Organization Studies in the Postmodern World*. London: Sage.

Collinson, D., Knights, D. & Collinson, M. (1990). *Managing to Discriminate*. London: Routledge.

Cooper, D.E. (1990). *Existentialism: A Reconstruction*. Oxford: Basil Blackwell.

Deetz, S. (1994). *Transforming Communication, Transforming Business: Building Responsive and Responsible Workplaces*. Cresskill, NJ: Hampton Press.

Ferguson, K.E. (1984). *The Feminist Case Against Bureaucracy*. Philadelphia, PA: Temple University Press.

Flax, J. (1990a). *Thinking Fragments: Psychoanalysis, Feminism, and Postmodernism in the Contemporary West*. Berkeley, CA: University of California Press.

Flax, J. (1990b). Postmodernism and Gender Relations in Feminist Theory. In L.J. Nicholson (Ed.), *Feminism/Postmodernism*. London: Routledge.

Freely, M. (1995). *What About Us? An Open Letter to the Mothers Feminism Forgot*. London: Bloomsbury.

Friedman, A. (1977). *Industry and Labour*. London: Macmillan.

Giddens, A. (1989). Response to my Critics. In D. Held & J. Thompson (Eds.), *Social Theory of Modern Societies: Anthony Giddens and His Critics*. Cambridge: Cambridge University Press.

Gore, J. (1992). What We Can Do For You! What *Can* "We" Do For "You". In C. Luke & J. Gore (Eds.), *Critical Pedagogy*. London: Routledge.

Gouldner, A. (1973). The Sociologist as Partisan. In A. Gouldner, *For Sociology: Renewal and Critique in Sociology Today*. London: Allen Lane.

Gramsci, A. (1971). *Selections from the Prison Notebooks of Antonio Gramsci*. London: Lawrence & Wishart.

Habermas, J. (1972). *Knowledge and Human Interests*. London: Heinemann.

Habermas, J. (1974). *Theory and Practice*. London: Heinemann.

Habermas, J. (1975). A Postscript to Knowledge and Human Interests. *Philosophy of the Social Sciences, 3*: 157–89.

Habermas, J. (1982). A Reply to my Critics. In J. Thompson and D. Held (Eds.), *Habermas: Critical Debates*. London: Heinemann.

Habermas, J.(1987). *The Theory of Communicative Action Volume 2*. London: Heinemann.

Habermas, J. (1988). *On The Logic of the Social Sciences*. Cambridge: Polity.

Hammer, M. (1994). Reengineering is *Not* Hocus-Pocus. *Across the Board*. September, 31, 8: 45–7.

Hammer, M. & Champy, J. (1993). *Reengineering the Corporation: A Manifesto for Business Revolution*. London: Nicholas Brealey.

Harding, S. (1986). *The Science Question in Feminism*. Ithaca, NY: Cornell University Press.

Hartsock, N. (1984). *Money, Sex, and Power: Toward a Feminist Historical Materialism*. Boston, MA: Northeast University Press.

Hearn, J., Sheppard, D.L., Tancred-Sheriff, P. & Burrell, G. (Eds.). (1989). *The Sexuality of Organization*. London: Sage.

Hopper, T. & Powell, A. (1985). Making Sense of Research into the Organizational and Social Aspects of Management Accounting: A Review of Its Underlying Assumptions. *Journal of Management Studies, 22*, 5: 429–65.

Jackson, M.C. (1982). The Nature of Soft Systems Thinking: The Work of Churchman, Ackott and Checkland. *Journal of Applied Systems Analysis, 9*: 17–29.

Jaggar, A. & Bordo, S. (1989). *Gender/Body/Knowledge: Feminist Reconstructions of Being and Knowing*. New Brunswick, NJ: Rutgers University Press.

Knights, D. & Willmott, H. (Eds.). (1990). *Labour Process Theory*. London: Macmillan.

Lukacs, G. (1971). *History and Class Consciousness*. London: Merlin.

Marcuse, H. (1964). *One-Dimensional Man: Studies in the Ideology of Advanced Industrial Society*. Boston, MA: Beacon Press.

Marshall, J. (1993). Viewing Organizational Communication from a Feminist Perspective: A Critique and Some Offerings. In S. Deetz (Ed.), *Communication Yearbook*. Vol. 16, Newbury Park, CA: Sage.

Marx, K. (1976). *Capital*. Vol. 1. Harmondsworth: Penguin.

Merchant, C. (1980). *Ecological Revolutions: Nature, Gender, and Science in New England*. Chapel Hill, NC: University of North Carolina Press.

Mumby, D.K. & Putnam, L.L. (1992). The Politics of Emotion: A Feminist Reading of Bounded Rationality. *Academy of Management Review, 17, 3*: 465–86.

Pfeffer, J. (1993). Barriers to the Advance of Organizational Science: Paradigm Development as a Dependent Variable. *Academy of Management Review, 18, 4:* 599–620.

Pringle, R. (1988). *Secretaries Talk.* London: Verso.

Putnam, L., Bantz, C., Deetz, S., Mumby, D. & Van Maanen, J. (1993). Ethnography Versus Critical Theory: Debating Organizational Research. *Journal of Management Inquiry, 2, 3:* 221–35.

Salaman, G. (1981). *Class and the Corporation.* Glasgow: Fontana.

Sievers, B. (1986). Beyond the Surrogate of Motivation. *Organization Studies, 7, 4:* 335–51.

Stark, D. (1980). Class Struggle and the Transformation of the Labor Process: A Relational Approach. *Theory and Society, 9:* 89–130.

Stirner, M. (1907). *The Ego and His Own.* London: Libertarian Book Club.

Taylor, F.W. (1911). *Principles of Scientific Management.* New York: Harper & Row.

Thompson, P. & McHugh, D. (1995). *Work Organizations: A Critical Introduction.* 2nd Edn. London: Macmillan.

Walby, S. (1986). *Patriarchy at Work.* Cambridge: Polity.

Weber, M. (1948). *From Max Weber: Essays in Sociology.* London: Routledge & Kegan Paul.

Weber, M. (1949). *The Methodology of the Social Sciences.* New York: Free Press.

Willmott, H.C. (1990). Beyond Paradigmatic Closure in Organizational Enquiry. In J. Hassard & D. Pym (Eds.), *The Theory and Philosophy of Organizations: Critical Issues and New Perspectives.* London: Routledge.

Willmott, H.C. (1993). Breaking the Paradigm Mentality. *Organization Studies, 14, 5:* 681–720.

INTRODUCTION TO PART III
Consulting in a political landscape

STEINAR BJARTVEIT

At times it seems as though the consultancy industry remains trapped in modernism. We can sense the ghosts of Fredrick Taylor and Henri Fayol looming in the background with their stopwatches and detailed plans. They hail from the time of great discoveries and inventions, a time where mysteries were unraveled and nature was conquered. It was the age of scientific method, when Man became God on this earth. With modernism came the unflinching belief that humans could control every aspect of their environment. We could reengineer or rearrange any of God's creations to make it work just the way we wanted it to. And then came the wonderful realization that our ability to control our environment was not limited to nature and all things mechanical – we could master sociology, psychology, and even business. Man himself could be decoded and managed. This was the basis for Fayol's guiding principle of plan, organize, command, coordinate, and control for all leadership (1967). And it was what caused Taylor to champion order and efficiency (even in the hotel bedroom and on the golf course) and crusade for a scientific approach to understanding administrative leadership (1980). Even today our livelihood is still firmly rooted in this tradition. The models we use reveal an analytical obsession with uncovering the fundamental principles and natural order of all things, and how they influence each other. Through rigorous attention to detail and theories of rationalization we will conquer the world – be it analysis of value chains or the balanced scorecard.

It has been suggested that organizational theory is dominated by two theoretical perspectives: cybernetic systems and cognitivism (Stacey, 2003). The first is based on the belief that the system – the totality – controls the individual. The second is premised on the belief that humans can and will follow rational decision models. These perspectives are rooted in modernism. They are the legacy of Fayol and Taylor. These perspectives are the invisible hand that governs all models of organization and strategic planning. They are the unspoken assumptions of all business truisms – not just for models of organization and strategy, but also for the manner in which consulting assignments are carried out. One of the prevailing descriptions for a consultancy process goes like this: entry-diagnosis-action planning-implementation-termination (Kubr, 2003). This is a description of a process that is based entirely on a rational decision model. This basic model pervades all the models used by the major consultancies. They're all fashioned on the same principles. We truly believe we can govern businesses and organizations, just as we believe we can manage the consultancy process.

So what could possibly be wrong with this? Isn't control and manipulation the name of the game for all consulting? Isn't this precisely the rigorous control that was championed in the previous section? One of the principal criticisms directed at modernism concerns the exaggerated and ill-founded belief in our ability to control all things. And our attempts to force this belief in rationality on our very existence. Rather than uncovering the principles of our existence – we desecrate them. Even Max Weber denounced what he termed the iron cage of rationality asserting that modernism would spawn "professionals with no spirit, hedonists with no heart" (1973, p.113). The same theme pops up again and again in films and books. From Chaplin's *Modern Times* to *A Clockwork Orange*, in *1984*, and even in *Harry Potter*! This is not to say that we should disregard all the models associated with modernism. Who could possibly deny the obvious progress we have achieved? But while modernism certainly brought us some major advances, we may have lost something along the way.

Over the past decade we have witnessed an increasing amount of criticism directed at the traditional models used in management literature (Brown & Eisenhardt, 1998; Mintzberg, 1994; Stacey, 2003). These are not light-hearted criticisms that deal with the shortcomings of particular models, but rather fundamental criticism of the assumptions on which these models are based. Do we simplify reality too much in our models – to the point where they might even be harmful? The proponents of chaos theory and complexity theory point out the dangers of using models that assume a stable and ordered existence – that bears very little resemblance to reality (Pascale, 1990; Russ, 1999; Stacey, 2003). If you swear by the consultant's traditional models you can forget all about innovation and change! This criticism is also directed at the non-political world of organizational theories. How can we possibly believe that senior executives can isolate themselves from the systems of which they are an integral part and make rational decisions – always keeping in mind what is best for the system? Such a view would make even Pollyanna blush. Because humans are quite simply not that mechanical and detached. Humans are political beings that will always champion their own interests – but this perspective is sorely missing from the models that consultants use.

This post-modernist criticism is clearly evident in the Scandinavian perspectives on organizational theory and on leadership. There are several research groups that have introduced this perspective into theories of organization and leadership, most notably at Stockholm and Lund (of which Alvesson's contribution in the previous section is a good example), but we have also seen some interesting contributions from Copenhagen and Oslo. The post-modernist criticism is more than just a critique of the oversimplified view of control found in most management literature – it goes to the very heart of the extreme positivistic tradition prevalent in the fields of organization and leadership. In fact, section II of this book could be seen as a tribute to the empirical and positivistic approach that brought the field of leadership from guesswork to science. The answer is hypothetic-deductive methodology. Karl Popper rules. However, academia is much more than this. The debate on positivism during the 1960s and 1970s revealed that there are some approaches within humanities and the social sciences that do not fit comfortably within the strict confines of a positivistic framework. However, this does not mean that consultants should revert to spiritualism and magical formulas. On the contrary, the academic requirements remain rigorous, but at the same time they also allow us to introduce concepts such as interpretation and understanding.

We usually associate hermeneutic analysis with the humanities and interpreting classical texts and as well as verse from the bible. However, these perspectives may provide a method for understanding social interaction (Alvesson & Sköldberg, 1994). The term hermeneutic is derived from the Greek God Hermes – the god that acted as messenger from Olympus. But how do we interpret messages from the gods? How do we interpret texts written thousands of years ago? You increase your understanding of the text by moving back and forth – from the parts to the whole and from the whole to the parts. By examining each part in detail, you gain insights that will have a bearing on your understanding of the whole. How can you grasp the *Iliad* without understanding the meaning of Priam's request to Achilles for the release of the body of his dead son? How can you appreciate this masterpiece without comprehending the very first sentence – that describes Achilles' rage? We gain understanding of social interaction in much the same way. The pieces help us to understand the whole, and the more we grasp the whole, the better we understand the pieces. Gradually your understanding increases, until you have reached a level of understanding beyond anything you might glean from an analyst's report. Some people suggest that this is the very essence of all consulting.

The humanities are more concerned with having a clear perception of one's own point of departure than with empirical research. You cannot interpret information neutrally. You are not a tabula rasa that observes and interprets what goes on around you with absolute neutrality and objectivity. Your understanding of what you observe will color your interpretation of events (Gadamer, 1989). Like it or not, you are prejudiced. Everyone is. The life you have lived, and the experiences you have had, will have taught you to understand and interpret events in a specific way. This might not be a problem if you are aware of your own prejudices and are able to view events from different perspectives. In fact, this may help you to gain new insights and open new horizons. As such, hermeneutic analysis is not just a method you can use to understand a specific case, it also touches upon the very heart of our existence. Because we are the one animal in the entire kingdom that is constantly searching for meaning and understanding.

This is why we have chosen to draw on some literature, in this section and the next, that is not customary in books on management literature. You will find references to Machiavelli, Shakespeare, Plato, and Aristotle. They have a very different point of departure from us, and if you are convinced that common sense is a recent phenomenon, you might not want to read these articles but rather concentrate on appropriate management articles in the acknowledged journals. We are, however, of the opinion that if a book has survived for 500 years, or even 2300 years, then this must be because it deals with universal issues that transcend the passage of time. Certainly it must resonate far beyond the context in which it was written.

In 200 years people will still be reading about Machiavelli's *Prince* and Marcus Aurelius' *Meditations*, but few will recall Michael Porter. We are standing on the shoulders of giants. People were thinking great thoughts long before our time, and they did so with such conviction and often from such an extreme perspective that it might seem frightening. But these people looked at things from a different point of view and with a tremendous clarity that can provide us with multiple perspectives that we can use to understand the issues that concern us. This is precisely why we feel that it is not enough for consultants to be familiar with the contemporary literature. They should also be well-versed in the classical literature and in the fundamental thinking that this literature rests on. This literature is a virtual treasure chest of insight that we can use to understand current issues. And in this, the post-modern age, this type of insight is a key component of what we choose to call wisdom (Sternberg, 2001).

The following chapters explore the problems associated with the oversimplified rational perspective of leadership and consultation. In chapter 7, Steinar Bjartveit examines some of the prevailing myths concerning leadership and shows how recent insights from chaos theory and complexity theory dispel these myths. He also considers what insights an old hand like Niccolo Machiavelli might have to offer us in our ever-changing and uncertain political environment. In chapter 8 Steinar Bjartveit and Göran Roos follow up on this by considering the consultation as a political scenario where the client uses the consultant for his or her own purposes. In chapter 9 Heidi Høivik assumes the opposite position and, using insights from Shakespeare's *Othello*, discusses how the consultant may harm the client, as Iago brought misery upon his charge.

What consultants should look for in this section:
- The consultant must search for meaning beyond the boundaries of traditional models and try to understand the political aspects of the assignment.
- The consultant must be willing to accept that hidden agendas are common in consultancy and realize s/he can use this to his or her advantage.
- The consultant must be aware of his or her own perspectives and of the manner and extent to which s/he influences others.

> **What clients should look for in this section:**
> - The best solution does not necessarily involve straightforward flowcharts and simple tweaks to the system.
> - The client must take care not to exert undue influence on the consultant and on the process itself – lest the leader becomes part of the problem.
> - The client must never allow him- or herself to be completely overrun by the consultant.

References

Alvesson, M. and Sköldberg, K. (1994). *Tolkning och reflektion. Vetenskapsfilosofi och kvalitativ metod.* Lund: Studentlitteratur.

Bjartveit, S. (2004). Machiavelli og ledelsesidealet. In N. Machiavelli, *Fyrsten.* Oslo: Bokklubben Jobb & Ledelse.

Brown, S.L. & Eisenhardt, K.M. (1998). *Competing on the edge. Strategy as structured chaos.* Boston: Harvard School Press.

Clegg, S.R. and Palmer, G. (Eds). (1996). *The politics of management knowledge.* Thousand Oaks: Sage.

Gadamer, H.G. (1989). *Truth and method.* (2nd revised Ed.) New York: Continuum.

Kubr, M. (2003). *Management consulting. A guide to the profession.* (4th Ed.) Geneva: International Labour Office.

Fayol, H. (1967). *General and industrial management.* Pitman.

Mintzberg, H. (1983). *Power in and around organizations.* Englewood Cliffs: Prentice-Hall.

Mintzberg, H. (1994). *The rise and fall of strategic planning.* New York: Prentice Hall.

Pascale, R. (1990). *Managing on the edge. How successful companies use conflict to stay ahead.* London: Penguin Books.

Russ, M. (1999). *The edge of organization. Chaos and complexity theories of formal social systems.* Thousand Oakes: Sage.

Stacey, R.D. (2003). *Strategic management and organizational dynamics. The challenge of complexity. 4th ed.* Harlow, England: FT Prentice Hall.

Sternberg, R.J. (2001). Why schools should teach for wisdom: The balance

theory of wisdom in educational settings. *Educational Psychologist, 36:* 227–245.
Taylor, F. W. (1980). *The principles of scientific management.* New York: W.W. Norton.
Weber, M. (1973). *Den protestantiske etikk og kapitalismens ånd.* Oslo: Gyldendal Norsk forlag.

Chapter 7 | In the realm of Fortuna

STEINAR BJARTVEIT

Introduction

Criticism of the consultancy sector has not been limited to its lack of a science. Concerns have been voiced over the theoretical basis for the models consultants wield and the interventions they propose. The consultant's toolkit is packed with simplistic 2-by-2 matrixes and flowcharts. They have contingency models for organizations of every shape and size, and key performance indicators for core competencies and competitive advantages. Most of these tools have been developed from classic theories of leadership and organizational theory. So, what could possibly be wrong with this theoretical foundation?

In recent years, questions have been raised about whether the assumptions, on which many classical theories of leadership are based, are entirely appropriate (Axelrod & Cohen, 2000; Brown & Eisenhardt, 1998; Mintzberg, 1994; Stacey, 2003). The critics would argue that if you swear by these classical theories, you run the risk of causing more harm than good. The theoretical foundation on which many of these theories rest is inadequate, and the perspective is too narrow and idealized. In the perfect world of these theories a balanced scorecard will always lead to Nirvana. But in our less than perfect reality, these models might not be appropriate.

In his 1994 book, *The Rise and Fall of Strategic Thinking*, Henry Mintzberg, one of the dons of strategic thinking, was sharply critical of the way strategic thinking is carried out in most organizations. Strategic thinking has not produced the desired results because it has developed into a bureaucratic planning system, usually headed up by a staff function. More recently, Mintzberg has warned companies against sending executives on classical MBA training programs because the subjects taught at many of these schools can be entirely inappropriate (2001). Ralph Stacey (2003) suggests that classical theories of leadership are founded on two traditions: cybernetic systems and cognitivist psychology. The first is based on the belief that there are guiding principles that govern the parties within a system, while the second is based on the belief that individuals within the system (primarily at senior levels) can liberate themselves from these guiding principles and make rational decisions that affect the system – and thus the individuals within the system. These models may be accurate to a certain extent, but they are not universal.

More recent perspectives, drawing on chaos theory and complexity theory, challenge the appropriateness of the traditional theories of leadership and organizations (Brown & Eisenhardt, 1998; Pascale, 1990; Stacey, 2003). They suggest that there are three states of existence. At opposing ends we find order and stability versus chaos and unpredictability. In the first state, all trains run according to schedule, teachers follow their guidelines, employees are predictable, and approved strategy is rolled out according to plan. At the other extreme the stock market is spinning out of control on a black Monday, the prison guards at Abu Ghair beat the people they have come to liberate, and, to the despair of every parent, children become obsessed with Pokémon figures. Both states are believable. Between these states there is an area of limited stability, where order and chaos coexist. The obvious question is: which one of these conditions most accurately represents human interaction? Certainly, at times we may experience all three states, but the prevailing one is the one in the middle – where things seem familiar, but are not necessarily predictable; where there is order, at least to a certain extent. Living in a continuous state of order and predictability, superbly illustrated in the motion picture *Groundhog Day*, would mean being condemned to relive the same day for all eternity: every morning you run into the same neighbor on your way to work; you attend the same staff meeting everyday at 11, and every evening you eat the exact same dinner (some people might suggest that this state is very real – it is called *suburbia*). Living in a continuous state of chaos would probably be like the picnic in *Deliverance*, with Jimi Hendrix and Janis Joplin along for the ride – not something most of us would enjoy. It is the in-between state that is typical for our existence.

What kind of existence are traditional theories of leadership predicated on? It would seem that the traditional theories are based on an existence characterized by order and predictability (Stacey, 2003). And in general, most of the models that consultants apply are based on these same, questionable assumptions. As such, this highly-ordered existence provides the basis for the unseen paradigm in leadership. But is this appropriate for real-world leadership?

The consultant's catechism

Within the traditional theories of leadership, there are a number of articles of faith that form the basis for the different styles of leadership as well as for the consultant's toolkit. We should take a closer look at some of these.

Believing in management-by-objectives and strategic planning

The traditional theories of management assume a state of order and predictability. Negative feedback is an intrinsic ingredient of this state. Any functioning system has feedback loops where one action may cause another action, which in turn has effect on the first action. This type of system is characterized by interdependence and reciprocal causalities, where negative feedback loops are intended to correct and prevent irregularities and return the system to equilibrium. In a sense, negative feedback works like an oven thermometer that has been set for a specific temperature – any deviations, above or below the desired temperature, are swiftly dealt with.

This type of homeostatic mechanism is characteristic of cybernetics – which is one of the fundamental principles of the current leadership paradigm (Stacey, 2003). Management-by-objectives, strategic leadership, and the balanced scorecard are all pillars of modern management literature. In reality these are cleverly disguised negative feedback systems. If you want strategic planning to pay off, you have to start with an internal and external strategic analysis of the organization's present state. And then you decide where you want the organization to go. The analysis of the gap between present state and desired direction form the basis for the strategic plan – full of goals, interim goals, and important milestones. Of course you will need an elaborate system of checks and key performance indicators that will light up in a brilliant shade red on the CEO's flight console should any deviations from the approved plan occur, allowing the CEO to intervene and correct these transgressions.

Sound familiar? Of course it does. But is this behavior natural for human beings? Certainly, humans have a penchant for making plans to guide their activities for everything from diets to quality-of-life programs, and even New Year resolutions. And sometime we achieve our goals. But the truth of the matter is that both weight-loss and quality-of-life institutions base their existence on a certain amount of fallback. Humans are quite simply not rational beings, and we don't always have the will or the ability to think of the long-term. We can adopt a very short-term perspective, be impulsive, and even downright stupid (Bjartveit & Kjærstad, 1996). When our diet crashes after three weeks of salad and vegetables, and we give in to the temptation of a massive wedge of devil's food cake, we don't necessarily correct for this with an even stricter regime of water and carrots. In fact, most of us would reason that once you have slipped, you might as well crash and burn. The temptation to "make up for all that starving" and wash the cake own with Coke and Lattés, and enjoy life, while you still can, is overwhelming. In principle this behavior is also characterized by a feedback mechanism – but this is positive feedback loop that is actually self-reinforcing in that feedback serves to increase the deviation. Basically, you are out of control, and eventually this cycle will lead to the chaotic and unpredictable state. But, then again, this type of behavior is also typical of the human condition. By and large, plans look great on paper.

As bad as this sounds, it could be worse. There is always the danger of throwing the baby out with the bathwater. The purpose of strategic planning is usually to identify new opportunities and develop a plan for taking advantage of these opportunities. Any deviations from this plan would need to be corrected immediately. However, there is much evidence that suggests the path to innovation often lies along the deviations. The management literature is rife with examples of deviation leading to innovation. The 3M's Post-It was the result of a failed program. The Polaroid camera was the brainchild of a little girl. The chocolate tail on the Krone-Is is the result of an unsuccessful attempt to line the inside of the cone with chocolate. These organizations adopted a different approach for dealing with deviations. If their managers had taken more business courses or hired more consultants, these successful innovations may never have seen the light of day. And this is why Henry Mintzberg (2001) advises against sending executives on MBA-programs – where they would be taught how to eliminate deviation – and thus stifle change and innovation. It is actually quite difficult to order creativity.

The motion picture *Forrest Gump* delights in innovation and positive feedback, and mocks our blind faith in rational models. Forrest succeeds because he listens to positive feedback. The scene where he has just been rejected by the woman he loves, illustrates this point. Forrest is sitting on the porch and recalls: "That day for no particular reason, I decided to go for a little run. So I ran to the end of the road. And when I got there, I thought maybe I'd run to the end of town. And when I got there, I thought maybe I'd just run across Greenbow County. And I figured since I'd run this far, maybe I'd just run across the great state of Alabama. And that's what I did." (Finerman, Tisch, Starkey, and Zemeckis, 1994)

And then he proceeds to run for three years, without stopping. He meets people that join him. He becomes a Messiah moving across the US at a jogger's pace. Suddenly, and without warning, he stops in the middle of the desert. His numerous followers nervously await what they assume will be the message from the quiet beacon they have followed through rain and sunshine. And what does Forrest say? "I think I'll go home now." What could this be, other than positive feedback? The story is a modern tale of creativity. The small-town fool that liberates himself from the confines of rationality.

The term "on the edge of chaos" is used to describe a system that, having been driven towards chaos by deviation, will tend to self-correct and move back towards equilibrium. In this context, innovation is the self-corrective behavior, and we could say that innovation was born out of chaos. But there is of course one hitch – you have very little control over the creativity that is fuelled by chaos. What emerges may be a wonderful, new concept that the world cannot do without or an entirely new approach to solving a universal problem, or it could be some destructive abomination. There is simply no way to govern the process, but rest assured it will be creative.

Belief in continuous change in an unsettled world

"Ours is the era of continuous change. The rate of change just keeps increasing." All consultants must know how to wield phrases like these – after all, much of current management speak is based on the certitude of these observations. These phrases may sound empty, but they do provide us with a perspective on the organization and its business environment. If the business environment is in a state of constant change, then the organization must learn how to keep pace in order to maintain equilibrium. In strategic thinking, this is precisely what is meant by: *the law of requisite variety* – the organization has to keep up with its environment in terms of momentum and complexity (Stacey, 2003).

But isn't this just a little Darwinism applied to the theory of the lifecycle of an organization? Organizations don't just adapt in response to changes in their environment. There must be some agents that are causing this change, and in doing so, creating new opportunities and challenges, both for themselves and for their environment. In this instance the causality is working in the opposite direction.

We could interpret Nokia's tremendous success in mobile telephones as an illustration of this principle. In a tough environment where the struggle to gain competitive advantage seemed to revolve around technology, Nokia chose to define the challenge somewhat differently. At Nokia, a mobile phone was not just a mobile phone. At Nokia they believed that the mobile phone was an ornament – an accessory that should be designed and marketed quite differently from a phone. An accessory is a fashion item, and as such it is characterized by unpredictability and positive feedback. You don't have to spend ages contemplating how to incorporate the latest technology into the next wave of mobile phones. But you do have to pay attention to fashion – spring, summer, autumn etc. Imagine what would happen if Valentino declared that they considered one of the dresses in their 1998 spring collection to be the best dress ever made – and that from now on, this would be the only dress they would make. You have to know which requirements are important and which are not, and you should aspire to more than just trying to keep up with the business environment. As part of the market, you can recreate it. Nokia created a fashion item aimed at the younger set that they hoped would change mobile phones as often as they changed their skirts or jeans. Who cares about technological perfection?

There is a very powerful interaction between an agent and the agent's competitive environment. The agent can shape the environment – or allow itself to be shaped by the environment. And even passive adaptation to the environment does have an effect on the environment – called The Red Queen Hypothesis (Ridley, 1993) in evolutionary theory. The term is inspired by a passage from *Alice in Wonderland*. When Alice encounters the Red Queen, they wind up in a footrace, but no matter how fast they run, they don't get anywhere – because the surrounding landscape races to keep up with them. The faster they go, the faster the landscape moves to keep up. And that is just the way it is in the real world. Every evolutionary step forward forces the environment to change just to keep up. Bad news for Nokia. The competitive edge they have worked so hard to achieve won't last forever. All they can be sure of is that their competitors will catch up. The only lasting competitive edge is the ability to continuously recreate the competitive landscape. Mere adaptation is not enough.

The belief in simple, linear relationships

And finally, there is the consultant's favorite tools: the 2-by-2 matrix and the flow chart. What would consultants and business schools talk about if they didn't have these tools that provide such wonderfully clear and concise descriptions of all plausible outcomes, and such unambiguous and proportional relationships between the action-variable and the effect-variable? In *The Matrix,* Neo was told: "You can take the blue pill or the red pill." However, for Neo, the consequences of his decision would be much larger. "You take the red pill, you'll stay in Wonderland and I'll show you how deep the rabbit hole goes." (Silver, Wachowski, and Wachowski, 1999)

A popular mantra in chaos theory is The Butterfly Effect. It may sound like the title of a B-movie, but it actually concerns the intriguing notion made so popular by chaos theory – that a single flap of a butterfly's wing in the rainforests of Brazil may turn out to be what causes a tornado in Texas. Not the kind of relationship you explain using a 2-by-2 matrix. The Butterfly Effect is based on research Edward Lorenz conducted back in the 1960s on a phenomenon he described as sensitive dependence on initial conditions. Lorenz was using computer simulations to study weather patterns, and quite by chance he stumbled across something that would turn out to have major implications for many different fields of research. Lorenz was running a weather simulation one day when the computer crashed just as it was nearing the end of the run. He had spent some time entering all the initial data and was loathe to start all over again, so he tried to see if he could get away with just reentering the data from the last few calculations made during the run prior to the crash – and see if the system would go on from there. So Lorenz meticulously entered this data – down to the 10th decimal point. To his surprise this run provided results that were very different from the first run. When he compared the two simulations he found that they started out following a similar pattern, but as they progressed, the variations between them increased – until they finally produced results that were completely different. Why? The underlying data should be the same. Well, at least down to the 10th decimal. It turns out that even minute differences – beyond the 10th decimal, can lead to different results. The single beat of a butterfly's wing. Don't place too much faith in the 5-day weather forecast. It is very difficult to predict the behavior of a system that is inherently unstable. The weatherman's best bet is to forecast partially sunny with the possibility of showers.

Some motion pictures have used this aspect of chaos theory as a main ingredient. *Sliding Doors* – featuring Gwyneth Paltrow – is a wonderful example of this. The main character's life follows completely different paths depending on whether or not she catches the subway. Having just lost her job, Paltrow's character is hurrying down one of the long escalators in London's Underground to catch the subway home. Part-way down the lengthy descent, Paltrow is held up momentarily by a little girl who is playing on the steps, and as a result she just misses the train – the doors slide shut right before her face. She is left, fuming, on the platform, and the scene ends with her wondering what to do. Then the film skips back to where Paltrow's character is hurrying down the steps, but this time the little girl's mother sees Paltrow coming and pulls her daughter out of the way – and Paltrow catches the subway. And from there on we follow what essentially turns out to be two different films about two entirely different lives. There is one, that seems quite miserable, where she catches the subway, and also, coming home from work at an early hour, catches her boyfriend in bed with his lover; and the other, which doesn't start too well either as she is mugged on her way up to grab a taxi and has her purse stolen. It is actually a little spooky. Think about your own life. How would your life have been if you hadn't gone to that party – or missed that meeting? Don't worry too much about it – just keep your eye on the flow chart. The blue pill or the red pill?

The significance of this type of phenomenon is that life is not as clear-cut as we like to think it is. What may seem like insignificant differences in initial conditions can lead to entirely different results. Bold predictions about relationships between cause and effect assume simplistic relationships in what is actually a capricious existence. Relationships are rarely linear. As we have seen, even the smallest variation can lead to exponential differences. You may have been trying to achieve something for the longest time, using all your might and effort – all to no avail. But then the smallest deviation, at the right time and place, something that might seem so insignificant that you just let it pass without giving it a thought, turns out to be just what was needed to get the ball rolling. These turning points are more important than finding a specific solution to a problem. Sometimes it is important just to get that ball rolling.

Obviously, these articles of faith, on which so much of traditional theories of leadership are predicated, are inadequate. They assume a stable and predictable existence. This may be appropriate in certain contexts, but where there is constant change and innovation, these theories simply do not hold up, because things are complex and unpredictable. At the same time, even though things may be unpredictable, they are still recognizable – so there is no giving up and leaving everything to chance. But, it does make things more difficult. Patterns may look similar, but you cannot count on them to be identical. Political agendas and irrational elements make things even worse. Pure chance and self-reinforcing processes may turn out to be significant. So how do we deal with chance? How do we provide management in the realm of Fortune?

The Prince and Fortuna

About 500 years ago Niccolò Machiavelli wrote what might be considered one of the most insightful books on leadership. What sets this book apart from the rest of management literature is the perspective of humans as being somewhat less than infallible. Machiavelli argues that humans do not always behave honorably and with the best of intentions. We do not always think of the common good. We do not fight for liberty, equality, and fraternity. In fact, we pursue our own personal interests – often to the detriment of others. *Ambizione* – is the inherent nature of man. We strive for fame, fortune, and power – we want to be admired and respected. Machiavelli did not consider original sin and the fall from grace the central themes of the bible. He found the tales that followed more interesting and revealing of the true nature of man. Cain beating Abel to death; Jacob deceiving Esau; Joseph being sold into slavery by his envious brothers. This, Machiavelli claims, is also the nature of man – and who can argue this? How can we explain all the evil that goes on in our world unless we accept that man does possess these immoral qualities? The human that

Machiavelli describes is neither Mother Theresa nor Mahatma Gandhi, but does in fact bear a striking resemblance to Homer Simpson. This person is selfish, shifty, and simple. Set against this, Pollyanna's faith in the good of man seems naive. Candide's hope that *all is for the best* fades. And the vision described in management literature of everyone coming together to rally around the strategic goals is just the pipedream of every business school graduate. We are individualistic, self-interested beings living in an unstable environment.

There are further similarities between Machiavelli and chaos theory. Machiavelli paints a political landscape where order and chaos coexist. This is the area of partial instability that exists between an ordered existence and utter chaos. This is what Machiavelli calls *Fortuna*. He has little faith in the suitability of decision science and management systems in Fortuna – where leadership alone is not enough. Chance plays a major role. "… I judge it to be true that Fortune may be mistress of half our actions, but that even she leaves the other half, or almost, under our control …" (Machiavelli, 1989, p. 90). Fortuna is the goddess that enriches our lives with chaos. She has been feared and coveted from Antiquity to Renaissance. She turns a mediocre manager into a CEO, and then crushes him while he is still euphoric. We cherish her when the wheel of fortune spins in our favor and fame and fortune befalls us, but we are left alone to seethe when the wheel spins against us and we are thrust unceremoniously into despair. The opening chorus in Carl Orff's *Carmina Burana* reveals her terrible price: "O Fortune, like the moon, you are ever changeable, ever waxing and waning." Machiavelli portrays her as capricious and even evil on occasion:

> "She turns states and kingdoms upside down as she pleases; she deprives the just of the good that she freely gives to the unjust … She times events as suits her; she raises us up, she puts us down without pit, without law or right." (Machiavelli, 1989, p. 746).

She is that cute, little girl in kindergarten, that beguiles adults and children alike, but who toys with us, and in rages of unchecked selfishness throws herself on the floor and wails until she gets to play Snow White in the school play. That is Fortuna.

Machiavelli even mocks our faith in control and management. J.G.A. Pocock describes how Machiavelli's portrayal of Fortuna is symbolic of a state of "… pure, uncontrolled, and illegitimated contingency." (1975, p. 156). In the realm of Fortuna there are no simple relationships. This realm, full of opposing interests and highly complex causal relationships, is the most unpredictable of all. But even there we can discern patterns. Relationships and causality can be detected. That is why Machiavelli wrote about it. It resembles a divine pattern in a secular chaos. And that is probably why Fortuna is a goddess.

One of the central themes of Machiavelli is that leaders place too much faith in Fortuna. Leaders tend to trust the upward momentum of the career system, and assume that the inherent elitism of this system will propel them to the top. Membership at the right Country Club matters more than great ideas and relentless drive. The incredulity of "how did I wind up as CEO, the board must have gone mad!" is almost a parody. Machiavelli despises weak leaders who are more concerned with furthering their own careers and negotiating huge pay packets than they are with running the organization and/or watching out for theirs employees. And he positively loathes the mercenaries that move from town to town, offering their services. Where does their loyalty lie? If you choose Fortuna for your companion, you will eventually find that she will abandon you. That is why you must defy this foul goddess. You need the courage to stand firm. Fortuna is not blind. She cannot be defeated, but she can be swayed. And it would seem that defiance brings her a certain sadomasochistic pleasure: "… it is necessary, in order to keep her under, to cuff and mauld her." (Machiavelli, 1989, p. 1992). If you ask her to tango (and hint some spanking), she might take you up. Machiavelli wants leaders to defy Fortuna.

And it is here we learn the essence of *The Prince*. The Prince Machiavelli portrays, is an innovator, *Il Principe nuovo* (Pocock, 1975). Here is a leader that has seized an opportunity to acquire power. He wants to make changes, and is not content to follow in the tracks of others. He dispels the old customs, but that also means that he cannot base his rule on the old traditions or on established authority. By initiating this process of regeneration he has thrust the system into a state of partial instability, a state of affairs characterized by political agendas and unpredictability more than anything else. This innovation offends some, and disrupts everyone. By daring to effect true leadership, he exposes himself to the vagaries of others. Unpredictability is inevitable whenever power is wielded or change is implemented. It is like waving Snow White's costume in front of a crowd of school kids. The Prince roused Fortuna.

So, how does one manage in the realm of Fortuna? Before Machiavelli, conventional wisdom would have followed the spirit of Boethius and suggested the need for the individual to reflect and be cleansed through *la vita contemplativa*. The postmodernistic version of this would be: "If it ain't broke, don't fix it," or BOHICA ("bend over, here it comes again"). Machiavelli would take the opposing view. First, he would argue that a leader should be measured by his deeds. *Vita attiva* – is the solution, not *vita contemplativa*. Delay is not an option. Investigations and delays are darkness – worse than death itself. Secondly, Machiavelli insists that leaders must have the ability to tailor their actions to the situation, and that this is where most leaders fail – because their scope is too limited and because they place too much faith in past success. Thirdly, Machiavelli argues that the leader must be able to restore order and bring Fortuna under control by introducing laws, power, and wisdom. Fortuna is like a river that has overflowed its banks and has flooded fields and swept away houses and trees – we need dams and dikes to bring her under control. We cannot let chaos run wild. Machiavelli emphasizes the importance of being able to restore order, even though this may be a long-term goal. However, this is not what Machiavelli considers the most important quality for a leader who is to survive in a complex and political environment. For this he mandates: *virtù*.

Virtù

When Machiavelli proposes virtù as the most important quality for a leader to possess, he is taking a pot shot at his contemporaries – as well as all those that follow, by mocking our politically correct perspective on leadership. There is an important difference between the way things appear and the way they really are. It is the gullible that believe in ideals like humility and compassion. When leaders bow their heads, they do so as hypocrites. They know the score; they know how to get what they want – *verita effetuale* – the efficient truth, as Machieavelli describes it. The Roman Empire becomes the ideal – but not the Rome of the emperors. It is the republican Rome that provides the heroes. This is where the principles necessary to create a global force are conceived. Machiavelli uses an entire book, *Discourses on Livy*, to explain, using layer upon layer of arguments and vivid portrayals, why the Roman republic was so hugely successful. They accepted the true nature of man, and his cruel existence, and used it for political purposes. The Roman republic was abundant in virtù, determination, boldness, recklessness, courage, generosity, and independency. To be virtuous does not mean being a picture of virtue. It means being both human and beast: *l'uomo e la bestia*:

> "You need to know, then, that there are two ways of fighting: one according to the laws, the other with force. The first is suited to man, the second to animals; because the first is often not sufficient, a prince must resort to the second. Therefore he needs to know well how to put to use the traits of animal and of man." (Machiavelli, 1989, p. 64).

So what animals should we try to emulate? The lion and the fox. The lion because it attacks Fortuna swiftly and decisively. The fox because it can outsmart Fortuna. Machiavelli's animal metaphors may seem simplistic, but they have much deeper connotations than is immediately evident. Using historical and contemporary examples, Machiavelli is able to show how leaders have overcome difficult circumstances, and he does this by using a number of concepts that have interesting links to a modern day perspective on leadership and human interaction.

The lion embodies courage, and Machiavelli cannot abide weak leadership. He is very critical of his former friend and supervisor, Piero Soderini – leader of the Florentine republic, who flees when the Medici sons descend on the republic. Machiavelli condemns Soderini to suffer in Limbo for all eternity: for Hell would not accept someone that coward and deceitful. On the other hand, he loves the epic heroes. Hannibal, who defies all odds and leads his army over the Alps to attack the Romans in their own backyard. Alexander, who marches into the vast and uncharted Asian continent to find the end of the earth. Caesar, who, with the gambler's motto *alea jacta est*, crosses the Rubicon and charges toward Pompei. "As for me, I believe this: it is better to be impetuous than cautious …" (Machiavelli, 1989, p. 92).

Current studies of leadership emphasize the importance of self-efficacy in leaders (Bandura, 1997). Self-efficacy means "… beliefs in one's capabilities to organize and execute the course of action required to produce given attainments" (Bandura, 1997, p. 3). Leaders have to believe they can make a difference. This does not have to be entirely true – merely believing that one can accomplish one's goals is sufficient. If the illusion is strong enough, it can become a self-fulfilling prophecy. Most of us would never perform the acts of bravery we have had to on occasion if we were aware of the odds against success. Faith can move mountains. This is precisely why narcissistic leaders can be so effective in all their self-centered infamy (Maccoby, 2000). Their faith in themselves is their primary force. And should doubt creep in, they would immediately loose their charm, as the sparkle would fade into darkness and paralysis would set in.

How does the lion defeat Fortuna? The lion approaches Fortuna in much the same way as we described earlier in chaos theory – by shaping its surroundings rather than allowing itself to be shaped by them. The lion represents the opposite of accommodation. They are quite simply savage and imprudent. A lion will solve a Gordic knot by chewing right through it. Lions seize opportunity when it presents itself to them. In the poem *Occasione*, Machiavelli relates these golden opportunities, windows of opportunities, and describes how most of us are not lion enough to seize these opportunities. Occasione is a Goddess. She never rests, and is hard to spot. Her face is covered by her hair, and this makes her difficult to recognize. Regret follows closely behind her. Those who do not seize Occasione will be themselves seized by regret. And those who waste their time daydreaming are unaware that Occasione has already passed them by. This is a fairly accurate description of the principle taken from chaos theory that you should take charge of circumstances rather than passively let them shape you. And we would expect lions to be better at this than squirrels.

Machiavelli wants leaders that want to achieve something. He has no time for the administrators that cautiously work their way up the career path towards the top. The prince-like qualities he requires are the stuff of leaders with great ideas, who have the will and conviction to carry them through to completion. As you can see, we are getting very close to the current discussion of leaders versus administrators (Zaleznik, 1977) and transformational versus transactional leaders (Bass, 1998). Machiavelli suggests that princes can lead people through *Gloria*. The desire to accomplish great and noble deeds can drive humans to act as well as to personal sacrifice. In the final chapter of *The Prince*, Machiavelli cries out for a leader that can drive the barbarians out of Italy and restore its honor. And once again we must consider the Roman ideal. The great heroes of the republic – Scipio, Cincinattus – seek just acts and noble deeds to carry out in the service of the republic. Gloria defines something that is larger than the self and its private ambitions.

But it is not enough to be a lion if you want to succeed. You also need to learn from the fox: "The one who knows how to play the fox comes out best …" (de Grazia, 1989, p. 65). Machiavelli praises the fox's qualities in several of his works – in both political analysis and in plays. The literary figure that emerges from this is a *confidence man* – a sly character that reads the social scene well and understands man's fundamental desires and darker sides (Rebhorn, 1988). We have all seen confidence men in movies like *The Sting* – that starred Robert Redford and Paul Newman. They play a pair of charming thieves that conned a major player without him even knowing he had been duped. As we sit there at the cinema and chuckle away at their cheek and self-assurance, we, the audience, are completely unaware that we too are being set up. The film leads us to believe that Newman and Redford, our charming heroes, are killed in a gunfight, but just as this starts to sink in and we feel the sadness and despair, they open their eyes, spit out the ampoules of red stain and rise from the dead. And we are left there, wondering how they pulled it off, and why we didn't see it coming. They are prototypical *tricksters* – the heroes of myths and legends that constantly outwit their "marks" (Rebhorn, 1988).

These fox-like qualities coincide with more recent theories of evolution that suggest that the development of human intelligence was in response to social challenges (Ridley, 1993). Intelligence was favored by natural selection because it improved our ability to manipulate and outwit others. This hypothesis has even been given its own name – in honor of its ideal: the Machiavelli hypothesis. The ability to outwit others requires cognitive complexity that necessitates the ability to think in abstract terms, the ability to act, and empathy. In this sense, the driving force of human intellectual development is the need for manipulation and trickery (Whiten & Byrne, 1997). This quality is evident in humans and to a certain extent in chimpanzees, but does not exist in other animals. If you find it hard to spot this trait in adults, then observe children. Long before they learn to master mathematical formulas they reveal a firm grasp of social intricacies. My own son showed signs of cunning at a very young age. At the age of six he was given his own TV so that he could watch his favorite videos in his own room when adults were watching the news on the TV in the family room – or his little brother was watching countless repetitions of *Postman Pat*. The joy was somewhat short-lived, as his younger brother soon demanded unrestricted use of this new TV. How did big brother deal with younger brother? It required a great deal of intellect, along with some acting, and a bit of manipulation. The following conversation took place on the way home from kindergarten: "Mommy, when we get home I'll run over to the TV and say I want to watch *Hercules*. That'll make Filip start to cry, and then you say: "No Mattias, it's Filip's turn to watch *Postman Pat*." And then I'll answer: "Well, OK," and while Filip is stuffing *Postman Pat* in the video I'll sneak off to my room and have my TV to myself." The plan was carried out, and each child happily enjoyed watching their favorite video. The manipulator was particularly happy. The deliberations he must have made concerning preconditions and consequences were quite complex. Ask the same kid the answer to 11 minus 7, and he will say 8! We have survived as a species that masters the skills of social gamesmanship and treachery, not as the producers of computer chips (Coismedes & Tooby, 1992).

Machiavelli wants leaders that are wise. Leaders that understand social interaction. He wants leaders that appreciate that humans are not created to participate in staff meetings, but rather for gossiping and influence peddling in the hallways (Dunbar, 1996). He wants leaders who recognize the need for putting a performance, and appreciate that leadership involves impression management (Giacalone & Rosenfeld, 1989). And above all, Machiavelli wants foxes, that have a few more tricks up their sleeves than lions, and that understand that sometimes you have to let Fortuna carry on and wait for her mood to change (de Grazia, 1989).

The fox will not allow himself to be taken in by rational decision models. It knows that the world is infinitely more complex than can ever be represented in a matrix. It can follow the chain of events and read the intentions of others. The fox does not follow a strict plan of attack, but rather it maintains a watchful eye and is prepared to deal with a number of possible eventualities – some more unexpected than others.

Fortuna is a river

What a coincidence! The most up-to-date perspectives on leadership bear a striking resemblance to 500-year-old advice intended for Princes. Or maybe this isn't such a coincidence after all? In *The Prince*, Machiavelli makes it very clear that he has no intention of trying to tell us how things should be. Even back then there was an abundance of books espousing the virtues of autocratic leadership, with a few words about compassion and humility thrown in for appearances. By clearly stating that he wished to describe things they way they are, Machiavelli turned everything on its head: "I have decided that I must concern myself with the truth of the matter as facts show it rather than with any fanciful notion." (Machiavelli, 1989, page 57). Machiavelli's advice applies to the real world – not to some illusion.

This is where Machiavelli dovetails with chaos theory and current theories of leadership – reality is complex, and there are no simple answers. Quite the contrary, simple answers may be wrong or even destructive. The challenge that leaders face today is leadership on the edge of chaos – they have to steer clear of the stifling restrictions of bureaucracy while avoiding the perils of chaos (Brown & Eisenhardt, 1998). The leader has to manage the balance between structure first and flexibility – in power struggles, and when faced with challenges of a more normative nature. This is the realm of Fortuna, where any sense of control is probably just an illusion, and the key is to know how to use influence. And where the advice of a 16th century author seems to make a lot of sense.

References

Axelrod, R. & Cohen, M.D. (2000). *Harnessing complexity. Organizational implications of a scientific frontier.* New York: Basic Books.

Bass, B.M. (1998). *Transformational leadership. Industrial, military, and educational impact.* Mahwah, New Jersey: Lawrence Erlbaum Associates.

Bandura, A. (1997). *Self-efficacy.* New York. Freeman.

Bjartveit, S. & Kjærstad, T. (1996). *Kaos og kosmos. Byggesteiner for individer og organisasjoner.* Oslo: Kolle forlag.

Brown, S.L. & Eisenhardt, K. (1998). *Competing on the edge: Strategy as structured chaos.* Boston: Harvard Business School Press.

Brown, S.L. & Eisenhardt, K.M. (1998). *Competing on the edge. Strategy as structured chaos.* Boston: Harvard School Press.

Cosimedes, L. & Tooby, J. (1992). The psychological foundations of culture. In J.H. Barkow, L. Cosimedes, and J. Tooby (Eds.), *The adapted mind. Evolutionary psychology and the generation of culture.* New York: Oxford University Press.

de Grazia, S. (1989). Machiavelli in hell. Princeton, N.J.: Princeton University Press.

Dunbar, R. (1996). *Grooming, gossip and the evolution of language.* London: Faber and Faber.

Finerman, W., Tisch, S., Starkey, S. (Producers) and Zemeckis, R. (Director). (1994). *Forrest Gump.* Paramount Pictures.

Giacalone, R.A. & Rosenfeld, P. (Eds.). (1989). *Impression management in the organization.* Hillsdale, N.J.: L. Erlbaum Associates.

Lorenz, E. (1993). *The essence of chaos.* Seattle: University of Washington Press.

Maccoby, M. (2000). Narcissistic leaders: The incredible pros, the inevitable cons. *Harvard Business Review,* January–February.

Marion, R. (1999). *The edge of organization. Chaos and complexity theories of formal social systems.* Thousand Oaks: Sage.

Mintzberg, H. (1994). *The rise and fall of strategic planning.* New York: Prentice Hall.

Mintzberg, H. (2001). Bjeffer mot MBA-studiet. *Dagens Næringsliv,* 17 September, p. 33.

Pascale, R. (1990). *Managing on the edge. How successful companies use conflict to stay ahead.* London: Penguin.

Pocock, J.G.A. (1975). *The Machiavellian moment.* Princeton, N.J.: Princeton University Press.

Rebhorn, W.A. (1988). *Foxes and lions.* Ithaca, N.Y.: Cornell University Press.

Ridley, M. (1993). *The red queen. Sex and the evolution of human nature.* London: Penguin.

Silver, J. (Producer), Wachowski, A. and Wachowski, L. (Directors). (1999). *Matrix.* Warner Bros.

Stacey, R.D. (2003). *Strategic Management and organizational dynamics. The challenge of complexity.* 4th ed. Harlow, England: FT Prentice Hall.

Whiten, A. & Byrne, R.W. (Eds.). (1997). *Machiavellian intelligence II.* New York: Cambridge University Press.

Zaleznik, A. (1977). Managers and leaders. Are they different? *Harvard Business Review,* May–June.

Chapter 8 | Hidden agendas

STEINAR BJARTVEIT
AND GÖRAN ROOS

The consultant – client relationship as a system

As a consultant, have you ever had the feeling that you have been sucked dry by the client? You have analyzed the case, cross-checked every reference and theory, and prepared your recommendations meticulously – but no matter what you say or do at the final presentation, your words fall on deaf ears. Or maybe not so much fall, they vanish – sucked into some kind of vacuum by God knows what. You find yourself and your good advice and well-prepared recommendations being sucked into some kind of nightmare that involves you approving interpretations that have nothing to do with your analysis and recommendations, and that you feel very uncomfortable with having to support. How could this happen? You can always write it off as a bad day at the office, or as inadequate preparation, but there is a more disturbing explanation. The client took control of you and your recommendations, and forced you to go along with things that you know deep down are unacceptable.

How does the client affect you as a consultant? Naive followers of simplistic models of causality may still believe that influence flows in only one direction in the consultancy process: the consultant intervenes on behalf of the client. It is quite clear: there is an aide and a client, an assignment and a service provider. However, some recent, and somewhat critical, studies of consulting suggest that the flow of influence is not a one-way street, but in fact flows in both directions (Fincham and Clark, 2002; Sturdy, 2002). This perspective finds strong support in *pragmatic communication theory* – a theory that was originally created by Gregory Bateson, and that has had a significant influence on subsequent thinking on communication and counseling (Bateson, 1972; Watzlawick, Bavelas, and Jackson, 1967). Pragmatic communications theory suggests that consultation involves more than straightforward counseling or support. The consultant-client relationship is a system within itself, and to understand what is going on in this relationship, it is necessary to examine the whole rather than the parts. The consultant and client each exert influence on each other, and their interaction leads to patterns that are repetitive and instantly recognizable – almost like habits or social customs.

Whether or not this is beneficial to the client depends a great deal on how the relationship develops. What often happens within this consultancy-system is that the client exerts more influence on the consultant than vice versa. We are not thinking of the more obvious factors such as mandate, allocation of resources, etc., but rather of the influence clients exert during the on-going interaction between client and consultant. Some of this influence is unintentional, and some of it may be rooted in the consultants' own vulnerability. And sometimes this problem is exacerbated by factors that lie outside the system – as is the case when consultants feel pressure from their own superiors to achieve high levels of utilization (percentage of available time that is billable to clients) and realization (percentage of target hourly list price that is realized within a specific project). If consultants speak their mind in opposition to the client, they may find themselves removed from the project – at the insistence of either the project manager or the client. Which may cause them to fall short of specified income targets – and which in turn means they may find themselves out of a job. This situation is not conducive to a frank and open discussion with clients.

Influence never stops. Accept it – the customer is running you! Some clients are so enthusiastic and convincing that they blow you away. They trample you and your level-headed analysis, and any objections you might have, and are not satisfied until you are reciting their gospel. You are loathe to shatter the illusion that they have created (… which will probably be shattered on its own accord in due time), and consultations are so much more pleasant when you go with the flow; when nobody looses face and no one gets upset (Argyris, 1990). But the client has taken charge of you, and it is doubtful whether this is a good thing for the consultation. Sometimes you will run into clients that created their own mess – their actions have been at best ill-advised, and possibly even destructive. Every instinct is telling you that you have to confront the client with the fact that it is his or her own actions that have led the firm astray, but the client is so obviously helpless and defenseless that you find yourself backing down. Some clients have a natural talent for looking so vulnerable and defenseless that they make Bambi look positively evil. Every time you summon the nerve to broach the difficult issues and suggest that you need to have a serious talk about the client's curious style of leadership, you find yourself looking at the saddest and most vulnerable pair of eyes you have ever seen, accompanied by the usual: "Is it serious? I suppose it is." And for some reason we often find it difficult to be frank in these situations, and we wind up comforting the client and telling them that, all things considered, they are not doing such a bad job after all. And *that* is something we do all too well. Damn their sullen faces and hangdog looks. Damn our own frailty.

But doesn't the client want help? Isn't that why he hired the consultant? Well, sort of. Systems theory suggests that providing help and giving advice are seldom straight-forward events. Sometimes it turns out that something that was not part of the original problem winds up being the toughest obstacle to overcome. When people struggle with a specific problem for long enough – without solving it, it is reasonable to assume that they have become part of the problem. This is not to say that the client *is* the problem, but rather that s/he may be standing in the way of a solution. The classical dilemma in this type of situation is the *more-of-the-same* solution (Watzlawick, Weakland, and Fisch, 1974). We are so thoroughly convinced that we have found the right solution, and are so enamored with it that we will use it over and over again, even though it doesn't seem to be providing the desired results. Strangely enough, the lack of success does not lead us to discard this solution, but rather to attempt a multitude of variations of the same solution. Sometimes the system becomes blind to other alternatives – and we do not learn from our mistakes. Quite the contrary – the lack of results strengthens our resolve and gives us stamina. We remain convinced despite repeated failure. So we brace ourselves and try one more time. The client tries over and over again – to no avail. Try again. It will work; it just needs a little more testing. This is obviously a case of the customer not being right, but he is standing firmly placed between us and a solution that might work.

In a perfect world, where client and consultant follow procedures based on theories of rational decision-making for solving problems, you may not encounter this problem. You can block out the noise and don your favorite consulting tools. However, in a complex and political reality, you will often run into a situation like this. The client does something to you. And this may not be for the better. However, you shouldn't avoid this type of assignment – but rather learn how to use this type of situation to make the project work. An assumed liability can turn out to be the greatest asset. Pragmatic communications theory suggests that the aide's best course of action is to create a new system: the consultant-client system, as a sort of experimental lab. New rules, new understandings, and new customs may emerge from this system – and be used in other systems where the client is also present. This similar to the principle that is used in therapy – which is by nature also a supportive relationship. By assuming the role of outsider, the aide can change the script, and something new may come out of this. However, it is common knowledge that the window of opportunity for the therapist is very brief. The therapist must establish rules and customs for a new game very quickly if he is to avoid being trapped in the client's world and constrained by the rules of the old game – the game that the client knows so well. If that happens, the therapist will himself require consultation in order to break out of the predetermined pattern. You should also take note of everything related to the client's behavior and influence. If those sad eyes are having an effect on you, just think what they are doing to everybody else! It is important to remember that your reaction to this behavior is not unique. In general, problems that arise in your interaction with the client may be indicative of the real problem that the client faces in relation to the rest of the organization. The ability to take a step back and observe your own interaction with the client is important because it will provide you with valuable information that you can use to help the client, and that is what consulting is all about.

Some books on consulting advise the client against relinquishing control of the assignment (Kubr, 1993; O'Shea and Madigan, 1997). We are tempted to give the consultant the same advice: never loose control of the assignment. In your want to get results; you will need a few degrees of latitude and some elbow room. Never allow yourself to be trapped into doing things against your better judgment. (This is not to say that the consultant is always right, or that the consultant should be given carte blanche to exert his or her own influence – consider the tale of Iago in the next chapter!) Thus, it is important to understand how the client influences you and what options you have.

Is the client aware of what s/he is doing? This problem can be approached from different angles, depending on whether or not the client is aware of the influence s/he may be having on others. In some cases the client may not realize what effect s/he is having on the consultant. The client may be caught up in his or her own realities and perceptions. And what can easily happen is that the client lectures the consultant on his or her view of reality and somehow expects the consultant to take this for granted. But in other cases clients may be fully aware of the influence they exert on others. They may exert this influence because they have a hidden agenda and need the consultant to accomplish this. In the next two sections we will take a closer look at each of these situations, because the client's behavior – whether it is conscious or not, will have consequences for the manner in which the consultant can provide help to the client. The first section adopts a social constructivist perspective to illustrate how social conceptions may entrap both client and consultant. The second section uses a conflict theory perspective – where clients are participants in a political struggle within the organization, and consultants are their weapon bearers. We will conclude by reviewing some possible courses of action the consultant could choose to deal with these tensions.

At first glance this chapter might give the impression that all consultants share an arrogant and know-it-all attitude – and even suggest that the blame for unsuccessful assignments rests entirely with the clients, who are either foolish, evil, or both. (In fact, Machiavelli (2004) even suggests that it takes a wise prince to appreciate good advice …). However, this is not our intention. As the following chapter (Høivik, 2005) describes, it is equally pertinent to speak of hidden agendas and of undue influence flowing in the opposite direction. But it is our opinion that it would be inappropriate to discuss models that rely on rational behavior from both parties. In any complex situation, where it is difficult to tell different versions of the truth, views of reality, and strategic frameworks apart, the consultant should be aware of how these things may influence the assignment. By the same token, it would be naive to disregard the fact that organizations are political, interests don't always dovetail, and that people aren't always working toward the greater good. The consultant wouldn't achieve much if his toolkit consisted entirely of models designed for situations characterized by enlightment and complete insight. Both clients and consultants have layers.

The social construction of truth

In the typical *more-of-the-same* dilemma, the client is unable to see his own contribution to the lack of success. You simply cannot see that you are standing in the way of a solution. You are unable to comprehend that it is precisely your well-founded understanding of the situation, and subsequent lack of innovative thinking, that leads every recommendation down the same route – to failure. In these situations, the client is unaware of the fact that s/he is inadvertently forcing the consultant to come up with endless variations on the same flawed solution. In fact, s/he may think s/he is giving the consultant necessary background information that will make the solution work, or that s/he is making sure the (greedy) consultant doesn't stray too far from his or her mandate and deliver something the client hasn't asked for. Let us examine the situations where the client is trapped in the organization's prevailing view of reality – and accepts this as a fundamental, and immutable, truth. Chapter IV – Coaching, deals with personal issues for the client as leader, and will explore the situations where the client's personal beliefs and conceptions may lead the project astray.

In their seminal book, *The Social Construction of Reality*, Berger and Luckmann (1966) describe reality as a social phenomenon, created through interaction between people. They adopt a phenomenological and social constructivist perspective that is based on man's unwavering confidence in established truisms and articles of faith. People seem to forget that they have themselves created these truisms and view the truth as something uniquely objective that exists independently of us. But what we call truth is indelibly linked to our interactions with others and with our surroundings. We are all convinced that we passively record the reality that surrounds us – in much the same way that a camera records what is seen through the viewfinder. But we are not passive recording devices. Man is always affecting his reality – and thus his perception of this reality. Man is driven by intentionality – the desire to search for meaning in all things (Bjartveit & Kjærstad, 1996). A life without understanding would be a life in darkness and chaos. This is the essence of man: we are doomed to search for meaning. Could you even imagine the opposite? Try looking at something – without trying to understand it! Good luck!

However, we often conduct this search for meaning in cooperation with others. Berger and Luckmann suggest that over time, interaction between people will give rise to patterns which in turn lead to habits being formed. It is just like two people moving in together for the first time. Two worlds meet, and they need to establish customs – for when they will eat, how they will eat, when they will watch TV, when they will, talk, how they will spend their Sundays, etc … Gradually a pattern that ensures stability and predictability will emerge. Berger and Luckmann argue that these patterns of actions become institutions … "whenever there is a reciprocal typification of habitualized actions by types of actors" (1966, p. 72). This is how we spend our Sundays (… which could be anything from lying in bed all day to taking a stroll in the park). But when habits become institutions, they assume objective qualities. That is the way things are. Try to remember your surprise and consternation the first time you spent Christmas with the in-laws (surely that is not the way you are supposed to celebrate Christmas!). And that is when the creation starts to exert influence on its creator. This is particularly evident whenever a new member joins an established reality – for instance, a new baby. The child will grow up in what he experiences as an objective reality. We even use this as an explanation whenever we explain why things are the way they are. The standard answer to all queries is quite simple: That's just the way thing are, sweetheart. That's the way people have spent their Sundays since the dawn of mankind. And that's that. Imagine their surprise when they eventually wander out into the world on their own – and discover a world full of alternative truisms. The truth is experienced as being objective and is internalized by new members.

Of course this perspective of established truisms is not limited to the world of families. It applies equally well to organizations. How do we create truisms in an organization? A social constructivist perspective has many similarities with the term organizational culture. Both models emphasize the fact that we fashion views and assumptions that are perceived as truisms. However, the social constructivist model is richer and more substantial. While organizational culture is limited to comparative dimensions of collectivism and masculinity, social constructivism also involves our experience of reality and truth. The social character of society and of organizations will give rise to different perceptions of reality. And the participants in this social reality perceive the truth as something real and objective. They are trapped by it, whether they are leaders or employees. That is the way of the world. This is the challenge that faces us. *Coke is it!*

As a result we cannot see the socially created world in which we live. We can simply not comprehend how Irakis could support Saddam Hussein, or even worse, why they would move even closer toward Islamic fundamentalism now that the tyrant has been removed and they have been given the opportunity to form a democracy. It must be due to ignorance and a stagnant civilization. By the same token we cannot understand how the American people could elect George W. Bush as president when people all over Europe groan in dismay every time Bush gives us that goofy smile and repeats his Saddam rhetoric on TV. Following the US presidential election in 2004, the *Daily Mirror* printed: "How can 59,054,087 people be that dumb?" on the front page. We are blissfully unaware of our own conception of reality – that makes it impossible for us to interpret these actions as anything but ignorant and misguided.

Some views of reality can be quite restrictive, especially when they are outdated or cannot provide an explanation for actual events. This aspect has been of major concern to organizational theorists. A company's strategies may be based on a well-meaning misinterpretation of the business climate – as in the case of the young Swedish entrepreneurs that started the internet retail site boo.com. They were just two of the countless number of pioneers that assumed that success on the internet was a given. Some of them managed to attract massive investments, and spent millions on promotional activities, but by the time they went online the public's interest had waned – leaving them with enormous debt and failed companies. Similarly, faith in technological competitive advantages can become almost fundamental, as was the case for the Swedish company ADDO, that manufactured the old fashioned "räkesnurran" (mechanical spin calculator), and was bought by Facit, another Swedish company – that firmly believed in the future of mechanical spin. Their out-dated view of reality caused them to miss out on the boom in electronics – which was instead dominated by Japanese rivals. There are a few other classical examples, such as when Ericsson discarded the mobile phone as a useless innovation; or when IBM boldly claimed that the world market for computers was, approximately, seven; or when DEC pondered why anybody would want a PC on their desks. It is not easy to catch a glimpse of the constructed reality in which each of us exists. Nor is it an easy undertaking to accept new perspectives of reality. Instead, we often resort to long-winded speeches and impeccable reasoning in defense of our favorite reality.

Berger and Luckmann (1966) call this type of explanation legitimizing, and as a consultant you would do well to listen carefully to these explanations, because the social order is revealed explicitly, albeit indirectly in these. Legitimization is second order institutionalization, and is created when an established reality must be explained to new members or defended. As such they reflect a need to reinforce reality as it is currently experienced. When you enter an organization as a consultant it may be difficult to identify the current institutions. But the legitimizations for these institutions will make themselves evident – in the form of explanations for why things are the way they are – and should remain that way. You can use the legitimizations to understand the client organization's social reality. This is how you identify the organization's inner life.

Berger and Luckmann (1966) describe four types of legitimizations: vocabulary, moral maxims, explicit theories, and symbolic universes. The *vocabulary* legitimates in itself. Language is power. Language governs the way opinions are formed. Just think how wonderful it is to toss around terms like investment, gains from synergy, motivation, and target figures. The act of using specific terms to describe certain phenomena will dictate meaning and exclude other interpretations. In Scandinavia this is evident in the many forms of the word snow: skare (snow where the top layer is melted, then frozen); newsnow, slush, and packing snow. It is kind of bizarre to watch films shot in LA when the plot requires snow. The first shot will be of nice, new, *cold* snow, but when the films cuts to the next shot, taken later when the snow is melting and the snow crystals are coarse and hard, it doesn't make sense. Don't they know what snow is? In the finished film these two sequences are supposed to be seconds apart and yet they look more like days apart to anyone who really knows snow. But even Scandinavians can be outdone when it comes to understanding snow – Eskimos have an even richer vocabulary when it comes to snow (Whorf, 1956) – which makes our reality seem comparatively modest. In fact this is a key element of the book *Miss Smilla's sense of snow* – which actually plays on the main character's keen sense of snow as compared to that of a native of Copenhagen. The police interpret a footprint in the snow on a rooftop as evidence that a boy has committed suicide. However, Miss Smilla, with her wonderful sense of snow, is able to see from the way the snow has been compacted under the footprint that the boy was running – fleeing from an assailant, and was chased off the roof. Murder; not suicide. So pay attention to the language people use. The expressions that the client organizations use, will reveal a great deal about who they are and what their reality looks like.

The second form of legitimization – *moral maxims or proverbs* – are even more palpable than vocabulary. Organizations and clients are inundated with these (... and consultant even more so). "You can't steer by looking in the rear-view mirror." "We live in the age of continuous change and must adapt even faster". "You have to earn before you can spend." These are all common-sense expositions – with absolutely no explanatory underpinning other than the actual phrases themselves. They don't even make an attempt to explain themselves – if you have to ask, then maybe you shouldn't be here. An executive-level discussion on strategy might thus consist of an endless exchange of business clichés, but no doubt the participants will be quite happy in the belief that their decisions are based on a thorough understanding of reality.

A more advanced form of legitimizing is called *explicit theories*. In this type of situation the client has attended a course or read a book. People have an incredible knack for reading literature that supports their own positions – so the theories that the client studies will tend to be in support of the organization's established world view. There is an unrelenting search for the magical silver bullet that will solve all problems – be it the Balanced Scorecard, Business Process Re-Engineering, or TQM, or anything else in the Heathrow Library of Management collection of simplistic solutions that purports to be the final solution to all evil. On a more serious note, this follows naturally from our tendency to look for theories that will support our views rather than challenge them. Scientific methodology teaches us that we can never really prove that a hypothesis is true, but merely "not reject" it, whereas in the course of a normal day most of us would claim that we can "prove" a hypothesis to be true. This phenomenon is evident in all simplistic management literature.

The most deeply rooted and advanced form of legitimizing is what Berger and Luckmann (1966) call *symbolic universes*. These permeate our lives and provide meaning to the institutional order of things and to the individual. These are the systems or truisms that we take for granted. We don't even think about them. They are true. Historically, Christianity has been a symbolic universe for the West. Once, Christianity provided order and meaning at both the macro- and micro levels, but it does so to a much lesser extent today. That doesn't mean that we don't have a symbolic universe today. In all likelihood, a new symbolic universe has replaced, or supplanted, the old symbolic universe as our view of reality has gradually evolved. So what symbolic universe describes our modern-day secularized society? Might it be that the market economy and faith in the stock market have become the great narratives of our time? Or, is it possible, in light of all the wars we have seen this past decade, that democracy has been sanctified and become the new faith that will solve all our problems? No doubt many will contend that the hedonistic pleasures of the individual are the one true god we all worship. The point is that it is difficult to recognize these legitimizations. We take them for granted, and that is all there is to say. The consultant has to spot these legitimizations, because in reality, this is the client lecturing you on his or her view of the world. And it is down this path s/he will drag you and your recommendations – until you convert to his or her view. More of the same is the name of the game, because they live in a social reality that leads them down the same path looking for solutions – time, and time again. The consultant must not yield to the temptation of becoming a member of the client's world, but rather stay impartial and try to understand how this view of reality is forcing the client down the same path to failure. And herein lays the great challenge. No one likes others messing with their perspective – there is a limit to what we will accept. And a confrontation that involves someone being told that their view of reality is misguided may be devastating (Bjartveit & Kjærstad, 1996). All sense of meaning disappears, and the sudden appearance of such a void is not accompanied by a celebration of freedom. Actually, it is quite the opposite; there are many theories that suggest this void will quickly be filled with anguish and anxiety (Heidegger, 1962; Kierkegaard, 1991). When the sky falls, chaos will reign. And we hate chaos. We want meaning. That is why anyone, even change agents, might be tempted to uphold the established truism, even when growth and development is what we really want.

Like pawns in a game

Paul Ricoeur (1974) emphasized the significance of suspicion when interpreting phenomena. Ricoeur's use of the term *hermeneutics of suspicion* is somewhat different from hermeneutics in the traditional sense – the human understanding and interpretation of the original meaning of texts and social actions (cf. part II). Ricoeur attempts to go beyond the obvious and often illusory, to identify a deeper meaning. Freud, Nietzsche, and Marx, are among the masters of suspicion. They sought to understand how seemingly innocuous details could have an effect on people in social events. Freud focused his attention on sex, Nietzshe on the will to power, and Marx on economics. And by the same token Ricoeur believes in suspicion, and wants to search for the hidden, and less than honorable, explanations. We must be willing to look beyond the obvious, beyond the Potemkin façade and the enthusiastic roar in honor of the Emperor's latest outfit. If we look beyond what is immediately apparent, we might find a deeper, and somewhat unpleasant, explanation for the phenomena we seek to understand. We must remain open to the possibility that there can be motives other than those stated that will explain someone's behavior.

In light of this we might ask ourselves whether the consultation itself could be interpreted as something more than just a supportive relationship. For a long time questions have been raised about whether consultants really have anything to offer clients, and criticism has been growing ever since (Alvesson, 1993; Fincham and Clark, 2002). By the same token we should ask ourselves whether the client is really just an innocent party in need of a helping hand. What motives do clients really have when they hire consultants? In the previous section we were concerned with what could be described as inadvertent manipulation borne out of helplessness. The client exerts considerable influence on the consultant, and unwittingly forces the consultant to adopt the client's own, inadequate perspective of reality. But we are talking about something different altogether here. As part of taking a critical look at the client as participant in the consultation we need to understand what the client really hopes to achieve by hiring a consultant. Based on the perspective of conflict theory, individuals will fight for their own interests – and as such power is at the heart of all social relationships (Wallace and Wolf, 1991). And this also applies to the client that hires a consultant. The consultant is hired as an external party to support the client and his or her interests – not necessarily the interest of the client's organization. Consultants can be of great help during power struggles. But such a motive would never be stated explicitly. The stated mission might not always be the true mission, but to actually put the true mission in words would violate social norms and customs. The true purpose of the consultancy must be concealed under layers of socially acceptable phrases like *right-sizing* and *tough talk*. Alternatively, the client may hire the consultant to do something that could contribute indirectly to achieving the client's goal. Rather than aide or counsel, the consultant is thus reduced to a *hired gun* – being used to accomplish some hidden agenda.

It would be difficult to make a list of all the possible hidden agendas clients could have. Instead, we would like to focus on four key categories of agendas that are of particular interest: contract research, alliances, cover-ups, and suppression. In these situations the consultant is hired to achieve something other the stated objective. In all four situations, the true nature of the assignment is kept from the consultant, and the consultant's expertise is used to achieve something other than the stated goal.

By *contract research*, we mean assignments – this could be different types of investigations or analyses, where the guidelines and limitations are so restrictive that there is really only one possible outcome. The client wants the analysis to provide clear recommendations – in support of his position. To ensure this result the client will usually restrict access to data, and be very clear about which alternatives s/he wants the consultant to explore and what results s/he thinks would be acceptable – or not acceptable, etc. What the client really wants is an expert opinion, from a credible, neutral third party, that is in fact tailored to support his or her position. A good illustration of this can be seen in the conflicting roles of Investment banks – where several recent court cases have forced the banks to alter their procedures. On the one hand, these banks serve as financial advisors, or suppliers, to a company, while on the other hand they employ analysts that give buy or sell recommendations on the same company. For some reason, banks seldom give sell recommendations for the shares of their major clients. There is also the case where the client really wants useless recommendations for what s/he sees as an insurmountable problem. It doesn't matter what you recommend, the client will say that either it's been tried before or that s/he cannot possibly try something like that. The more exasperated you get, the happier the client gets. What the client is really looking for is confirmation from the expert that the problem is impossible to solve. Because this will prove that the problem can be attributed to factors beyond control and remove any suspicion that the client (the leader) him- or herself is part of the problem. This is the complete opposite of the situation where the leader is lauded for something s/he has absolutely nothing to do with (Meindl, Ehrlich, and Dukerich, 1985). Or, in other words: "I'm not the only one struggling with this problem, even those expert consultants couldn't come up with a solution, so don't look at me."

While contract research is usually linked to reports and recommendations, *alliances* are more common at the implementation stage of an assignment. When conflict arises and parties face off against each other, the consultant is called in, as mercenary, to reinforce this or that position. And strategic counsel becomes aide-de-camp in the struggle for higher ground in the fight over whose view of reality will prevail. In reality, development programs for management teams, where the different conflicting positions on important matters are supposed to be aligned, actually wind up helping some participants in the struggle for power within a team.

Consultants can also be used for *cover-ups* – to cover for the client's own ineptitude. Essentially, the consultant comes in, winds up taking over the whole process and accomplishing something that the client would never have been able to do on his or her own. The difference between this and a regular assignment is subtle – the main purpose of the cover-up is to protect the image of the client. Sometimes the consultant is just there to make the client shine and conceal the cracks in the client's facade, while other times s/he may actually take over some of the client's duties. There have even been cases where consultants are called in to convince employees and the general public that management is better than it really is. Inept senior executives will let the consultant present what is essentially all the consultant's own work and then step forward and receive the applause – thus taking credit for something they had no part in. The consultant may also be called in to squash a revolt in the making – and to convince everybody that it is human to err – and even more human to forgive. Thus allowing the client to survive another day and avoid being fired. In these situations the hidden agenda is concerned with protecting the client's position – a position for which s/he, in reality, is not qualified to have. The consultant and the client are not creating anything; they are just giving the old stuff a fresh coat of paint.

The final category of hidden agenda is subjugation. There is an element of subjugation in all hidden agendas, but this particular form of subjugation goes on at the top levels of the organization. This is large-scale subjugation of the regular employees. Sometime clients will hire a consultant to carry out tasks that they don't have the stomach for themselves – and for which the client uses the consultant to distance him- or herself from the unpleasantries involved. The consultant carries out the mission – with cool professionalism and surgical precision. Downsizing is a good example of this type of situation – where the executives calling the shots would prefer not having to meet the soon-to-be-unemployed face-to-face and let the consultant take their place. There are also situations that no one wants to have their name associated with – this could be hostile takeovers or brutal restructuring, where it is best for all parties involved if the evil mastermind behind these actions leaves the organization once the mission is carried out. The consultant may be used as a bulldozer during implementation, but also comes in handy as scapegoat after the project is completed. There are more subtle forms of subjugation – they may not be unpleasant or seem coercive, but they do affect employees' perception of reality. For what exactly is a motivational seminary? We can trace the history of these events all the way back to the Roman Coliseum – bread and circus have become attitudinal massage. Entertain and pacify employees – and they might forget all their troubles and complaints. It is less about motivation, and more about manipulating perceptions and sentiments. The consultants have become the gladiators – in a well-rehearsed performance designed to control and subdue the masses. There is really very little motivating involved.

In each one of these situations, the consultant is being used to accomplish something other than the client's stated objective. The consultant is deliberately being exploited. Is the consultant aware that s/he is being used? From a conflict theory perspective it would be naive to pretend that this type of manipulation didn't occur from time to time. The client will always try to influence the consultant. S/he has got his or her own interests to take care of. But it might also be somewhat naive and just a little bit bull-headed to think that the only decent course of action is to terminate the assignment. There are other options – that might be more beneficial to the consultant, to the client, and to the client's organization. Let us examine a few of these options.

Countermeasures

Milan Kubr (1996, p. 8) defines management consulting as: "… an independent professional advisory service assisting managers and organizations in achieving organizational purposes and objectives by solving management and business problems, identifying and seizing new opportunities, enhancing learning, and implementing changes." This should be our point of departure when we consider the consultant's possible courses of actions when excessive or inappropriate pressure from the client threatens to disrupt the assignment. First, Kubr's definition emphasizes the consultant's role as advisor – with an obligation to give the client the best possible advice. Regardless of how the client tries to influence the consultant, the consultant should always keep in mind what is best for the customer. This is, however, a lot more difficult to carry out in practice than it may sound. Neither puppets nor self-appointed moralists will get very far in this type of situation. Puppets will applaud the client at every turn, while the moralists tend to get a little self-righteous and forget all about the client's needs. Second, it is the duty of the consultant to assist the organization to achieve its objectives, which means that they cannot assist in actions that are at odds with the plans and objectives of the organization. The consultant must not become a political factor – helping a prince that is only out to further his own career and powerbase. And neither should the consultant quietly accept assumptions that could damage the organization and prevent it from reaching its goals. Third, the consultant is an independent professional service provider – which implies that the consultant should have his or her own code of ethics that states what should, or should not, be done. The consultant should not willingly carry out assignments that violate this code of ethics. Integrity is at the core of professionalism – but integrity should be judged from your actions, and not by the code of ethics you claim to swear by (Maister, 2004).

In light of these circumstances, which may apply to any consultancy assignment, we would like to suggest the following possible courses of action for a consultant who is being pressured by a client: close your eyes, accept the client's agenda, establish your own hidden agenda, or terminate the assignment. The consultant uses these forms of intervention in the client-consultant system to move the system in a direction that is acceptable for the consultant. Even though the client is an active participant in this system, s/he really should consider any actions that may improve the performance of this system – with an eye to providing his or her organization with the best possible help. The four alternatives we have listed do not explicitly take the client's mindset into account – that is whether or not the undue influence is the result of deliberation or desperation. Three of the options are suitable for both deadlocked social constructions and political agendas, whereas the fourth, accepting the client's agenda only applies to political influence.

The first option is to close your eyes and block out the client's influence. This option is recommended when other interventions against undue influence would probably wind up making things even worse. This is particularly appropriate if the manipulation concerns relatively minor or harmless issues. Or, it could be that although some of the client's perspectives might be somewhat twisted, they are rather harmless. What could the consultant possibly hope to achieve by creating even more confusion inside the client's head? Ibsen would back us on this one – not all things need to be brought out into the open and analyzed. In Ibsens play *The Wild Duck* (Ibsen, 1991); two aides disagree on the best course of action. Gregers Werle wants to help Hjalmar Ekdahl in his time of need by confronting him with his own shortcomings, while Dr. Relling argues that it is best to leave well enough alone. Dr. Relling warns Werle that his stubborn insistence on taking away a person's "life lie" may cause more harm than good. Righteousness and the truth do not always assure a positive outcome – something Ibsen illustrates masterfully in his play. An enthusiastic Monty Pythonistic "Get it all out in the open" does not do the trick. Sometime these admonitions can exacerbate the problem and lead to self-perpetuating deviations (cf. Ch. 4). The consultant has a moral obligation to consider these issues. It should be pointed out that the ability to overlook awkward dilemmas is something that most consultants seem to have. So this option might not be new to anyone.

The second alternative is to accept the client's hidden agenda – to the extent that it does not violate the principles we discussed previously. It could be that the client's hidden agenda is a perfectly acceptable assignment, which the client would feel uncomfortable having to put in words. It is perfectly legitimate to help a client win an internal struggle for power, or to bolster a leader's popularity – but there are obvious limits to how directly a client could, or would, state these objectives. Once the consultant has accepted the client's agenda, there are two options. The consultant can accept the client's hidden agenda –without actually stating this explicitly – leading to an I-know-that-you-know-that-I-know-what-you're-doing situation. The rationale for this is simply that an open and frank discussion of the true nature of the assignment would make matters worse.

There are very strong emotional reactions linked to the issue of loosing face in public in our culture (Argyris, 1990). If the client looses face in a confrontation over the true nature of the assignment, s/he could become very defensive and even obstructive, and this could get in the way of the assignment. Thus, it makes more sense to avoid an open confrontation and find some level of understanding that works for both parties. Alternatively, it could be that an open dialogue may be acceptable, and that, and the hidden agenda, can be explicitly accepted. This depends on how well the relationship between client and consultant is developing, and on the nature of the assignment. A delicate hand is required when the subject of hidden agendas is raised, and especially so if the nature of the assignment should change as a result of this subject being raised. There is much to be gained, in the form of trust and momentum, if such an open accord can be reached. The client-consultant system changes for the better, and is open to new discussions. This is similar to the long-term process of leadership coaching. As trust grows between leader and coach, and if the relationship is perceived as beneficial, the client may start to open up and reveal some difficult issues, which may not be at the heart of what was the original focus of discussions, but may have been blocking progress all the same. This takes the relationship to a new level, and the coaching a large step forward.

A third alternative would be for the consultant to develop his or her own hidden agenda in response to the client's – implying that the consultant views the influence from client as detrimental to the organization – and to the achievement of its goals. The boundaries that the client puts in place are so restrictive that the consultant can no longer close his or her eyes to this, and s/he creates a hidden agenda of his or her own to deal with this. If it is the client's fixed ideas on important issues that stand in the way of considering new ideas or developments, then the consultant will have to do something about this in order to accomplish the assignment's objective. The consultant creates a new agenda that will have an indirect effect on the original goal. But this poses the question of whether this hidden agenda, which is in effect a new objective that the client is unaware of, constitutes a breach of the original contract – and its stated goals. As long as the main objective remains unchanged, and this new agenda's only purpose is to achieve the main objective, this type of action can be justified, although the consultant alone is responsible for making this decision. This type of indirect intervention is quite common in psychotherapy, especially in cases that seem to have reached an impasse when it is inappropriate to target the client head on (Watzlawick, Weakland, and Fisch, 1974). If all it took to achieve the goals was a logical and well-meaning piece of advice to be delivered across the boardroom table, then consulting would be a cinch. You need to become more confident as a leader! See the things you are not really noticing! Be spontaneous! Try not to tremble! Sometimes the consultation needs to focus on the soft intervening factors that determine behavior.

In some cases, the consultant may reveal his hidden agenda to the client (which thus means that it no longer is a hidden agenda), but this requires a delicate touch. If the client comes to realize how some of these intervening factors are actually getting in the way of what s/he is trying to achieve, this may take the relationship to the next level and pave the way for future consultations. On the other hand it is easy to see that the confrontational approach may put the client on the defensive, in which case open confrontation is not advised. If this seems to be the case, the consultant will have to keep this intervention hidden for the client. This may sound somewhat crude and dubious, but consultants are often forced into this type of indirect, hidden intervention. It is quite common for consultants to try to give misguided leaders a little extra advice or direction – without coming out in the open about it, in the hope that the client will start to think about certain issues. These are hidden, indirect interventions, that the consultant conducts of his or her own accord, based on a desire to help the client.

The final alternative is for the consultant to terminate the assignment. This could happen when the consultant feels it is impossible to continue with the assignment, given the level of pressure being exerted by the client. Rumor would have that is a highly uncommon event in the world of consulting and that consultants will sell their soul for a good fee. But in this case there is an ethical reason to consider termination – based on the principles we used to define consultation. Sometimes you have to pack up and leave. But we must emphasize that terminating a contract is in itself a fierce intervention – that no doubt will have an effect on the client. The client-consultant system is terminated. The consultant cannot just climb up on his or her high horse and speak of categorical imperatives and ethical standards. Even when termination seems like the only course of action, the consultant still has a moral obligation for what this intervention does to the client. The best case scenario would be that this makes the client change his or her ways, in which case this would be the best possible intervention. Worst case scenario is that the termination causes the client to feel embarrassed and abandoned – which may lead to even more destructive behavior. So what is the best way to help the client?

In each one of these approaches, the consultant is intervening against the client's influence (even in the case where s/he chooses to close his or her eyes to what is going on). You arrive at these types of interventions based on rational models of problem solving. These problems are highly complex, and will truly challenge the consultant's powers of reasoning, because it is the consultant's responsibility to deal with these issues. In the dialogue *Gorgias* (Platon, 1977) Socrates passes the most insidious judgment of all time over the consultancy sector. The target of Socrates' criticisms was the Sophists – the consultants of Antiquity, who offered advice and education to the young, aspiring men of Athens (Field, 1970). But Socrates' criticisms are equally relevant today. The essence of Socrates' criticisms concerns the responsibility the consultant has to the client. Do you assume responsibility for what happens to the client when the assignment is over? This is the true ethical dilemma for consultants. There is no right or wrong decisions here. Sometimes it is right versus right – or wrong versus wrong. But you cannot *not* have an influence.

Sleep-test

If you accept that the relationship between consultant and client as a system where the parties interact with each other, both openly and secretly, consciously and unwittingly, you must also accept that this will have a bearing on your analyses and interventions. A relationship involves interaction, and you cannot escape the fact that you exert influence and are yourself the object of influence. Do you really appreciate what this game entails? Can you handle it? Dealt with in the appropriate way, the client's hidden agendas and attempts to influence your actions can actually provide you with valuable information that you can use to accomplish the assignment – and achieve the stated goals. On the other hand, you may be sucked into a struggle that you cannot escape from, or, you may intervene in such a way that you damage the relationship.

Aristotle claimed that for a person to make sound, ethical decisions in difficult situations such as the ones we have described, this person must be knowledgeable of the four cardinal virtues: fortitude, justice, prudence, and temperance. Our reasoning must go beyond our own selfish interests and take in to account the common good. Measured against this standard the modern-day consultant will not fare well. Can you look at yourself in the mirror, knowing what you have done? Can you sleep at night? These were Aristotle's simple requirements. The sleep test may sound naive, but it is all the same a firm measure of the moral standard of our actions as consultants (Badaracco, 1997). An individual's emotions may provide more moral guidance than isolated intellectual reasoning. But that requires that the individual is conscious of what is going on in his surroundings, and of how s/he, as a consultant, exerts influence on these surroundings.

References

Alvesson, M. (1993). Organizations as rhetoric: knowledge-intensive firms and the struggle with ambiguity. *Journal of Management Studies,* 30(6), 997–1015.

Argyris, C. (1990). *Overcoming organizational defences: Facilitating organizational learning.* Needham Height, MA: Allyn and Bacon.

Aristoteles (1999). *Den nikomakiske etikk.* Oslo: Bokklubben Dagens Bøker.

Badaracco, J. L. (1997). *Defining moments. When managers must choose between right and right.* Boston: Harvard Business School Press.

Bateson, G. (1972). *Steps to an ecology of mind.* St. Albans: Paladin.

Berger, P. & Luckmann, T. (1966). *The social construction of reality. A treatise in the sociology of knowledge.* London: Penguin Books.

Bjartveit, S. & Kjærstad, T. (1996). *Kaos og kosmos. Byggesteiner for individer og organisasjoner.* Oslo: Kolle Forlag.

Field, G. C. (1970). Sophists. In N. G. L. Hammond & H. H. Scullard (Eds.), *The Oxford classical dictionary.* Oxford: Oxford University Press.

Fincham, R. & Clark, T. (2002). Introduction: The ermergence of critical perspectives on consulting. In T. Clark & R. Fincham, *Critical consulting. New perspectives on the management advice industry.* Oxford: Blackwell Business.

Heidegger, M. (1962). *Being and time.* Oxford: Blackwell.

How can 59,054,087 persons be so dumb? (2004, November 4). *Daily Mirror,* p. 1.

Høivik, H.W. (2005. Consultants as destructive confidants and the unethical 'games that people play'. In S. Bjartveit & G. Roos (Eds.), *Scandinavian perspectives on management consulting*. Oslo: J.W. Cappelens Forlag.

Ibsen, H. (1991). *Vildanden*. Oslo: Gyldendal.

Kierkegaard, S. (1991). *Begrepet angest*. København: DSL/Borgens Forlag.

Kubr, M. (1993). *How to select and use consultants. A client's guide*. Geneva: International Labour Office.

Kubr, M. (Ed.). (1996). *Management consulting. A guide to the profession*. 3rd ed. Geneva: International Labour Office.

Machiavelli, N. (2004). *Fyrsten*. Oslo: Bokklubben Dagens Bøker.

Maister, D. (2004). Professionalism in consulting. In L. Greiner & F. Poulfeldt (Eds.), *Handbook of management consulting. The contemporary consultant. Insights from world experts*. Mason, Ohio: Thomson, South-Western.

Meindl, J.R., Ehrlich, S.B. & Dukerich, J.M. (1985). The romance of leadership. *Administrative Science Quarterly*, 30, 78–102.

O'Shea, J. & Madigan, C. (1997). *Dangerous company. The consulting powerhouses and the businesses they save and ruin*. London: Nicholas Brealey Publishing.

Platon (1977). *Gorgias*. København: Gyldendal.

Ricoeur, P. (1974). *The conflict of interpretations: Essays in hermeneutics*. Evanston: Northwestern University Press.

Sturdy, A. (2002). Front-line diffusion: The production and negotiation of knowledge through training interactions. In T. Clark & R. Fincham (Eds.), *Critical consulting. New perspectives on the management advice industry*. Oxford: Blackwell Business.

Wallace, R.A. & Wolf, A. (1991). *Contemporary sociological theory. Continuing the classical tradition*. 3rd ed. Englewood Cliffs, NJ: Prentice Hall.

Watzlawick, P., Bavelas, J.B. & Jackson, D.D. (1967). *Pragmatics of human communication*. New York: Norton.

Watzlawick, P., Weakland, J. & Fisch, R. (1974). *Change. Principles of problem formation and problem resolution*. New York: Norton.

Whorf, B.L. (1956). Science and linguistics. In J. B. Carroll (Ed.), *Language, thought and reality: selected writings of Benjamin Lee Whorf*. Cambridge, MA: MIT Press.

Chapter 9

Consultants as destructive confidants and the unethical 'games that people play'

HEIDI VON WELTZIEN HØIVIK

Truth is a powerful weapon. People may not think so but it is very powerful. And truth – like anything that is powerful – can be frightening or reassuring, depending on which side you are on. If you're on the side of truth, it's very reassuring – you have its protection. But if you're on the side of untruth – then it is very frightening.

Aung San Suu Kyi[1]

In business schools students are often exposed to case studies that present them with an engaging narrative, displaying a problematic situation in business that requires decision making. The primary goal of this type of exercise is to develop three main skills: The first is to be able to give an accurate account of the case, the second is to 'imagine' options available in real life situations, and the third is to test rational, analytical tools and skills for decision making. However there is an even more compelling reason to engage students in activities that stimulate their imagination. Adam Smith, often called the "founder of modern economics", though he was a moral philosopher, emphasized the role of what he calls the "judicious spectator" as indispensable to proper reasoning on economic policy matter. Indeed, Smith himself gave considerable weight to literature as the source of moral guidance. In his work, *The Theory of Moral Sentiments,* Smith writes (I.I.4.6):

"The spectator must... endeavor, as much as he can, to put himself in the situation of the other, and to bring home to himself every little cir-

---

[1] quoted in: Judith A. White (1998). Leadership through compassion and understanding. *Journal of Management Inquiry* 7, 286–293.

cumstance of distress which can possibly occur to the sufferer. He must adopt the whole case of his companion with all its minutes incidents; and strive to render as perfect as possible, that imaginary change of situation upon which his sympathy is founded." [2]

Smith's advice of course is to be both *judicious* in the moral sense of the word and a *spectator*, using rational detachment in order to develop special capabilities as human beings.

Literary works lend themselves well to the cultivation of emphatic imagination with rational arguments and illustrate that rational arguments without imagination are blind. Imagination here means the ability to envisage another person's life and to view circumstances from a holistic perspective. For consultants this ability is of the utmost importance. They need to develop personal skills by learning how to wrestle with complex situations. Perhaps no other "business cases" can be as rich in narrative textures as for example Shakespeare's tragedies.

Shakespeare's *Othello* is a tragedy of human frailty and toxic relations that lead to the tragic death of others. In this drama people bring death on others through lies, deception, hatred, and loss of control.

Othello is about truth and how truth can be maliciously manipulated. It is also about power and vulnerability, trust and risk, envy and resentment, intellect, and emotions, and it is about a consultant being the most destructive confidant. It is also about ethics and morality, loyalty and human dignity, and values like honesty, honor, and integrity.

The sobering reality of destructive relationships depicted in this play shows that it always takes at least two people in a relationship, where one trusts and the other usurps this trust, to bring about destruction. Both Othello and Iago are equally responsible and complicit in their destructive relationship. While Othello seems to need the relationship the most, Iago needs to demonstrate his brilliant intellect and his power by usurping and manipulating others. The game he plays with other people is caused by his distorted sense of superiority and a yearning for satisfaction. To him, those who have undervalued him are mere "fools". They are stupid, and they are like puppets in his hands, made to suffer at the mere motion of a finger,

---

[2] quoted in: Martha C. Nussbaum (1995). *Poetic Justice: The Literary Imagination and Public Life* (p. 73). Boston: Beacon Press.

while all the time believing that he is their true and honest friend.[3]

The following analysis of the play sets out to investigate the following: Does Shakespeare's *Othello* have relevance for managers in today's business world? What can consultants and confidants of people in power learn from the play? How does Iago serve Othello as either confidant or consultant? What are his strategies, and why and how is he so successful in manipulating Othello?

To answer these and other questions, the article is structured according to the following thematic issues: Vulnerability, trust and risk, envy and resentment, and professionalism as a consultant and confidant. At the end of the chapter I shall try to view the characters' thinking and behavior from an ethical point of view and draw some conclusions relevant to the business context.

Vulnerability

Let us begin with conceptualizing vulnerability, as it is closely linked to trust:

> "The notion of vulnerability is complex and slippery. Most simply, to be "vulnerable" is to be susceptible to being wounded, liable to physical hurt. More generally being vulnerable is being susceptible to some harm or other. One can be vulnerable to man-made or natural harms: one can also be vulnerable from actions or omission."[4]

Let us look at an example from Goodin (p. 118): "A is more vulnerable to B (1) the more control B has over outcomes that affect A's interests and (2) the more heavily A's interests are at stake in the outcomes that B controls. B is defined as having 'less control' the more likely it is that the outcome will occur (or not occur) whatever B does ..."

As we can see here, vulnerability can be interpreted in terms of a lack of control which one agent might have vis-à-vis another agent with regard to the fulfillment of the first agent's interest.

Closely linked to vulnerability are two related concepts – susceptibility

---

[3] http://www.theatredance.com/othello/main.html
[4] Goodin, R.E. (1985). *Protecting the Vulnerable* (p. 118). Chicago: The University of Chicago Press.

and disadvantage. According to Brenkert, vulnerability is distinct from susceptibility, in that a person might be susceptible to something or someone and still not be vulnerable to that thing or person.[5] *Susceptibility* merely implies that one is "capable of being affected, quite easily" by something or someone. It is true that one who is susceptible may also be vulnerable. Clearly, one who is vulnerable is susceptible. But one need not be vulnerable if one is susceptible, since one's susceptibility may not be to some form of harm. An overweight and under-exercised adult might be susceptible through flattery or positive remarks, to certain suggestions made by friends, to exercise more and moderate food intake. But this person would not be vulnerable to such suggestions. Hence, vulnerability and susceptibility are different, according to Brenkert (p. 8).

Disadvantage, on the other hand, "refers to those who are unequal … Because of characteristics that are not of their own choosing, including their age, race, ethnic minority status, and sometimes gender".[6]

Let us now test these concepts with regard to the character of Othello. To what extent does Othello make himself vulnerable? How does he place himself in a situation where his vulnerability is exposed?

Vulnerability always occurs in a particular context. In Shakespeare's drama *Othello* the armed forces, the military, is such a context, just like the market would be for business people, where certain forms of competition and norms for behavior exist. The strongest and/or the smartest wins and does this quite often by exploiting the vulnerability of the others, the "enemy" or the weaker competitor.

On a deeper level, what are Othello's incapacities or qualitatively different experiences that make him vulnerable?

According to Brenkert (p. 11) there are four specific characteristics of vulnerability which can be distinguished:

Physically vulnerable – susceptibility due to physical or biological condition.

Cognitively vulnerable – lack certain levels of ability to cognitively process information or to be aware that certain information was being

---

[5] Brenkert, George G. (1999). Marketing and the Vulnerable. *BEQ 9*, 7–20, p. 8.
[6] Andreassen, A.R. (1993). Revisiting the Disadvantaged: Old Lessons and New Problems. *Journal of Public Policy and Marketing, 12,* 270–275, p. 273.

withheld or manipulated in deceptive ways. People lacking education or other forms of sophistication.

Motivationally vulnerable – person who could not resist ordinary temptations and/or enticements due to their own individual characteristics.

Socially vulnerable – persons whose social situation renders them significantly less able than others to resist various enticements, appeals, or challenges which may bring them harm.

With regard to Othello, his *physical vulnerability* is his skin color. He is black. The play bears the subtitle: The Moor of Venice. He is fully aware of this vulnerability due to his skin color, and he knows that he needs to work extra hard to be recognized and accepted by others:

> *Her father loved me; oft invited me;*
> *Still question'd me the story of my life,*
> *From year to year, the battles, sieges, fortunes,*
> *That I have passed.*
> *I ran it through, even from my boyish days,*
> *To the very moment that he bade me tell it;*
> (I,III)

And when Iago manages to place the first seed of suspicion into Othello's mind he again expresses his inferiority:

> *This fellow's of exceeding honesty,*
> *And knows all qualities, with a learned spirit,*
> *Of human dealings. If I do prove her haggard,*
> *Though that her jesses were my dear heartstrings,*
> *I'ld whistle her off and let her down the wind,*
> *To pray at fortune. Haply, for I am black*
> *And have not those soft parts of conversation*
> *That chamberers have, or for I am declined*
> *Into the vale of years,—yet that's not much—*
> *She's gone. I am abused; and my relief*
> *Must be to loathe her. O curse of marriage,*

That we can call these delicate creatures ours,
And not their appetites! I had rather be a toad,
And live upon the vapour of a dungeon,
Than keep a corner in the thing I love
For others' uses. Yet, 'tis the plague of great ones;
Prerogatived are they less than the base;
'Tis destiny unshunnable, like death:
Even then this forked plague is fated to us.

(III, scene 3)

Othello's *cognitive vulnerability* is caused by his personal character traits that are heavily shaped by his past history of which he reveals only a glimpse. He is a romantic and does not feel at home in Venetian culture or society. There is mystery surrounding his descent, his upbringing, his wanderings in vast deserts, and his experiences among marvelous peoples. He refers to magic handkerchiefs and prophetic tidings and thus shows a belief in superhuman or magic powers. His is the world of imagination and tales with which he charmed Desdemona:

Wherein I spake of most disastrous chances,
Of moving accidents by flood and field
Of hair-breadth scapes i' the imminent deadly breach,
Of being taken by the insolent foe
And sold to slavery, of my redemption thence
And portance in my travels' history:
Wherein of antres vast and deserts idle,
Rough quarries, rocks and hills whose heads touch heaven
It was my hint to speak,–such was the process;
And of the Cannibals that each other eat,
The Anthropophagi and men whose heads
Do grow beneath their shoulders. This to hear
Would Desdemona seriously incline:

(I, scene 3)

He even sees poetry in pride about a glorious war. His reality has different multi-dimensions and history. As the philosopher Hans-Georg Gadamer has said:

"In fact history does not belong to us; we belong to it. Long before we understand ourselves through the process of self-examination, we understand ourselves in a self-evident way in the family, society, and state in which we live. The focus of subjectivity is a distorting mirror. The self-awareness of the individual is only a flickering in the closed circuits of historical life. That is why the prejudices of the individual, far more than his judgments, constitute the historical reality of his being."[7]

Othello is unaccustomed to the manipulative tactics and wit displayed by Iago. He may sense it, but he seems incapable of cognitively processing the information Iago passes on to him.

He is *motivationally vulnerable* because he has a very strong sense of pride and honour. He is proud of himself and his military achievements, and especially proud of the honourable appearance he at least presents. He states this in his defense when accused of having bewitched Desdemona:

> *That I have ta'en away this old man's daughter,*
> *It is most true; true, I have married her:*
> *The very head and front of my offending*
> *Hath this extent, no more. Rude am I in my speech,*
> *And little bless'd with the soft phrase of peace:*
> *For since these arms of mine had seven years' pith,*
> *Till now some nine moons wasted, they have used*
> *Their dearest action in the tented field,*
> *And little of this great world can I speak,*
> *More than pertains to feats of broil and battle,*
> *And therefore little shall I grace my cause*
> *In speaking for myself.*
>
> (I, scene 3)

His vanity and pride make him project an image of being powerful, accomplished, humble, and moral at all times. When his pride and vanity are injured, Othello does not react with reason, only with emotions. There are only two realities in his world: the reality of the battlefield character-

---

[7] Hans-Georg Gadamer (1989). *Truth and Method* (pp. 276–77). Rev. trans. J. Weinsheimer and D. Marshall. New York: Crossroad.

ized by control and competence, and the reality of emotions, like love and magic. If both these realities break down, there is only chaos. His only resort is rage and despair.

Othello's *social vulnerability* is equally obvious: He is a stranger in the Venetian world of citizens. His black skin also determines how Othello perceives himself as a rough outsider. Othello's race and background set him apart, and make him painfully self-conscious. Carefully looking after his reputation, he seeks reassurance that he is regarded as equal to white people. He constantly asks Desdemona to verify this to him:

> *It gives me wonder great as my content*
> *To see you here before me. O my soul's joy!*
> *If after every tempest come such calms,*
> *May the winds blow till they have waken'd death!*
> *And let the labouring bark climb hills of seas*
> *Olympus-high and duck again as low*
> *As hell's from heaven! If it were now to die,*
> *'Twere now to be most happy; for, I fear,*
> *My soul hath her content so absolute*
> *That not another comfort like to this*
> *Succeeds in unknown fate.*
>
> (II, scene 1)

He allows himself to be flattered by Iago who knows how to take advantage of Othello's vulnerability. This is morally unacceptable as it causes harm to another person. If we believe that Iago does this knowingly – and there is evidence for believing this – it is morally unacceptable. The most poignant conversation of the play is:

> OTHELLO *What dost thou think?*
> IAGO   *Think, my lord!*
> OTHELLO *Think, my lord!*
>   *By heaven, he echoes me,*
>   *As if there were some monster in his thought*
>   *Too hideous to be shown. Thou dost mean something:*
>   *I heard thee say even now, thou likedst not that,*
>   *When Cassio left my wife: what didst not like?*

>   *And when I told thee he was of my counsel*
>   *In my whole course of wooing, thou criedst 'Indeed!'*
>   *And didst contract and purse thy brow together,*
>   *As if thou then hadst shut up in thy brain*
>   *Some horrible conceit: if thou dost love me,*
>   *Show me thy thought.*
> IAGO   *My lord, you know I love you.*
> OTHELLO   *I think thou dost;*
>   *And, for I know thou'rt full of love and honesty,*
>   *And weigh'st thy words before thou givest them breath,*
>   *Therefore these stops of thine fright me the more:*
>   *For such things in a false disloyal knave*
>   *Are tricks of custom, but in a man that's just*
>   *They are close delations, working from the heart*
>   *That passion cannot rule.*
>
>   (III. Scene 2)

Trust and risk

At this point in the drama, Othello has a true choice of either trusting Iago or disregarding the allegations. He chooses to trust Iago and asks him to provide proof.

At this point Iago has become his trusted confidant and consultant. A mutual relationship based on friendship, love, trust, and loyalty is established as far as Othello is concerned.

Othello and Iago enter into a contractual relationship where both know that above all trust is at stake. The concept of trust is widely discussed in a variety of disciplines. I have selected the definitions below as they are of relevance to the discussion in this paper and because they are also closely linked to vulnerability, reliance, dependence, and risk.

Curral says that trust is reliance on another person under conditions of dependence and risk. The willingness of a party to be vulnerable to the actions of another party based on the expectations that the other will perform a particular action important to the trustor, irrespective of the ability to monitor or control that other party:[8]

---

[8] Curral, S,C. (1990). *The Role of Interpersonal Trust in Work Relationships* (unpublished doctoral dissertation, Cornell University).

"Being vulnerable … implies that there is something of importance to be lost. Making oneself vulnerable is taking risk".[9] Annette Baier[10] offers two outcome directed definitions: "Accepted vulnerability to another's possible but not expected ill will (or lack of good will) toward one"[11] and "reliance on others' competence and willingness to look after, rather than harm, things one cares about".[12]

Baier also proposes that the integrity of trust relationships can be tested by determining whether either party is manipulating the other, by preying upon the qualities of the other in ways that require concealment if the relationship is to be continued.[13]

Based on these propositions it seems obvious that there are positive expectations expressed with trust. And there is both reliance and risk involved by giving the trustee the opportunity to do harm.

This definitely places moral responsibility on the trustee. A consultant or confidant, as a trustee, has unspecified and discretionary responsibilities and can easily go beyond the boundaries in the relationship with his or her client. Due care is essential in maintaining a trusting relationship. With due care we refer to knowing and respecting the boundaries that the consultant must not exceed.

Iago goes beyond the given boundaries as a soldier and subordinate to Othello, by questioning his authority. Not knowing what is going on "behind his back", reduces Othello's authority and competence as commander and husband.

Othello (like many CEOs in business) is dependent upon trust. He must trust both his soldiers and his wife. His trust is tied to certain expectations that the people he trusts will behave in a certain preferred way that promotes and sustains his authority and power. It is important for him to feel secure with regard to the loyalty of his men and his wife.

He also has a professional need to know that he can rely on his men. Their loyalty may determine life or death in war. This is part of his professional "project" so to speak as 'General of the Venetian army'. His trust is

---

[9] Mayer, D. and Schoorman, D. (1995). An Integrative Model of Organizational Trust. *Academy of Management Review, 20 (3),* 709–734.
[10] Annette Baier (1994). *Moral Prejudices.* Cambridge, MA: Harvard University Press.
[11] ibid p. 99
[12] ibid p. 128
[13] ibid p. 123

based on factual evidence, often revealed by action during a military action. He alone is in charge of this military "project", and his professional reputation and image as general are at stake, if he is betrayed.

Trusting his wife is very different in that this says something special about another person. Othello's trust involves feelings of being certain of his wife's love and his own expectations in this regard. It is not based on evidence alone. Trust has to be rewarded by the trustee. The trustee alone is capable of damaging the trustor. Othello is more vulnerable in this relationship because there is another element of asymmetry. The trustee has power over the trustor. Desdemona is not in a 'professional relationship' with Othello; her trust and being trusted is based on true emotions, feelings, and genuine love. It is within her power to harm Othello's confidence in these feelings.

Envy and resentments

Friedrich Nietzsche in *On the Geneaology of Morals* once said:

> "(The man of resentment) loves hiding places, secret paths and back doors, everything covert entices him as his world, his security, his refreshment; he understands how to keep silent, how not to forget, how to wait, how to be provisionally self-deprecating and humble".[14]

Iago is resentful because Othello, the general, has undervalued him and has promoted his rival Cassio instead of him. In addition he has married Desdemona. Iago expresses this with the following words:

> *Three great ones of the city,*
> *In personal suit to make me his lieutenant,*
> *Off-capp'd to him: and, by the faith of man,*
> *I know my price, I am worth no worse a place:*
> *But he; as loving his own pride and purposes,*
> *Evades them, with a bombast circumstance*
> *Horribly stuff'd with epithets of war;*
> *And, in conclusion,*

---

[14] quoted in Solomon (1993), p. 242.

> *Nonsuits my mediators; for, 'Certes,' says he,*
> *'I have already chose my officer.'*
> *And what was he?*
> *Forsooth, a great arithmetician,*
> *One Michael Cassio, a Florentine,*
> *A fellow almost damn'd in a fair wife;*
> *That never set a squadron in the field,*
> *Nor the division of a battle knows*
> *More than a spinster; unless the bookish theoric,*
> *Wherein the toged consuls can propose*
> *As masterly as he: mere prattle, without practise,*
> *Is all his soldiership. But he, sir, had the election:*
> *And I, of whom his eyes had seen the proof*
> *At Rhodes, at Cyprus and on other grounds*
> *Christian and heathen, must be be-lee'd and calm'd*
> *By debitor and creditor: this counter-caster,*
> *He, in good time, must his lieutenant be,*
> *And I–God bless the mark!–his Moorship's ancient.*
>
> (1, scene 1)

Solomon in *Ethics and Excellence* describes how envy and resentment can be viewed as 'corporate poison' in business, but this is also true for the situation which Shakespeare describes in *Othello*. Envy and resentment "affect the health of the organization the way a slow acting poison affect the health of an individual ... Envy and resentment are both obsessed with the idea that one has been slighted or denied his or her due. The difference between them is that envy desires what one does not have – usually power, position, or material goods – whereas resentment is aimed at the person, the process, at the justice of the matter." [15]

Resentment leads to outrage, a feeling of being cheated, "whereas envy includes lust and scheming, resentment prompts us to dig deeper, condemn, build a case and feigning cooperation but in fact sowing the seeds of disruption".

---
[15] Solomon, pp. 243–45.

> RODERIGO By heaven, I rather would have been his hangman.
> IAGO But there's no remedy: 'tis the curse of service,
> Preferment goes by letter and affection,
> And not by old gradation, where each second
> Stood heir to the first. Now, sir, be judge yourself,
> Whether I in any just term am affined
> To love the Moor.
>
> (1, scene 1)

"Envy is not just covetous; it is also malicious and potentially destructive." (p. 243).

> *Though I do hate him as I do hell-pains.*
> *Yet, for necessity of present life,*
> *I must show out a flag and sign of love,*
> *Which is indeed but sign.*
>
> (I, scene 1)

Iago feels a deep resentment towards Cassio and is envious of Cassio's promotion and of Othello for having gained the love of Desdemona. He is consumed by a desire to inflict pain on others in return for what he considers a slight. This passionate desire, easily recognizable in how Shakespeare allows Iago to 'word' it, is at the same time deceitfully hidden by the fact that most statements Iago makes are not believable.

This puts not only Othello but also the audience in a state of not knowing what is true or untrue. The audience is being confused on purpose, partially to show how "subjective" Iago's judgements are and also to show that he may turn out to be a victim of his own desires. Iago's psyche is complex and even troublesome for him. As he plays games with other people around him, he at once enjoys and despises his own actions.

In fact, I would venture to describe Iago as a man setting out on a project that seeks to fulfill his desire, but who is at the same time fully aware of the horror of this desire. Unconsciously he is trying to vanquish his own resistance by inventing reasons for the project, and by appealing to and relying on his rational intellect.

His resentment is aimed at Othello's eminence and success. Iago despises his own dependence on Othello. His disappointment at the loss of the lieutenancy is replaced by an irresistible lust to initiate a game and by the prospect of satisfying a sense of power. This is achievable by masterminding Othello through an intricate and hazardous game of intrigue, lies, and slander.

Only once Iago admits something of the truth. It is when he uses the phrase "to plume up my will in double knavery". To "plume up the will", to heighten one's sense of power or superiority – this seems to be the unconscious motive of many acts of cruelty which evidently do not spring chiefly from ill-will – and which therefore puzzle and sometimes horrify us most.[16]

Professionalism as consultant and confidant

Let us now move to the second target of the paper, analyzing the learning potential between the role as a consultant and the figure of Iago in Shakespeare's Othello.

According to Bowie, people in business must view themselves as professionals, and the service motive must dominate[17]. The question therefore becomes: Do the definitions of professionals apply for consultants as well? A look at what is meant by "professionalism" may help us understand where consultants as a "new profession" should belong.

There are two accounts about the nature of a profession: One view of the professions, the "functionalist" approach holds that the professions are, by their nature, self-conscious communities whose members know the norm that is attached to membership of that community and who identify themselves to each other and to outsiders as members of that community. A profession is a distinct type of occupation, like medical doctor, lawyer, or engineer. "The members possess specialist, theoretical knowledge and practical skills that are meant to solve real human problems. Professions have an altruistic orientation or rather a sense of social responsibility"[18]. Most of these professions have 'Ethical Codes' for their profession.

The other view can be called the "power" approach. It views the pro-

---

[16] http://www.theatredance.com/othello/main.html
[17] Norman Bowie (1988). The Profit Seeking Paradox. In N. Dale Wright (Ed.), *Ethics of Administration*. Provo, Utah: Brigham Young University Press.
[18] Andrew Brien (1998). Professional Ethics and the Culture of Trust. *JBE February*, 391–409, p. 396.

fessions as little more than "conspiracies against the laity". In this view, the professions are a "semi-mythic construct, fashioned by members of an occupation for the purpose of obtaining social and economic advantages, who then successfully persuade the rest of society to accept their construct and honor their claim for special protection and privileges."[19]

In this view professions are monopolies based on self-interest, and the pretense of being altruistic is merely a trick to maintain their privileged position. And since there is no unified view shared by its members, there are no "Codes of Ethics" regulating the behavior.

This first view stresses that to be truly professional – e.g. as a consultant, in particular – the motivation is or should be something more than just making money. The professions' service should aim at fulfilling an obligation to society. This is still a problem for business managers and consultants. "Medicine, law and engineering are professions", says Henry Mintzberg, a management professor at McGill University. They demand mastery of a core body of knowledge. Business is different. Business schools instruct students in the mechanical skills of accounting, financing, and marketing. But the essence of business – taking sensible risks, creating valuable products, motivating people, and satisfying customers – lies elsewhere and cannot be taught in a classroom. "Leadership" as Mintzberg puts it, "is not a profession".[20]

Iago, as Othello's consultant, definitely uses the "power" approach for a personal gain. His power is his intellect and his insight into the psyche of people. He has power over Othello, by being white, by being a Venetian, and by being "a friend and confidant" of many of the other men who fatefully believe in his 'honesty'. He knows how to use his power with ingenuity and artistry. He is quick and versatile and knows how to deal with sudden unforeseen difficulties. He makes full use of all opportunities as long as they fit into his scheme. He enjoys what I would call playing a game with other people as though they were puppets on a string. He has no scruples using Roderigo or Cassio, nor his wife, in his game. He has a remarkable strength of will and seldom seems to be led astray by emotions or affect. He remains true to his own nature. Let us see for example how he deals with Roderigo:

---

[19] Newton, L. (1982). The Origin of Professionalism: Sociological Conclusions and Ethical Implications. *Business and Professional Ethics Journal 1*, 33–43, p. 34.
[20] Robert J. Samuelson (1990). *Newsweek, May 14* (quoted in Solomon, 1993, p. 140).

> RODERIGO What should I do? I confess it is my shame to be so
> fond; but it is not in my virtue to amend it.
> IAGO Virtue! a fig! 'tis in ourselves that we are thus
> or thus. Our bodies are our gardens, to the which
> our wills are gardeners: so that if we will plant
> nettles, or sow lettuce, set hyssop and weed up
> thyme, supply it with one gender of herbs, or
> distract it with many, either to have it sterile
> with idleness, or manured with industry, why, the
> power and corrigible authority of this lies in our
> wills. If the balance of our lives had not one
> scale of reason to poise another of sensuality, the
> blood and baseness of our natures would conduct us
> to most preposterous conclusions: but we have
> reason to cool our raging motions, our carnal
> stings, our unbitted lusts, whereof I take this that
> you call love to be a sect or scion.
>
> (I, scene 3)

Does this not indicate that Iago has little regard for true emotions like love? All that matters has to be governed by will and reason. This seems to be the power he believes in. In his world absolute egotism is the only rational and thus the proper attitude. Conscience or virtue, values like honor or respect for others do not exist. He denies their existence because he claims the world around him does not practice these virtues. And those who still may believe in these values, he considers honest fools capable of betraying both themselves and others. Only when he realizes that he too is betrayed by Emilia, his wife (V, scene 2), does he show true emotions and indignation he previously so vehemently has refused to accept. In many ways he is not consistent in his beliefs, and one may wonder whether he therefore becomes a victim of his own constructed reality that turns out to be an illusion. He is full of spite against true and honest goodness or love in other people. Goodness irritates his intellect, he sees it as a weakness, a stupidity – he mocks Roderigo. Desdemona's true love for Othello does not fit into the world he has constructed for himself, a world where egotism is dominating, nothing else. By endearing himself as Othello's confidant, he becomes a dangerous consultant who usurps his 'power' by pulling Othello into his own distorted version of reality. He makes full use of his vulnerability and misuses his trust.

Before we conclude, let us review how business consultants can improve their reputation by focusing on ethical conduct.

Competence and integrity are fundamental in the ethical codes of most professional organizations, and have recently become more commonplace in the consulting profession as well. Perhaps the most essential requirement for consultants in ensuring competent practice, is a thorough understanding of their own limitations. Consultants should be able to assess the extent of their own knowledge, skills, relevance, and experience relative to the particular demands of a given consulting project. Equally important, consultants must be acutely aware of personal and interpersonal traits and inclinations that might influence their perception, judgment, decisions, and actions. In almost every contact with a client, consultants will face potential ethical dilemmas concerning issues like confidentiality, conflict of interest, possessing privileged information, imbalance of power – to name a few. Often ethical issues in a consultation are related either directly or indirectly to values, value conflicts, and their potential impact on the process and outcome of a consultation. Warwick and Kelman (1973)[21] defined values as "individual or shared conceptions of the desirable, that is 'goods' considered worth pursuing" (p. 146). Values are fundamentally related to ethics. "At its core, ethical responsibility requires a full consideration of the process and probable consequences of intervention in the light of a set of guiding values" (p. 379). Conflicts of values are a natural occurrence in consultation, as would be expected in any situation involving multiple parties with diverse and often competing interests and priorities. The consultant often must choose between conflicting values. It is essential that such difficult choices be made with the client, preferably based on ethical guidelines and not on subjectivity.

Consultants also have an ethical responsibility to consider potential value conflicts arising between themselves and clients that might impede their ability to work effectively together. At what point does the incompatibility of consultant-consultee values threaten their ability to work effectively together? And how much responsibility must the consultant accept for the impact of intervention on those who will be affected by it?

---

[21] Warwick, D. and Kelman, H. (1973). Ethical issues in social intervention. In G. Zaltman (Ed.), *Processes and phenomena of social change* (pp. 377-417). New York: Wiley Interscience.

Iago does not seem to care. These are fundamental issues for consultants and are ethical issues at the very core.

Some ethical issues in consultancy are further complicated by the fact that a consulting relationship involves three parties: the consultant, the consultee, and the consultee's organization, in this case Othello's army. It is difficult to consider members of the affected organization of the consultee to be part of the consultation agreement since they are not present, do not have the opportunity to articulate their own priorities, and often do not even know that a consultation is taking place. In Shakespeare's *Othello*, several innocent people are hurt or even have to die because of Iago. This indicates that often neglected and tragic difficulties may arise from the impact of a consultant's advice on individuals with whom s/he may have little or no direct contact. The overall quality of the relationship that exists between a consultant and a client is important for the success of any consulting engagement. Any assessment, including an ethical evaluation of the assistance provided by any consultant, is rooted in the quality of the relationship. This is best manifested by a good communication processes. Communication between client and consultant about objectives and expectations is vital to ethical conduct.

Finally let us review the ethical style of thinking and acting we witness in *Othello*.

According to Robert C. Solomon in *Ethics and Excellence*, there are seven distinct ethical styles of thinking and acting[22]. The following approaches appear to be most prevalent in practical situations:

1. Rule governed: thinking and acting on the basis of rules and principles, with only secondary regards to circumstances or exceptions.
2. Utilitarian: weighing probable consequences, both to the company or the professional and to the public well-being.
3. Loyalist: evaluating all decisions first in terms of benefit to the profession, the institution, the company, and its reputation.
4. Prudent: long-term self-interest through identification with the profession, and the institution or the larger social good.
5. Virtuous: every action is measured in terms of its reflection on one's character.

---

[22] Robert C. Solomon (1993). *Ethics and Excellence* (p. 255). Oxford: Oxford University Press.

6 Intuitive: making decisions on the basis of "conscience" and without deliberation, argument, or reasons.
7 Emphatic: following one's feelings of sympathy and compassion. "Putting oneself in the other's place" is the modus operandi.

However, according to him there are also a few *degenerate styles* which are not uncommon variations of the above. In other words, even decent ethical styles can go awry. As a matter of fact some seem to be relevant for the present discussion.

1 Rule-governed compulsive: being so caught up in principles that even the point of the principles is lost from the view.

In this regard Iago's pride is hurt and he feels that he has not been treated by Othello with principles of fairness and justice:

2 Utilitarian perplexed liberal: finding so many possible consequences and complications that action becomes impossible and inaction the only moral source.

Iago's only utility is his own revenge. He stages a "game" in which all others become puppets and realizes too late the consequences of his actions. He cannot prevent events that are no longer under his control from happening. These events are not caused by rational or intellectual decisions but are brought about by emotions such as love and hate.

3 Loyalist hominoid: in office circumstances, the technician who has lost all sense of social context and even of his or her own well-being.

Also this degenerate style applies in Othello. He seems to have discarded all need and understanding of the social context he is part of because he becomes totally immersed in his project of 'masterminding a game'.

4 Prudent gamesman: thinks of a profession solely in terms of self-advancement and treats all rules and laws – including moral principles – as mere boundaries of action. Ethical problems for the gamesman are mainly obstacles, opportunities, and challenges.

Again we find ample evidence in the play of how moral principles are discarded by Othello. His world is the world of "games", where no rules or laws exist other than those that serve his purpose.

5. Virtuous heroic: in which every action is self-consciously a reflection of extraordinary virtues and abilities, and in which any course of action that is routine or ordinary is not to be seriously considered.

Iago's pretence to have a need to restore his vexed honor and his extreme pride and reliance on his intellect let him seek a course which undermines what at the beginning could be understood as reasonable outrage over being passed over.

6. Intuitive mystical: making decisions on the basis of invariably cosmic intuitions, often with cloudy references to the "whole earth" or "cosmic harmony" without further justification and with as little references to practical realities as possible.

Othello is the only one who believes in mystical truths and falls victim in believing in the magic power of the 'handkerchief'. When the "handkerchief" is found with Cassio, no logical explanation is acceptable to Othello. Rage, despair, and madness are what he resorts to.

7. Emphatic sentimental or maudlin: having so much sympathy that it becomes impossible to look after one's own or the profession's self-interest.

Othello again is the victim of becoming overly sentimental, ignoring both his self-interest as general and husband. He falls victim to his "passions".

Conclusion

What can we learn from seeing these degenerated ethical styles of thinking and acting in Shakespeare's play both as individuals and as consultants or confidants in business?

Firstly, Shakespeare was a genius in mastering such character descriptions as Iago and Othello, who are relevant even today.

Secondly, let us quote William Hazlitt[23] who has summarized this better than anyone else: "It has been said that tragedy purifies the affections by terror and pity. That is, it substitutes imaginary sympathy for mere selfishness. It gives us a high and permanent interest, beyond ourselves, in humanity as such. It raises the great, the remote, and the possible to an equality with the real, the little and the near. It makes man a partaker with his kind. It subdues and softens the stubbornness of his will. It teaches him that there are and have been others like himself, by showing him as in a glass what they have felt, thought, and done. It opens the chambers of the human heart. It leaves nothing indifferent to us that can affect our common nature. It excites our sensibility by exhibiting the passions wound up to the utmost pitch by the power of imagination or the temptation of circumstances; and corrects their fatal excesses in ourselves by pointing to the greater extent of sufferings and of crimes to which they have led others.

Tragedy creates a balance of the affections. It makes us thoughtful spectators in the lists of life. It is the refiner of the species; a discipline of humanity."

The habitual study of poetry and works of imagination is one chief part of a well-grounded education. A taste for liberal art is necessary to complete the character of a gentleman.

Science alone is hard and mechanical. It exercises the understanding upon things out of ourselves, while it leaves the affections unemployed, or engrossed with our own immediate, narrow interests. *Othello* furnishes an illustration of these remarks. It excites our sympathy to an extraordinary degree.

The moral it conveys has a closer application to the concerns of human life than that of almost any other of Shakespeare's plays. 'It comes directly home to the bosoms and business of men.'[24]

As we have seen, Iago is both a confidant and a consultant to Othello. His motivation is highly subjective – injured pride and a lust for revenge. However, his means are strategic manipulation. The most striking feature is his inability to envision the outcome of the games he plays with other people's feelings and desires. His obsession with his own goal renders him blind and emotionally cold to the world and the people around him. His

---

[23] http://absoluteshakespeare.com/guides/othello/essay/othello_essay.htm
[24] op.cit.

goal is to destroy the relationship between Othello and Desdemona who have just been married. True love between two people does not seem to exist for Iago. At the same time Iago falls victim to his own 'hubris', believing in his own superior intellect and outstanding ability in judging others. He uses people as a means to his own end, and that is unethical.

Viewing Iago's "strategic behavior" and comparing it to what can be observed in the business world, one is tempted to refer to the following: Top management surround themselves with people who are likely to agree with them most of the time. They do not see that some "confidants" or "consultants" in reality are not serving them but rather their own goals. Managers can fall victim to such confidants who interpret or construct reality for them in a way that can be far from the truth. In the role as confidants or consultants they can exert power over manager by exclusively presenting the superior strength of a certain technical knowledge and expertise, regardless of whether it is suitable for the organization or not. Consultants – both internal and external to the company – can also 'obtain evidence' from other parts of the organization and then use this 'proof' to manipulate decision making. Iago needed the handkerchief, which Othello had received from his mother and given to Desdemona, in order to be "trusted".

In the hands of confidants and consultants, managers, like all other human beings, are vulnerable and have to rely on trust. Moral and ethical considerations such as not using people only as a means to an end are often ignored or disregarded with bleak reference to the amorality of business.

The honor code in the military demands extreme loyalty and trust and should not be compromised. This can be compared to the goal of business: profit maximization to which the loyalty of all employees is owed. "Telepathy-goal obsession" can become a state of mind in business. Individual ethical or moral judgment and concerns, the inner voice, have to give way or be silenced for the sake of reaching a set of economic targets. The goal obsession itself can be rationalized by referring to the "rules of the game". Excuses can be made also by referring to 'we're only doing what everybody else is doing'.

Shakespeare allows Iago to succeed with "the game he plays". Yet, he also shows us the tragic consequences his "success" has for himself and for others.

The ethical and moral lesson here is: A military or a business organization has a set of rules or scripts, implicit codes of honor and conduct which are man-made. They are constructed to achieve an objective. As the play shows human beings for various reasons, can misuse and manipulate these rules in order to achieve personal objectives.

The most frightening or even scary part is that this can be done in a way that looks perfectly trustworthy and correct, even though it may rest on a darker set of motives or desires. As spectators of *Othello* we can both admire and despise Iago at the same time as the play unfolds before our eyes. As in the movie "Wallstreet", the main character is both a hero and a despicable manipulator who promotes "greed is good".

Last but not least, the processes we are involved in and the emotions we are experiencing when viewing Shakespeare's *Othello,* should help us to become morally more mature.

References

Andreassen, A.R. (1993). Revisiting the Disadvantaged: Old Lessons and New Problems. *Journal of Public Policy and Marketing, 12,* 270–275.

Baier A. (1994). *Moral Prejudices.* Cambridge, MA: Harvard University Press.

Bowie, N. (1988). The Profit Seeking Paradox. In N. Dale Wright (Ed.), *Ethics of Administration.* Provo, Utah: Brigham Young University Press.

Brenkert, George G. (1999). Marketing and the Vulnerable. *Business Ethics Quarterly, 9,* 7–20.

Brien, A. (1998). Professional Ethics and the Culture of Trust. *Journal of Business Ethics, February,* 391–409.

Curral, S.C. (1990). *The Role of Interpersonal Trust in Work Relationships.* (unpublished doctoral dissertation, Cornell University).

Gadamer, Hans-Georg (1989). *Truth and Method.* Rev. trans. J. Weinsheimer and D. Marshall. New York: Crossroad.

Goodin, R.E. (1985). *Protecting the Vulnerable* (p. 118). Chicago: The University of Chicago Press.

http://absoluteshakespeare.com/guides/othello/essay/othello_essay.htm

http://www.theatredance.com/othello/main.html

Mayer, D. and D. Schoorman (1995). An Integrative Model of Organizational Trust. *Academy of Management Review, 20 (3),* 709–734.

Newton, L. (1982). The Origin of Professionalism: Sociological Conclusions and Ethical Implications. *Business and Professional Ethics Journal 1*, 33–43, p. 34.

Solomon, Robert C. (1993). *Ethics and Excellence*. Oxford: Oxford University Press.

von Weltzien Hoivik, Heidi (2004). The concept of moral imagination – an inspiration for writing and using case histories in business ethics? *Journal of Business Ethics Education, Vol. 1, Issue 1,* 31–44.

Warwick, D., & Kelman, H. (1973). Ethical issues in social intervention. In G. Zaltman (Ed.), *Processes and phenomena of social change* (pp. 377–417). New York: Wiley Interscience.

White, Judith A. (1998). Leadership through compassion and understanding. *Journal of Management Inquiry 7*, 286–293.

INTRODUCTION TO PART IV
The consultee

STEINAR BJARTVEIT

The most important component in management consulting is the manager that is receiving the consultant's advice – the *consultee*. A consulting assignment is never just about finding a solution to a business challenge. The executive – the client – the person receiving the advice is a major part of the assignment. An executive cannot be considered as separate from the system that s/he runs – and is an integral part of (Stacey, 2003; Watzlawick, Bavelas, & Jackson, 1967). The executive is part of the system and is influenced by the system, and as such, leadership cannot be separated from the person that is performing the leadership. The leader's susceptibility to influence and his or her own character will have a bearing on how s/he runs the system – and allows him- or herself to be run by the system. The person executing leadership, the client, will always be a major factor in any consultation. You cannot believe that leadership is important without believing that the person executing the leadership is important.

Today's leaders have received a great deal of attention from the media – that focuses on the leader as either hugely successful or a terrible disaster. At times it seems as though the media swears blindly by the Great Man Theory – that stipulates that leaders have inordinate amounts of influence on the organization's performance (Khurana, 2002). The media tends to give leaders too much credit for success – and for failure (… and the size of pay packets and severance packages tend to rise and fall in tune with their stardom). In reality the leader does not have that much influence. There are other factors, such as market forces, technological development, competition, and government regulation – that are equally important. But this focus from the media makes it tougher on leaders. There is little room for making mistakes or even lack of success. The top executives are more vulnerable than ever. And if the leader does have to step down, s/he is forever marked as incompetent or weak, and the chances of making a return to the top level are small. A great number of executives will experience this type of personal and professional crisis – being forced to step down, deservedly or not. They may be forced to take the fall for poor results, or may be sacrificed as part of reorganization. Never has the spotlight on the leaders shone brighter.

As a result of these recent developments, the consultancy industry has increased its focus on leadership development. Executive coaching has emerged as a highly profitable field in consulting (Executive Coaching, 2003), but in many ways there have always been elements of leadership development in consulting. The traditional approach to leadership development has been based in psychometrics and in trait theories (Robbins, 2004; Yukl, 2001). This has lead to a dramatic increase in the use of personality tests for selection and development of leaders. As mentioned in chapter 2 – many of these tests have come under criticism for a lack of validity and reliability. However, consultants have also used system- and psychodynamic approaches (Killburg, 2000) and solution-focused models (de Shazer, 1985). Consultants have typically focused on behavioral issues or on solving specific problems.

One of the perspectives on leadership that has emerged in Scandinavia is based on humanistic thinking and has its roots in humanism and existentialism. Scandinavian philosophers and authors such as Kierkegaard, Løgstrup, and Ibsen, in addition to other European influences, have been very influential for the development of humanism, and this is why the humanistic perspective differs quite significantly from mainstream American leadership. At present there are groups at Uppsala, Copenhagen, and Oslo conducting research into humanistic leadership. Some of the topics being explored, resonate in the current literature on leadership, and the attempts to link classic perspectives on leadership with organizational theory may give rise to new insights.

Traditionally the consultant has approached the leader with a *Know Thyself* mantra, and in many ways this reflects the current infatuation with the individual and the individual's self-fulfillment. We must get in touch with our masculine and our feminine selves – as well as our hidden and unconscious selves. We must be in touch with body and soul – discover excitement and live our lives in one long sigh of pleasure. However, our postmodern interpretation of Know Thyself may differ somewhat from the original intention of those who inscribed it on the temple of enlightment – Apollo, at Delphi: gnothi seauton. Even Cicero thought there was a need for some clarification:

> "For I do not suppose the meaning of the maxim is that we should know our limbs, our height or shape; our selves are not bodies, and in speaking as I do to you, I am not speaking to your body. When then Apollo says, 'Know thyself', he says, 'Know thy soul.'" (1945:61–62).

Thus, in a humanistic and existentialistic perspective, Know Thyself is not limited to self-centered, introspective sentimentality. Nor is it a baseline for self-improvement. Apollo had something else in mind – that was equally important for leaders and followers. Cicero says: "Know your soul", "… because the soul needs the soul to see". Kierkegaard (1991) develops this further and finds greater meaning in the term *choose* oneself rather than *know* oneself. So what is the existential claim?

Ibsen leans heavily on Kierkegaard. We often find Ibsen's leaders and heroes struggling with deep, inner conflict (Kittang, 2002). They find themselves caught in existential dilemmas where they have to choose between being all that they can be – or fading from existence. "I must! I must! A voice deep in my soul urges me on, and I will heed its call." This is the opening line of Ibsen's play *Catilina*. This is his declaration. There is something Nietzsche-like about Ibsen's heroes. The have the will to power – the will to achieve more in life. This is evident in the play *The Pretenders*, where two leaders fight for the throne in Norway (Bjartveit, Eikeset, and Edvardsen, 2005). Both won the throne, but only one of them knows why. The young Håkon wants to unite Norway – not into a kingdom, but into one people, while his rival, the Duke Skule has only one ambition: power. And this is what causes him to despair even in victory. He wanders the halls at night, and although he is exhausted he cannot sleep, because something is keeping him awake: Håkon's great vision. Håkon has the will and the drive to achieve more. He possesses the idea that defines him as a leader and as a person. And this is why the people follow him.

Skule wonders: "Can an heir to the throne assume the throne in the same manner as he adorns the royal gown?" Ibsen's existential challenge dovetails with one of the ongoing debates on leadership. Is there a fundamental difference between a leader and a manager (Zaleznik, 1977)? Are we in the process of degrading the role of leader into some institutional figure – devoid of relational and creative aspects? Recently, several authors have emphasized the need for leaders that base their leadership on personal convictions (Bass, 1998; Collins, 2001; Gardner, 1995; Weick, 1995) or on a strong identity. Leaders are not hired to fill a position before they move on to the next step in their career. Leaders create meaning. If a leader is to have an impact on a firm's performance, s/he must have a strong sense of conviction or a personal belief in wanting to be a leader. Sensemaking, preparedness, and practical wisdom all go hand-in-hand with excellent results. And this is not quite what they teach at MBA-schools.

But there is an obvious risk in being a leader. There are few positions where it is easier to get lost in the demands of the role. Status, career, and peer reviews take priority. Either that or it gets so windy at the top that the only chance of survival is to hunker down on the executive floor. Once again we find traces in Scandinavian literature of topics that are highly relevant for leaders even today. At what point does the desire for world fame overpower the instinct of remaining a mere subject? When do we hide behind irony or boredom – to avoid having to face ourselves? One of the most Norwegian (or, Scandinavian, some would argue) of them all is Ibsen's Peer Gynt. He wanders from one fairy tale to the next, from illusion to illusion, never having to face himself. Until one day, when he has to do some soul searching and slowly peels back the layers of his person, in much the same way as he would peel an onion – only to find that he, just like the onion, has no core. Ibsen wanted to castigate Scandinavians (especially his fellow Norwegians). They were a people prone to cowardice and flight. A people that sought refuge in conventional opinion and in accepted social games. And even a troll can be a Mountain King.

Why do you want to be a leader? Why should anyone let themselves be lead by you? These are the questions that slash right through any blueprint for leadership or MBA-course. Leadership is a matter of understanding yourself and who you are, what you want to achieve, and what sense you create – this gives others something to follow. On the other hand you can always adorn a royal gown and assume the role of manager.

In the final section of this book there are three chapters that explore the humanistic and existentialistic foundation for Scandinavian theories of leadership. Bråkenhielm and Hansson contemplate the differences between authoritarian and humanistic leadership – and consider what implications this may have for leadership and for consulting. Bjartveit and Eikeset take a closer look at leadership development, drawing on the perspectives of both Dante and Kierkegaard. Finally, Fogh Kirkeby defines leadership in terms of the event, in which leadership is no longer defined as the person that assumes the role of leadership, but rather as an entirety that the leader must prove him- or herself worthy of.

> **What consultants should look for in this section:**
> - The consultant needs to focus more closely on the leader's understanding of him- or herself, beyond the usual self-improvement programs and feedback sessions.
> - The consultant must dare to see the leader as more than just an entity that needs help, and become a companion for this leader.
> - The consultant must take care to build a relationship over time, and be willing to stick with the client – even though this may not always seem worthwhile.
>
> **What clients should look for in this section:**
> - The leader must be willing to accept that s/he is one of the main elements of any solution and that this may involve considerable self-reflection.
> - When the leader becomes the object of the consultation, it is often difficult to obtain immediate results.
> - Leadership involves recognizing that you are part of something more than your own career and short-term performance.

References

Bass, B.M. (1998). *Transformational leadership. Industrial, military, and educational impact.* Mahwah, New Jersey: Lawrence Erlbaum Associates.

Bjartveit, S., Eikeset, K. & Edvardsen, E. (2005). Ledere med og uten kongstanker. *Dagsavisen*, 21 February.

Cicero (1945). *Tusculan disputations.* Cambridge, Mass.: Harvard University Press.

Collins, J. (2001). *Good to great. Why some companies make the leap ... and others don't.* New York: Harper Business.

de Shazer, S. (1985). *Keys to solution in brief therapy.* New York: Norton.

Executive Coaching. Corporate therapy. (2003). *The Economist.* November 15.

Gardner, H. (1995). *Leading minds. An anatomy of leadership.* New York: Basic Books.

Khurana, R. (2002). *Searching for a corporate savior. The irrational quest for charismatic CEOs.* Princeton: Princeton University Press.

Kierkegaard, S. (1991). *Enten – Eller II.* København: Gyldendal.

Kilburg, R.R. (2000). *Executive coaching. Developing managerial wisdom in a world of chaos.* Washington: American Psychological Association.

Kittang, A. (2002). *Ibsens heroisme. Fra Brand til Når vi døde vågner.* Oslo: Gyldendal.

Robbins, S.R. (2004). *Organizational behaviour.* 11th ed. Englewood Cliffs, NJ: Prentice Hall.

Stacey, R.D. (2003). *Strategic management and organizational dynamics. The challenge of complexity.* 4th ed. Harlow, England: FT Prentice Hall.

Watzlawick, P., Bavelas, J.B. & Jackson, D.D. (1967). *Pragmatics of human communication.* New York: Norton.

Weick, K.E. (1995). *Sensemaking in organizations.* Thousand Oaks, California: Sage.

Yukl, G. (2001). *Leadership in organizations.* 5th ed. Englewood Cliffs, NJ: Prentice Hall.

Zaleznik, A. (1977). Managers and leaders. Are they different? *Harvard Business Review,* May-June.

Chapter 10
View of human nature, leadership, and consulting

CARL REINHOLD BRÅKENHIELM
AND BENGT HANSSON

Most leaders with a few years personal experience in management, and who are still keen to develop their leaderships skills further, have realized that there are no simple methods, no quick fixes or other short-cuts to becoming a first-rate leader. Simply making some slight alterations to your personal style and learning how to communicate more clearly will not suffice. If leadership development is going to work, it has to focus on the leader's inner self, personal values, and perspective on human nature, and it must advance emotional maturity. What is the current state of leadership? Are emotional values considered important for leaders? And how does all this affect the role of the business consultant? We will try to provide some answers to these questions.

Autocratic versus humanistic leadership

What is the measure of a good leader? Are some standards more predominant than others? These questions are very complex and require knowledge from several different fields, and most attempts to provide answers have fallen short. In his book, *Företagsledning och Machiavelli* (1968), Anthony Jay examines Machiavelli's theories and finds that they are remarkably pertinent to modern management. Jay suggests that there are considerable similarities between the renaissance states described by Machiavelli – and the business corporations of today. Current styles of leadership seem to reflect Machiavelli's ideal of power and of autocratic leadership. Jay has attempted to analyze modern corporations, such as IBM, General Electrics, and BBC – using Machiavelli's methodology, which involves approaching a relatively common issue and examining how others have dealt with this issue previously. Jay is highly critical of many of the current theories in management that are founded in sociology and in business theory.

To be a humanistic leader means to take the needs and requirements of people into account in your style of leadership. All economic activity is based on selling products and services to businesses and consumers – products and services that will somehow *enrich the buyers' lives*. As such, all product- and service development should be aimed at satisfying the customers' ever-changing desires. It is a well-known and well documented fact that employees report greater job satisfaction and perform better when they feel they can have an influence on the tasks they are to perform, are given responsibility for achieving their goals, and feel that they are acknowledged and appreciated. To promote this, organizations should design workflows so that they take the needs of employees into account to a much greater degree than is currently the case. Over the last decade, the debate seems to have focused less on soft issues and more on hard issues like financial strategy and structure. From this we must assume that senior management has little knowledge, and even less interest for, organizational issues. (Ekman, 2002; our highlight).

We can think of businesses, organizations, and states as organisms. Today, companies have an extensive experience with the inner workings of this organism: men and women with personal experience at running this business; leaders that are strong and leaders that are weak, and leaders that are sensible, stupid, tolerant, or tyrants; inner conflicts and external struggles; the challenge of organizing for battle or for creating stability and tranquility.

Most theories of leadership revolve around the issues of systems theories, work studies, cost control. … But despite this, leadership can be an intriguing, and even epic, topic of study, well worth a closer look. The prevailing view is of businesses as social institutions with customs and norms, status groups and pecking order, and many sociologist and political scientists have studied businesses using this perspective. However, organizations can also be political institutions – autocratic or democratic, peaceful or hostile, liberal or patriarchal (Jay, 1968).

The Machiavellian perspective on leadership subsumes what we have chosen to term the idea of "autocratic" leadership. We have used quotation marks to make it clear that we have no intention of passing moral judgment on this idea of leadership. In its purest form this theory of leadership assumes that managing a business or political organization cannot de done within the bounds of what is considered morally justifiable behavior. Bertold Brecht has illustrated this in rather dramatic style in *The Good Person of Setzuan*. Three gods descend to earth. The only person that shows them compassion and offers them shelter is the prostitute Shen Te. The gods give her some money – so that she may escape from a life of prostitution and open a tobacco shop. And that is when the misery begins. The kind-hearted Shen Te is repeatedly conned and exploited by others, and her benevolence is thoroughly put to the test. In order to save herself from further anguish, and her tobacco shop from ruin, she decides to disguise her self as her strong-willed and unyielding male cousin Shui Ta. Brecht's play is a story of survival in an existence that even the gods find harsh. An existence that necessitates double standards, deceit, and foul play just to keep oneself from going under. For a another interpretation of autocratic leadership, we encourage you to check out Oliver Stone's *Wall Street* (1987), which we will be taking a closer look at shortly.

A somewhat more agreeable variety of "autocratic" leadership assumes that the leader of a business in a competitive environment will tend to stay within the boundaries of what is morally acceptable – unless it is bad for business, in which case morals will loose out to profits. An example of this could be when the interests of an employee must give way to what is best for the company.

At the other end of the scale from autocratic, we find "humanistic" leadership. In its purest form, humanistic leadership means that a leader must at all times be a fair and just person. There are different forms of humanistic leadership, but we will not get into the details here (see Sundman, 2004, for a further discussion). A more tenient form of humanistic leadership involves the leader giving priority to moral concerns over business considerations should these be in conflict. Double standards, deceit, and foul play, are not permitted even though they may benefit the firm.

In recent years there has been an increased focus on the importance of a leader's personal growth for the development of good leadership skills, and the benefits to the leader of having a life outside the company. Although it could be suggested that the latter has more to do with the leader's own personal well-being and longevity as a leader than with any direct impact on performance as a leader.

With the emergence of the knowledge economy, we have seen an increased tendency to think of organizations as organisms where the values and psychological characteristics of the people that make up the organization determine what goes on within the organism. In a knowledge organization, the individual is the company's main asset – hence the term intellectual capital. During the second part of the 1990s, the Institute for Personnel and Corporate Development published several studies of organizations based on the perspective of human capital (see Bo Hansson, 2003). The issue of democracy in the workplace – the formal relationship between manager and employee – received a lot of attention in Sweden during the 1970s and 1980s. This debate gave rise to legislation that granted employees a certain level of formal influence. Some changes in the styles of leadership and negotiation have been evident as a result of this legislation, but the desire for clear and distinct leadership soon reemerged in the form of demands for clear communication from manager to subordinate and a clear definition of the leader's authority and areas of responsibility. During the 1990s the view of the leader as business person was obvious in all the down-sized organizations, the bonus programs for senior executives, and in the arguments used to justify pay increases for executives. This can be interpreted as a regression to "autocratic" leadership – albeit in a more human form. In his book *Himmel och helvete. Om företagende, makt och ledarskap* (2002) Bo Ekman, a well-known executive and business consultant (SIFO Management Group) who started his career back in the 1970s, discusses the latest developments in management theory and practice.

Ekman's reflections may be taken in support of the "humanistic" perspective on leadership. There has been some progress towards more democracy in the workplace in Sweden over the last couple of decades, but this seems to be more the exception than the rule. Could it be that fundamental values held by leaders, and by the organizations they lead, do not really reflect on the humanistic approach when it comes to actually running the business? There is Bo Ekman's description of a "humanistic" leader:

> A humanistic leader accepts people for what they are and gets results by making people work together. A humanistic leader is not inherently evil, moral, or immoral. *This all depends on the leaders' own set of values, and to what extent these leaders are true to their values in the execution of their duties* (Ekman, 2002; our italics).

The term "humanistic" leadership does not seem to have gained as much support as "clear leadership". Perhaps the current leadership ideal is closer to the "autocratic" style than the "humanistic" ideal?

The humanistic leader and perspective on human nature

In this section, we will attempt to describe a barely discernible, but quite fundamental, area of conflict between the "autocratic" and the "humanistic" approaches to leadership. Different leadership ideals may base their legitimacy on a variety of factors, but one of the most defining aspects of any style of leadership, and one that provides legitimacy, is the underlying view of human nature. In reality, leadership ideal and view of human nature are inextricably intertwined, but to get a closer look at the view of human nature that underlies a leadership ideal, we will attempt to separate the two. An excellent theoretical point of departure is Göran Collste's doctoral thesis *Power, moral, and humans – an analysis of conflicting values in the debate on democracy in the workplace* (1984). This is how he introduces his study:

> "In this study I will address the issue of how businesses should be run. This involves a discussion of different types of administration, and as such our views on human nature will play a significant role. Whatever perspective we have on the needs and qualities of human beings will greatly influence our attitude towards democracy. The qualities necessary to be a part of a democracy include the ability to acquire knowledge and the ability to apply this knowledge to political issues. One also needs the ability to evaluate the moral aspects of these political issues and act in accordance with the intentions of a specific political position. One also needs finally, one needs a certain amount of what Mill calls "humanity" – the ability to look beyond personal interests and see what's best for the community." (Collste, 1984, p. 49).

In other words, leaders should base their style of leadership on fundamental human needs such as: security, sense of community, self-respect, understanding and continuity, self-realization, and autonomy; in addition to the principles of organizing that allow business profits and personal growth to coexist. Collste refers to a number of organizational psychologists that have a needs-based point of departure for their theories – Erich Fromm, Abraham Maslow, and Douglas McGregor, and who have made calls for a new form of leadership (p. 213). All three stress the importance of the organizational climate for the individual's mental health. Maslow advocates a more elitist view of human nature – he places a great deal of emphasis on the obvious variations in intelligence and qualities among humans and argues that only the truly competent should be allowed to lead others. McGregor's position is much less elitist, and he displays a confidence in the ability of employees to resolve important issues. Collste (1984) summarizes: that it seems logical to assume that many of the factors underlying human self-respect would get a boost if the employee were allowed to take part in decisions pertaining to his or her own work environment. His or her sense of independence and freedom would benefit from his or her being given the opportunity to take part in decisions that affect his or her working conditions. His or her self-esteem would no doubt receive a boost if s/he were entrusted with the responsibility of participating in decision processes – rather than merely being subjected to the consequences of decisions made by others.

Collste notes that a perspective of human nature is often an implicit, and even unwitting, premise underlying one's political standpoint. In order to identify the perspective of human nature underlying each of the different positions on democracy in the workplace that the various involved parties assumed, Collste applied the following set of questions:

1 What human needs should be met? Is it the material needs connected to consumption that are most essential? Or is it the psychological and social needs, such as feelings of community and influence that are most important?
2 What constitutes the ideal personality?
3 Should humans act individually or together as one to achieve their goals?
4 What human qualities are emphasized – egoistical or altruistic?
5 Is it the inequalities between humans in terms of individual abilities that is emphasized – or the equalities?
6 Are humans seen as active and creative or as passive and disinterested in what goes on around them (Colste, 1984, p. 26)?

Based on the answers to these questions we can identify the perspective of human nature underlying the humanistic and the autocratic styles of leadership. The humanistic style of leadership is characterized by a perspective of human nature that
1) emphasizes the materialistic, psychological, and social needs
2) has a multitude of ideal personalities
3) emphasizes human individuality
4) underscores her altruistic intentions
5) epitomizes an egalitarian perspective of unity
6) views humans as active and creative.

The normative question

Collste has devised a set of principles of normative ethics in order to make a case for the humanistic perspective over the autocratic perspective. He uses this humanistic view of human nature as a basis for judging the various arguments forwarded by different interest groups during the debate on democracy in the workplace that took place in Sweden during the 1980s. His normative theory is founded on a theory of human needs. The reasoning behind this is his belief that positions on moral issues should be based on a perception of what alternative will be most beneficial for the individual's well-being, as well as being most favorable in terms of providing opportunities for personal growth and self-realization. He argues that these are the most important criteria for judging positions on moral issues (p. 48). A perspective on the nature of people may include assumptions about needs and opportunities, what could be described as characteristic of human nature, and beliefs concerning what constitutes good behavior. Thus, a perspective on human nature may consist of beliefs that are based on reality as well as beliefs rooted in personal values (Collste, 1984, p. 51).

It is beyond the scope of this article to provide an in-depth analysis of Collste's normative ethics. We would instead like to focus on one of the fundamental principles of a humanistic perspective of human nature – the *principle that all human beings are of equal worth*. This is the main principle underlying the humanistic perspective, so if it doesn't hold up, the whole perspective looses its credibility.

We will not get into the long and somewhat complicated history of the humanistic perspective of human nature, but instead provide a brief description of the essence of this view (for a more thorough review, see Bråkenheim, 1994). Simply put, the humanistic perspective contains two different components. First there is the belief that humans have a unique moral standing, and deserve to be treated with the outmost respect. There are many things that are worthy of our respect, but none are as important as human beings. This does not necessarily mean that we are above everything else in the universe. However, in our world, on this planet, it is human to think that human beings have more worth than all other creatures. Second, the humanistic perspective implies that all humans – every single member of the human race – have this special worth. This is not simply because they belong to the species homo sapiens. We have to distinguish between the claim that all members of the human race have special worth and are important, and the claim that they have this worth simply because they belong to the human race. Although the humanistic perspective is founded on the former, it does not imply the latter.

There are a number of criticisms aimed at the first component of the humanistic perspective. One of the major objections comes from animal rights organizations – and from the philosophers that have laid the foundation for these movements. Animals, it is contended, have the same worth – and thus the same rights, as humans. This view has spread far beyond the rosters of animal rights groups. Scholars at the Uppsala University have conducted some research on issues related to faith and ideology – and several studies have revealed that fully 2/3 of all Swedes do not agree that humans have a higher worth than all other creatures. Humans should not be considered above all other living things (see also Nils Uddenberg's article in *Världsbild och mening*, 2001).

A different, and more radical, approach is that of denying the concept of worth altogether. The case could be made that no entity has value in itself – only for the life of the larger society. Jack London's novel *The Sea Wolf* provides an excellent portrayal of this perspective. The novel tells the story of an idealistic young man who, through a series of unfortunate events, winds up on a ship run by Captain Wolf Larsen. One day the young man gets into a conversation with Larsen on the value of life. The captain ends the talk with the following reflection:

"Do you know, the only value life has is what life puts upon itself; and it is of course overestimated, since it is of necessity prejudiced in its own favor. Take that man I had aloft. He held on as if he were a precious thing, a treasure beyond diamonds or rubies. To you? No. To me? Not at all. To himself, yes. But I do not accept his estimate. He sadly overrates himself. There is plenty more life demanding to be born. Had he fallen and dripped his brains upon the deck like honey from the comb, there would have been no loss to the world. He was worth nothing to the world. The supply is too large. To himself only was he of value, and to show how fictitious even this value was, being dead, he is unconscious that he has lost himself."

Albert Schweitzer is a firm proponent of the opposite view, as is exemplified by the following excerpt:

"… I am life that wants to live, surrounded by life that wants to live. Since I am the will to live, I reaffirm my own life, which is not the same as saying that I will continue to exist without pondering the mystery and the value of this existence. When I reflect upon what life is, I feel obligated to respect all the will to live that surrounds me just as I would respect my own …" (Quoted from Lönnebo, 1964, p. 153).

There is a third possibility, that lies somewhere between Wolf Larsen and Schweitzer: not all life has the same worth. Some forms of life have more worth than others. But this does not necessarily mean that humans have the greatest worth. The value of any life does not relate to rationality, intelligence, or language – but to the capacity for suffering. We can find this capacity in other higher species. By this measure, a young and healthy monkey, living safely within the pride, would have more worth than a human being that is sick and dying. At least, this is how Peter Singer (see Singer, 1995, p. 182) reasons.

In our opinion, none of the three perspectives that challenge the concept that humans have more worth than other creatures seem convincing. Humans occupy a special place in the natural order of things and should be treated in accordance with the UN declaration of human rights. In his *Till kritiken av det praktiska förnuftet.*, written in the 18th century, Immanuel Kant (2004) provides a compelling argument for this view. Human self-determination is based on our ability to reason, a faculty that exists only in humans, and this is what gives humans a special worth that should not be violated by treating the individual only as a means to an end – for economical, political, religious, or other purposes. Kant was well aware of the fact that in different situations humans need to rely on each other in order to further the common good – or to run a business. But this must be achieved without violating the individual's autonomy or self-worth. The implications of this view of human nature are evident in the UN's Universal declaration of human rights (1948) – which cover freedom of opinion, freedom of speech, and freedom of religion. Kant's way of thinking also has serious implications for the way we evaluate leadership in business. Since humans can reason, and have the power of self-determination, it is morally wrong to view humans merely as manpower or as one element of the firm's competitiveness. It is quite simply wrong to seek to dehumanize that which has its own self-purpose.

But is this perspective of human nature realistic in the business world? Doesn't a successful CEO in a capitalistic and global economy have to be autocratic – and compete with every means available? Once again, we encounter the issue raised in Bertold Brechts *The Good Man of Setzuan* – is it possible to behave morally and be a capitalistic at the same time? Of course it is possible. In fact, we would argue that unless business leaders can achieve profitability and competitiveness while aspiring to moral clarity in terms of human worth, capitalism will not be tenable in the long term.

Once you accept that human beings are, in moral terms, above all other creatures, the question of whether all humans are of equal worth immediately arises. Do *all* humans have equal worth? This forces one to ask what the term worth really means. Most people accept the notion of equal worth – but what practical implications does this belief have? In a study conducted during the 1980s, Anders Jeffner tried to get at the heart of this issue by posing some questions related to health care issues. How should we prioritize among people with different health care needs – if demand outstrips supply? The study (among a representative sample of the adult population of Sweden) was designed to press respondents to choose between different alternatives in health care issues:

"Even though it is our goal to provide care for everybody, we are sometimes faced with having to choose between patients because we simply do not have the capacity to treat everyone (an example of this might be a shortage of dialysis machines – used to treat patients with kidney failure). If the situation should arise, that we have to choose between two patients, despite all our attempts to avoid this, and only provide care to one – who do you think this should be?"

Respondents were given five situations where they had to decide who was to receive care and who was not, or respondents could opt out and let the patients draw lots. Here are the results:

Priorities in health care. N=521 Percentages
We have to choose between a young woman, less than 30 years old, and an older woman – more than 70 years old.
If all else is equal – who should be provided with care?

The young woman should be given priority	74%
The older woman should be given priority	3%
Draw lots	10%
Undecided, don't know	13%

We have to choose between a Swede and a foreigner
If all else is equal – who should be provided with care?

The Swede should be given priority	29%
The foreigner should be given priority	0%
Draw lots	47%
Undecided, don't know	24%

We have to choose between someone who has taken good care of him- or herself and someone who has let his/her health deteriorate.
If all else is equal – who should be provided with care?

The one who has taken care of him- or herself	49%
The one who has let his/her health deteriorate	0%
Draw lots	47%
Undecided, don't know	24%

We have to choose between a parent with young kids and someone with no children. Who should be given priority?
If all else is equal – who should be provided with care?

The parent	65%
The person that doesn't have children	1%
Draw lots	18%
Undecided, don't know	16%

We have to choose between an executive who is vital for a company on which many jobs depend and a regular employee. Who should be given priority?
If all else is equal – who should be provided with care?

The executive	9%
The employee	9%
Draw lots	53%
Undecided, don't know	29%

First, we should take note of the fact that a majority seems to accept the notion of prioritizing among patients in need of care. Hardly anyone was willing to give priority to the older woman, to the foreigner, to the deadbeat, or to the childless adult. In fact it was only when being asked to choose between an executive and an employee that a majority left the decision to chance. It is possible that had the questions be posed somewhat differently, a greater number of respondents would have chosen to leave the decision to chance. However, even taking this into account, the pattern that emerges is clear, and is quite similar across different groups of respondents – there are no differences between people living in cities or in the country side. Nor are there any significant differences between different age groups either (Calltorp & Bråkenheim, 1990, pp. 35–37).

But why should some people have more worth than others – and be more deserving of health benefits? Age doesn't strike us as a just criterion – especially when we take into account the fact that the elderly have paid a substantial amount of taxes in the course of their lifetime that have gone to the public health system we have in the Nordic countries. Could we use a merit-based approach? It would seem not. Sickness and poor health strikes randomly – we have no way of knowing who will live a healthy, carefree life, and who will be plagued by ill health. Therefore, it would seem useful to use personal merit to determine who should receive health care, and who should not?

There are other objections to the principle of equal worth. Small children don't really possess self-determination, and neither do those afflicted with dementia or Alzheimer's disease and who no longer have the ability to rationalize – which according to Kant is the basis for worth as humans. However, these objections are not necessarily fatal. We protect children because they are on their way to becoming self-determining individuals. And the elderly should be regarded in light of their significant contribution to our sense of community.

Rather than challenge the notion of equal worth, we could affirm it. But why should we believe that all people have equal worth? Actually, there are a number of different reasons. The most obvious, and appealing, seen from many different perspectives, is quite simply that if we don't believe in equal worth – everybody looses out. If we chose to apply an elitist morale and implement differential treatment among people, our society would rapidly become brutal and intolerable. History is rife with examples of these experiments – some quite recent, such as Nazism and apartheid. Both of these examples are of such an undesirable character that they pose the question of whether there might be more than just practical reasons for the equal worth perspective. At the Nürenberg trials that followed in the wake of the 2nd World War, the Nazi society – with its explicit ranking of human worth, was condemned as intolerant and cruel. The Nazi leaders were all charged with crimes against humanity – and convicted. The Nazi destruction violated and negated something more fundamental than just a few simple societal rules. It is not easy to identify exactly what this is – but human worth or human dignity comes very close; acknowledging that human dignity has value in itself and is beyond objective measurement. Is there any basis for such a moral realism? Yes, if we allow for the fact that individuals develop and grow in close relationships with others. This sense of community may be losing some of its significance, but it is still an important part of what gives each member of the human family a sense of worth (Bråkenhielm, 1994, ch. 4).

This perspective could also have some religious connotations. God loves all humans, and we are all equal before God. Or as they say in Sweden: we are all a bit weird before God. The problem with using religion as a basis for judging human worth is that this is only meaningful to those who place their faith in religion. For this, and other reasons, it seems preferable to find a basis that transcends religious belief.

Human nature and the business consultant

In this third, and final, section, we will pose the question: How does all this affect the business consultant's profession?

For the business consultant, knowledge of the client's – often the CEO's – perspective of human nature is usually underrated. An individual's view of human nature is often evident when you study his or her behavior, or the way certain words are used to describe experiences, values, and attitudes. Sometimes it is enough just to understand his or her perspective; other times it may be necessary to introduce some change – and this is why it is imperative that the consultant acquires knowledge of the leader's view of human nature. The likelihood that the consultant will complete an assignment successfully increases greatly if s/he gains some knowledge of the prevailing culture – and the probable tensions between different views of human nature – within an organization. Oliver Stone's *Wall Street* (1987) provides a very realistic illustration of the tensions that may exist within an organization. An ambitious, young trader (played by Charlie Sheen) is drawn into the world of industrial espionage – by Wall Street legend Gordon Gekko (a role that got Michael Douglas an Oscar). But, the trader soon comes to realize that the price he has to pay for all the easy money is too steep – and his dream becomes a nightmare. You can imagine the predicament of a business consultant if s/he got sucked into this kind of struggle for power. In cases like that, knowledge of the law and personal integrity may not be enough – excellent social skills, including the ability to perceive where others stand on important moral issues, is also necessary.

We would like to use Chris Argyris' distinction between single-loop learning and double-loop learning to shed some further light on this issue. Learning often comes about as a result of mistakes – that are corrected. Whenever errors occur, people begin to look for new ways of doing things, within hidden presuppositions – goals, values, plans, and procedures are all taken for granted. This is what Argyris, and his colleague Donald Schön, describe as *single-loop learning*. An alternative approach would be to take a closer look at existing boundaries and assumptions. This would be what is called *double-loop learning*. This type of learning can be more fundamental – as deep seated beliefs and assumptions may be shifted – which in turn may require new strategies and new outcomes. Argyris and Schön claim that when the error detected and corrected permits the organization to carry on its present policies or achieve its present objectives, then that error-and-correction process is *single-loop* learning. Single-loop learning is like a thermostat that learns when it is too hot or too cold and turns the heat on or off. The thermostat can perform this task because it can receive information (the temperature of the room) and take corrective action. *Double-loop* learning occurs when error is detected and corrected in ways that involve the modification of an organization's underlying norms, policies, and objectives. (Argyris & Schön, 1978, p. 2-3).

The differences between the two types of learning can be illustrated in this way (see http://www.infed.org/thinkers/et-schon.htm):

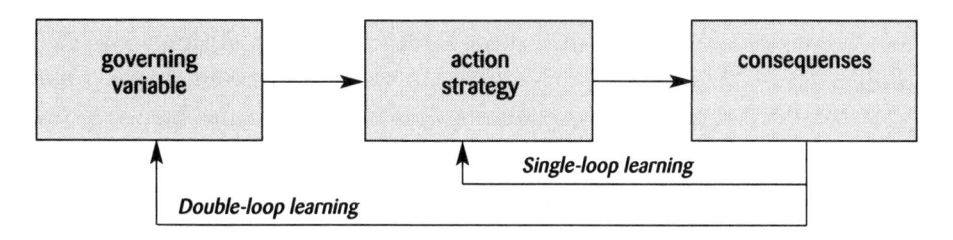

```
┌─────────────┐     ┌─────────────┐     ┌─────────────┐
│  governing  │ ──▶ │   action    │ ──▶ │ consequenses│
│  variable   │     │  strategy   │     │             │
└─────────────┘     └─────────────┘     └─────────────┘
       ▲                   ▲                    │
       │                   │  Single-loop learning
       │                   └────────────────────┘
       │     Double-loop learning
       └────────────────────────────────────────┘
```

Single-loop learning is evident whenever goals, values, and boundaries, and – we would like to add – perspectives on human nature are taken for granted. In many different types of consultancy assignments, the consultant – and the client – are faced with the question of whether organizational changes, educational programs, and development programs for personnel should involve single-loop learning or double-loop learning. If the latter is the case, the consultant cannot avoid the issue of management's, as well as employees', view of human nature.

The business consultant will often form a close relationship with management. Executives often hire consultants to assist in difficult decisions – this could mean large-scale reorganization, but it could also involve a specific program of development for certain members of staff. The organization may not have the necessary competence to carry out a reorganization or to develop an educational program – and relies on the consultant to provide expert knowledge. In situations like these there is no way to avoid the question of management's perspective of human nature, as it may be a deciding factor. The consultant may find him- or herself in a dilemma –

being used as a pawn in organizational power play. There are quite often hidden agendas involved in a consultancy assignment – as Anderson points out in his book *The Consultant's World* (1998). The perspective of human nature is usually part of what is hidden from the consultant – and this may actually be part of the problem.

Let us take a brief look at the role of education for these issues. The American researcher James Rest, whose major field of study was moral cognition, devised a method for measuring moral reasoning development – that is an individual's ability to identify and relate to moral issues. Rest developed the Defining Issues Test (DIT), in which subjects are asked to respond to several questions on moral issues related to a story. One of the conclusions Rest was able to draw from extensive use of this study was that there is a strong relationship between education and moral development. This is not a universal truth – but those with higher education tend to score better on the DIT than those with lower levels of education. This finding is of course open to interpretation, but Rest suggested that it had more to do with exposure to the educational environment than with the content of any specific educational program. This suggests that it is not so much what is taught at high schools and universities that matters, but rather that institutions of higher learning (the higher the better) "promote reflections and self-discovery, and this does actually affect moral thinking" (Rest, 1986, and Sivberg, 1993).

We should also take note of another issue. According to the New Testament, Jesus warned his disciples "why behold you the sliver that is in thy brother's eye, but consider not the beam that is in your own eye?" Management's perspective of human nature is important, but so is that of the consultant. The consultant should ask him- or herself: What is *my* perspective on human nature? What are the fundamental needs of the individual? What are my personal ideals? Am I an individualist or a collectivist? Do I tend to emphasize the good or the bad in people? Do I notice the differences or the similarities between people – in terms of qualities and competencies? Are people generally creative and active – or are they passive and indifferent to change?

A recent study on leadership ideals among Swedish executives conducted by Bengt Hansson (2004), uncovered a range of leadership ideals and perspectives on human nature. Both the politically incorrect, autocratic perspective, and the politically acceptable, but rather impractical, humanistic perspective are represented in Swedish business. Whether or not the findings from this study are representative of Swedish executives in general – or for that matter Scandinavian and even European executives, needs to be explored further.

Conclusion

This analysis raises a number of important questions – some with far-reaching consequences. Certainly one of the most interesting questions is whether leadership in business is different from that of leadership in government, or from leadership in a nonprofit organization? Should the leader of a public hospital run his or her organization differently than a leader of a privately-owned hospital? Our view is that a nonprofit governmental organization in certain respects should be run differently than a business in the private sector. However, in both cases, leadership should be based on the same view of human nature – as both cases involve people that are working to make the lives of others richer and more secure. And that view should be based on the notion of equal worth among all humans.

References

Andersson, L. (1998). *I konsultens värld.* Lund: Studentlitteratur.

Argyris, C. & Schön, D. (1978). *Organizational learning: A theory of action perspective.* Reading, Mass.: Addison Wesley.

Bråkenhielm, Carl Reinhold (1994). *Människan i världen. Om filosofi, teologi och etik i våra världsbilder.* Uppsala: Almqvist & Wiksell.

Bråkenhielm, Carl Reinhold (Ed.). (2001). *Världsbild och mening.* Nora: Nya Doxa.

Calltorp, Johan & Bråkenhielm, Carl Reinhold (Eds.). (1990). *Vårdens pris.* Stockholm: Verbum.

Collste, G. (1984). *Makten, moralen och människan. En analys av värdekonflikter i debatten om medbestämmande och löntagarstyre.* Uppsala: Almqvist & Wiksell.

Ekman, B. (2002). *Himmel och helvete. Om företagande, makt och ledarskap.* Stockholm: Ekerlids förlag AB.

Hansson, B. (2003). *Skapar investeringar i FOU, utbildning och arbetsmiljö/*

hälsa några värden i företaget? Resultat från humankapitalmätningen 2002, HKM rapport 03/01, IPF, Uppsala.

Hansson, B. (2004). *Människosyn och ledarskap. Är ledarideal från Markus Aurelius respektive Machiavelli synliga och relevanta i vår tid?* PM augusti 2004, Uppsala universitet.

Jay, A. (1968). *Företagsledning och Machiavelli,* Stockholm: Wahlström & Widstrand.

Kant, Immanuel (2004). *Till kritiken av det praktiska förnuftet.*

London, Jack (1953). *Varg-Larsen.* Stockholm: B. Wahlströms bokforlag.

Lönnebo, Martin (1964). *Albert Schweitzers etiskt-religiösa ideal.* Uppsala universitet.

Rest, James (Ed.). (1986). *Moral development. advances in research and theory.* New York: Praeger Publishers.

Singer, Peter (1995). *Rethinking life & death. The collapse of our traditional ethics.* Oxford: Oxford University Press.

Sivberg, Bengt (1993). *Professional judgement. A theoretical model and multi-experiments in nursing professional judgement.* Lund: Lund University Press.

Sundman, Per (2004). The just manager – a good manager. Unpublished article.

Uddenberg, N. (2001). Article in *Världsbild och mening.*

Chapter 11 | Dante's journey

STEINAR BJARTVEIT AND KJETIL EIKESET

Midway in the journey of our life

If it is true that it is the first sentence of a book that is the most important, you should take a moment to enjoy this one:

> "Midway in the journey of our life
> I found myself in a dark wood
> For the straight way was lost."

Midway in life, and off course. An experience as common to us now as it was in the 14th century – when Dante's *The Divine Comedy* (1970, p. 3), one of the masterpieces of literature, was written. As we passed into the current millennium, *The Divine Comedy* was declared to be the finest work of the previous millennium. This book has kept readers spellbound and enchanted for centuries. It has had a discernible effect on art, philosophy, theology, and even on the lives of individuals. The number of books and studies made about this book can be measured in kilos. Researchers have devoted their entire professional careers to understanding and interpreting this work. Givonanni Boccaccio was the first *Dantisti*. T. S. Elliot maintained that there were only two authors worth spending any time on: Shakespeare and Dante.

Dante's book tells of a journey. He finds his way out of the forest and spots a rise in the distance – where he thinks he might find serenity and savior. With fresh hope he starts to climb the hill, but he is foiled in his attempts. A leopard bounds forth and blocks his way. Dante is frightened, but is still set on reaching the top. Then a lion appears and, lifting its head and roaring, it frightens Dante back. Dante is despondent, and then the most frightening of the three animals appears. "A she-wolf which appeared in its leanness to be charged with all cravings and which has already made many live in wretchedness." Dante is forced to retreat – step by step back to the dark woods. But just then his rescuer arrives. He eyes the figure of a man. Dante does not know where this figure has come from, but calls out in desperation, and the man answers him. He is not from the land of the living, but rather from the kingdom of the dead, and he is sent to help Dante. Something about the figure strikes a chord with Dante, and slowly it dawns on him that the figure standing before him is his ideal poet, the model and inspiration of his verse – the Roman poet Virgil. And Virgil offers Dante advice: If you wish to reach the top of the hill, you must take another road: through Hell, Purgatory, and Paradise. It is for your own good, and I will guide you.

Midway in the journey of our life. Dante's epic story has been the subject of many interpretations. The book provides the foundation for layer upon layer of understanding. Dante is highly critical of his contemporaries – of political figures and of theological beliefs. The journey has obvious religious undertones, but it is also a tale of Dante's own journey towards greater self-knowledge. It is quite common in literature for travelogs to describe two concurrent journeys: the physical journey that actually takes place; and the emotional journey that inevitably shows the protagonist growing through trials and tribulations. It could be Odysseus searching for Ithaca, or Captain Willard's hunt for Colonel Kurtz in *Apocalypse Now*. The first sentence in the book sets the scene for what is to follow. The poet Dante tells the story of Dante who must wander through Hell and Purgatory to obtain forgiveness and salvation

La Divina Commedia is in many ways quite similar to another influential autobiography: *Augustin's Confessions* (Freccero, 1986). Just like Augustin, who bears all and tells us how the act of acknowledging his own true nature gave him greater self-knowledge and changed him forever, Dante tells a story of upheaval and change. Dante encounters some of his contemporaries, as well as other known historical figures, in his wanderings through Hell and Purgatory, and some of these meetings upset him more than others. These figures serve to confront the poet Dante with the traveler Dante – the questions he raises go straight to his soul. Dante is forced to acknowledge his own true nature in this way many times in both Hell and Purgatory. *La Divina Commedia* is "the story of how the self that was becomes the self that is". (Jacoff, 1986:xii). As such, the story is timeless – equally relevant for our time. Dante's many encounters with the fates of his contemporaries and with his own sins is not that different from similar encounters that people have today. Perhaps these encounters are even more vivid than they were 700 years ago. Alone and way off course, in a dark wood – midway through life.

… I found myself

So what can present day consultants and leaders learn form a 700-year-old Italian poem? The question is rather – what is there not to learn? Dante's journey is the tale of the individual's search for meaning. The story is about understanding a person's actions both in a broader and in a more immediate context – as opposed to current understanding of the role of leadership as something set apart from the person playing the role. Today, the role of leadership is often seen as being purely instrumental – and we tend to overlook the personal and human qualities necessary to carry out the role of leader. Leadership has become something that can be taught through MBA schools and leadership development programs. And this has somehow become an all-embracing education: if you can make it there, you can make it anywhere. This implies that the leader is merely an all-purpose tool that may enjoy a long and prosperous career, moving from one executive position to another. But the role of being leader cannot be divorced from the person playing the role – as this instrumental view would have us believe. First, leadership is not just a position in the hierarchy – it is a social relation (House, 1974). Leadership positions are not just handed out to anyone, a person has to show him- or herself worthy – within a specific social context. Second, different social contexts require different personal qualities and social skills (Goleman, Boyatzis, and McKee, 2002). It is naive to assume that a few MBA-courses or a one-week get-to-know-yourself program is sufficient preparation for the ever-changing demands of an organization. Third, leadership is something quite different from management – and unfortunately today's leadership schools are more geared towards teaching management (Zaleznik, 1977). This is despite the fact that studies on leadership have shown that transformational leaders are the most effective, and that they differ greatly from traditional managers (Bass, 1998). Fourth, this type of leadership requires far greater self-knowledge than is emphasized in traditional leadership programs (Conger & Kanungo, 1998; Collins, 2001). Leadership requires an existential understanding of yourself as an individual – in terms of who you want to be and what you want to accomplish.

One of the requirements that have emerged in all the studies and literature on leadership might seem innocuous at first glance. Leadership is not a role that can be acted out according to a script. Leadership demands engagement, emotional commitment, and personal conviction – a responsibility that you assume because it concerns something you feel you should contribute to. Leadership involves the will to accomplish something, and the determination to fight for it and for the responsibility of being leader. The obvious question that arises is fundamental: "What do I want to accomplish by being leader?" The good news is that leaders don't have to look far and wide to find reasons for their leadership. The bad news, or rather – the uncomfortable truth, is that the leader must search inside him- or herself for the answers. This shift in focus – from external factors to internal qualities is characteristic of modern literature on leadership. Leadership has become much more personal – the leader's views and personal qualities are important. Leadership is no longer mechanical, technical, or economical – it is interpersonal. And it has become a much more personal issue for the leader as well. For what if you don't know? What if, as in the case of Dante, you find yourself midway through life and lost in the woods. The bad news is that you won't find any answers in a book. There are no answers to be found – in theories of management, in job descriptions, or in your mandate. Dante was perfectly familiar with all these things. He had studied well. He had been a leader in Florence. But even so, he found himself alone, and lost in the dark woods. What he had lost, and what he recovered in a strange place midway through life – was himself. This is by no means an easy way out – Dante had to go through Hell, and beyond. This requirement – knowing who you are, may seem innocuous, but for most it is the toughest one they will ever face.

Thus, there is one item of knowledge that neither Dante nor today's leaders, can expect others to provide – self-knowledge. To put it in economic terms: you cannot outsource an existential understanding of who you are and what you want to accomplish. There is quite simply no external measure for this as it concerns our inner being. Søren Kierkegaard makes a very clear distinction between the inner and the outer in terms of knowing oneself (1994). If is true, as the literature on leadership would seem to assume, that leadership involves an element of personal character that implies that the leader's relationship to him- or herself cannot be stripped away and replaced by an operative or by a superficial role, then this moves the field of leadership straight into the philosophy of existentialism. Existence means to come forth, to stand out, to appear – to assume existence or character, to become real. Kierkegaard's thesis is that man's existence is entirely personal, and that it cannot be copied. The responsibility for my outlook on life lies with me; all choices are mine, and no theories or truths can make any difference. Personal convictions must be based on personal choices related to one's own existence, and the only path available is the inner. This entails much more than simply acting out roles – because at least then, we are aware of what we are doing, and any disparity is evident. The only way *to exist in truth*, is to make your own choices about your own existence.

Kierkegaard doesn't stop there. In his *Concluding Unscientific Postscript*, Kirekegaard states that *subjectivity is the truth*. The pseudonym he uses is Johannes Climacus. In Greek climax means to ascend, and Johannes ascends to heaven in pursuit of heavenly vision. It does not exist in the speeches, views, theories, or writings of others. Just look at the title – the terms necessary to define truth are wholly unscientific. Kierkegaard does this to emphasize that this topic is subjective – as opposed to the cut and dried truths of objective science. Because the topic at hand is not really a topic – it is about what it means to exist as a person, as a subject in your own life. For Kierkegaard, words like *sincerity* and *passion* are closer to truth than anything else. Passion is the fire that burns within, and makes a person assume his or her identity and give it worth, that make a tremendous difference (Thielst, 1999, p. 35). This passion, this sincerity, means to be concerned with oneself and one's own fate. While recognizing that, this is a responsibility one has to oneself. To look inside oneself and tell yourself who you are, is what Kierkegaard's existential landscape is all about. To exist in truth, *to be that particular individual*, and not to be everybody else. According to Kierkegaard man should be eternally concerned with himself and his own life. The questions is: how?

You choose. Because if it is so that we are concerned for our own existence, the choices we make will be significant for us – and we will want to make these choices. These choices cannot be made for us by others. The individual chooses for him- or herself – this is characteristic of the ethical view of existence, rather than the passive, observing manner of the onlooker. One prefers to make choices for oneself – rather than being indifferent and unconcerned. It is actually a choice between choosing and not choosing. It's making the choice that is vital, not what decision one makes. Søren Kierkegaard had his literary breakthrough in 1943 with what has been described by many as his masterpiece: *Either – Or*. The title is a brilliant summary of his philosophy – you cannot have it both ways. To exist is to choose. We choose to want to choose. For if it is so, that we are concerned with ourselves, these choices will be important. And if these choices are important to us, we start to see the world in a manner that Kierkegaard describes as "Absolute Difference" (1991, p. 208). An individual does not choose good over evil, but simply taking these things into account, suggests that some things mean more than others. "My either-or does not suggest the choice between good and evil, but rather the choice to accept both good and evil – or reject them altogether." (1991, p. 159). Thus, one has begun to assume responsibility for oneself and one's own life, and can choose to rediscover oneself. As a result, the person that always chooses is all s/he is, and all s/he can be. We are the synthesis of the essential and the possible, of the choices we have made and the freedom to choose. That is all. But it does mean that we may find we have made the wrong choices, and that we are off course, and all alone in a dark forest.

Kierkegaard is concerned with exactly the same thing that Dante encounters midway in life. How does one relate to oneself? How does one think about oneself? What should be important in my life? Can I justify my actions? Have I made choices? Is this me? Is this the way I am supposed to be? The potential here is enormous – and so is the responsibility. But herein lies also the burden, and Kierkegaard has felt the burden himself. His definition of the self is so succinct that no psychologist has ever surpassed him in potency or vitality: "The self is a relation which relates to itself, or that in the relation which is its relating to itself. The self is not the relation but the relation's relating to itself." (Kierkegaard, 2004, part I).

Confused? Don't worry, or perhaps that is precisely why you should. What Kierkegaard describes as being human, is pure motion, the faculty for contemplation, and for self-awareness. To be in truth, to be in subjectivity, is human when it relates to itself as a relation. When it experiences itself, as being identical to self. Identity means that one is the same as one is – and this implies so very much. That I am, here and now, everything I am, and everything I can become. Depending on what choices I make. You would have to search far and wide to find a definition more powerful, positive, persistent, and obligating than this. Wonderful, isn't it? And just a little unnerving, like Dante must have felt.

For this is what Dante requires of himself. He is concerned with the personal issues in his life. There are some things that cannot be left to others: Dante's relationship to himself. This is the fate and the greatness of man: we are responsible for both our own choices and our own view of ourselves. This is the requirement that resonates through the literature on leadership as an imperative. A leader must have personal convictions, and assume responsibility for these choices. A leader does not need to hide behind others, blame others, or copy predecessors – the leader uses him- or herself as a mainstay and as a point of reference. But choosing what to believe in, something that you can live with and stand up for, requires a great deal of courage. This is the existential landscape in which Dante has lost his way. He has to reclaim himself. And the road goes through self-knowledge. There are no insurance policies or guaranties that cover a life lived. Kierkegaard and Dante alike recognize the insecurity of being alive. We understand life looking backwards, but we live it going forwards.

In deciding to journey through Hell and Purgatory in order to understand himself and his life, Dante is devoting himself to a vivid understanding of himself as a human being. Who he is and what choices he makes, will have consequences for Dante in this life and in the afterlife. *La Divina Commedia* is the story of someone coming to terms with himself – with a happy ending (that is why it is called a comedy). He has lost himself in life. Once he has endured a series of encounters with the souls of the dead – and been confronted with himself, he can continue with his life in the land of the living.

… I think and deem it best that you should follow me

The poet Dante sends the traveler Dante on his journey through Hell, Purgatory, and Paradise. But he does not send him on his way all alone. The poet Dante creates aides that will guide the traveler safely on his journey. The first aide to appear is Virgil, who comforts Dante when he is lost and despairing after encountering the three beasts on his way up the hill. Virgil guides Dante through Hell and most of the way through Purgatory. Beatrice takes over from Virgil, and Bernard of Clairvaux from her.

For the poet Dante these aides serve several purposes. They represent different qualities: Virgil is common sense; Beatrice is love. They are literary figures that move Dante, and the story, forward. They are the running commentary that makes sense of what is happening – for both traveler and reader. But they also appear literally to guide Dante and keep him company. As Dante, the poet, sees it, Dante, the traveler, cannot make it on his own. On such a journey, one cannot travel alone. And this is why Dante creates for himself first-rate aides that provide him with the best help he could envision. He needs somebody to explain things, to support him, to chastise him, and to keep him moving. His aides help him to keep moving when he stumbles. "Therefore I think and deem it best that you should follow me" (Dante, 1970, p. 11), says Virgil. And Dante, not entirely convinced, but somewhat hopeful, is ready to follow.

The classic role of counselor has been brought back to life in the recent literature on leadership. It has of course been given a new, and trendy, label – it is now referred to as executive coach. But we can trace the roots of this form of counsel a long way back in history and mythology. The Centaur Chiron advised the young Achilles; Maecenas counseled Augustus; Raleigh aided Elizabeth, and Gandalf followed Aragon through the mines of Moria. These are all long-term relationships that have formed between leader and counselor. Something quite apart from the short-term relationship between leader and consultant within the boundaries of a defined project. Traditional counsel emphasizes both the task that is to be undertaken, and the person who is to undertake the task.

Today, in the age of therapy, the role of counsel is often linked to psychotherapy (Kilburg, 2000; Berglas, 2002). A form of coaching on the couch – and defined by the customs and roles inherent in psychotherapy. The counselor is in reality the healer. And it is sometimes hard to tell executive coaching apart from life coaching or various forms of psychotherapy. While executive coaching may include elements of psychotherapy, it would be inappropriate to suggest that it is part of psychotherapy (Fitzgerald & Berger, 2002). Executive coaching is much more than psychotherapy.

Definitions of executive coaching usually include two elements: the client's performance, and the client's personal growth (Flaherty, 1999; Kilburg, 2000; Fitzgerald & Berger, 2002). The former is reminiscent of the traditional role of counseling, while the latter borders on psychotherapy. However, the focus of executive coaching is both performance and performer. It involves much more than a regular consultation because the person, in the capacity of being leader, is afforded more focused attention. Coaching assignments often follow in the wake of a regular consultancy assignment when a relationship of trust and respect forms between consultant and client. But the nature of this assignment is very different, as the client and his or her goals now become the focal point, and the client's leadership performance the primary measure. This implies a long-term relationship. Executive coaching does not lend itself to the quick-fix or to step-by-step techniques. Quite the contrary – it is the relationship between coach and client that forms the basis for learning and achievement. There is an expectation that coaching will result in increased on-the-job performance for the leader, and this is one area where coaching differs from psychotherapy. Coaching is very pragmatic in the sense that the client will expect to feel the benefit of coaching manifest itself in the execution of his or her duties as leader. This implies that, in addition to relational and psycho-therapeutical skills, the coach is expected to have a working knowledge of the client's field; the organization and the management team. In some cases, specific industry knowledge might even been required.

As such, we do not need coaches that are psychotherapists or consultants that provide expert advice within a narrow field. We need companions. The Human Resources technocrats will never dominate this field. "… coaching is a principle-shaped ontological stance and not a series of techniques." (Flaherty, 1999, p. 13). Executive coaching is something entirely different. It is a relationship where the client learns about him- or herself, not through any transfer of knowledge or insightful interpretations, but simply by embarking on a journey to encounter one's own self.

Kierkegaard uses a similar model for the role of aide – based on a Socratic model where the focus is always on the client or main character. The purpose of any Socratic model is to get the subject to contemplate his or her own terms, motives, and reasoning. But in an existentialistic perspective the personal supersedes the factual, because the person's own point of departure and growth are "the subject itself". And this development, this motion, must come from within, and not from others. The aide cannot tell the client what to think, what to choose, or what to do. What the aide can do, is to create the most favorable conditions for contemplation, choice, and action to take place. In a sense it is like midwifery. The midwife does not give birth to the child. The use of the midwife analogy is pertinent and deliberate; Kierkegaard defines this as *maieutikk*, and describes this as an impulse or desire towards responsibility.

The relationship is asymmetrical in that the responsibility for interpretation, decision, and action must always rest with the client. Just how does the coach contribute to the leader forming stronger convictions and self-determination? The coach will encourage the client to make choices, and to accept that responsibility for all interpretations and the actions based on these interpretations is the client's – and that these actions will have consequences. Taking a closer look at the consequences of decisions made and actions carried out, will be an important part of the process, but it is even more important that the client starts to appreciate that these decisions, and the actions, based on them, define his or her character. The client will also learn that once you accept responsibility for the consequences of your actions, you start to make more conscious and considered decisions. Beneath all this there lies the movement towards the subjective, towards the personal as something that obligates. The best thing a coach can do, is encourage soul-searching, self-definition and the will to make choices: "The maieuthic drive from A to B is liberating in that it contributes to developing B as a person with conviction." (Næss, 1994, p. 25, our translation). In other words, the client is best served by a coach that paves the way for self-examination and stronger convictions. If an intervention leads to greater personal involvement and responsibility for the choices that need to be made – it is a success. And this is precisely what Virgil does! The many personal encounters Dante experiences in the Inferno are in fact situations where Dante is put on the spot and forced to make choices. Dante is faced with the responsibility for interpreting and dealing with this situation.

Measured against the standards of today, in this age of therapy, Virgil is not exactly the epitome of the professional coach. He is not that well groomed and actually commits a few therapeutic blunders along the way. He makes some strange choices, and he puts into words things are best left unsaid. Still, he is Dante's first choice of companion. If Dante is going to go through Hell, this is the character that he wants to guide him. This is the spirit that will introduce Dante to a "who's who" of the dead, and literally unearth the souls that Dante must encounter. Virgil emerges as a shining authority, but at the same time maintains his humanity. It is clear that Dante admires Virgil, but he is also to hold up Virgil as a standard that he wants to surpass. What starts out as master-apprentice relationship, gradually develops into a relationship of equals that culminates when they reach Purgatory, and Virgil lets Dante proceed on his own. "The temporal fire and the eternal you have seen, my son, and are come to part where I of myself discern no farther onward." (Dante, 1973, p. 301).

Let us follow them on their journey and take a closer look at some of the most significant encounters.

... deep Hell does not receive them

As Dante passes through the gates of Hell, he enters the Devil's waiting room. This is a truly original and completely absurd setting where Dante encounters souls that will forever remain in Limbo – not admitted to Hell. There are so many of these indistinguishable figures – Dante has never seen this many souls. He had never envisioned that so many people had ever lived. These souls are forever doomed to follow behind a banner. Who are these people? Virgil is loathe to tell – there is nothing to be learned here. Move on! But Dante is terrified by the sheer number – and the fact that he recognizes some of these souls. What is this endless procession, here before the river Styx – that must be crossed to get into Hell proper? Finally Virgil answers Dante:

> "Such is the miserable condition of the sorry souls of those who lived without infamy and without praise … The heavens drive them out, so as not to be less beautiful; and deep Hell does not receive them, lest the wicked have some glory over them." (Dante, 1973, p. 27).

These are the souls that have never made any choices. The ones that have never stood for anything. And just as they fed off others their entire life, they must now suffer the eternal misery of having wasps, maggots, and mosquitoes feed off them as they wander around in circles.

The spectacle of the Devil's waiting room should be equally terrifying in our day. In many ways, for most people, this is as far as they will get. These are the ones with no cause, not known for suffering a good cause or a scandal in a bad one. These worthless souls have achieved so little that Heaven refuses to accept them, and Hell wants to be rid of them. These people have never taken a stand on anything. They have lived minor lives, and are doomed to suffer minor discomfort for all eternity. And no names are mentioned, because these souls are not worthy of having their own names. At the same time, they are the majority of us.

Before we even make it into Hell, Virgil is forcing us to confront things we would rather not. If this is as far as most people get, what about leaders? The ones that should go forth, and lead us into the future with great confidence? Think again. Just think how easy it is to wilt under the pressures to conform and the fear of becoming unpopular; the need for ingratiation and the desire to gain power. For, as we all know, the toughest job is carrying the torch. Merely following behind, until something better comes by, is the easy part. The easiest piece of advice you can give to a leader is quite simply: never stay long enough in one job to allow your results to catch up with you. Move on. Leave the scene of the crime. Turn like the wind inside a wheel, and follow the path of least resistance. This advice flies in the face of the current thinking on leadership that emphasizes the need for leaders with strong personal convictions. But, unfortunately, this advice is very practical, quite common, and utterly state-of-the-art. These fair-weather fans and incidental followers, that only serve to slow others down, are everywhere, even among leaders.

The problem with these figures is that they have never made decisions for themselves, but always followed others – as they now must follow the meaningless banner. Giacomo Oreglia (2001) argues that this is the gem of Dante, his prose most fitting of our time. Dante put forth this critique of modern-day society 650 years too early! For this cycle is as much a symbol of our time as it was of Dante's. This cycle tells the story of how these useless, always middle-of-the-road people, who never take a stand on issues and merely follow in others' footsteps, are despised by one and all. They are the *Neutrals*. The real concern with those that always follow, is that they don't see this as a problem. Nothing means much to them, things are generally agreeable, and life is without major sources of aggravation. The indifferent are not passionate about much, and hardly aware of their own existence. Making choices is really not called for, because everyday there are so many things that one can chase after! When forced to account for themselves they meekly submit that there isn't enough time to do everything, otherwise they would of course be doing this or deciding that. As soon as they have done a little more following.

It is hard to find a more fitting critique of our modern society. So little time and so much to do, and so many choices to make, that we simply cannot make our minds up what to choose. Least of all what choices to make for ourselves. Taking charge of your own life, now that is a big responsibility. It is easier to look to the right or look to the left, than to look inside oneself. This is one of the things that Kierkegaard laments modern man, and he uses a lot of space in his writings to describe what he sees as man evading his own existence and shrinking from important choices. It might be easier to understand what it means to choose for oneself and to take a stand, if we can understand what this does not mean. Kierkegaard's psychological descriptions of how we abstain from making choices as being the antithesis of the meaning of human existence, are ingenious. And this helps us to see why there are so many people lost in this pre-Hell, or the Devil's waiting room. For the indifferent are the most numerous.

Kierkegaard's descriptions of people were masterful, and he often ventured out into the streets of Copenhagen for what he called his "people-bath". Back in the 1840s, Copenhagen was a metropolis full of people going about their lives – not unlike our modern cities. The first character that Kierkegaard describes is the *Bourgeois*. He is always well-groomed. He is well-off, and is making a very comfortable living – from numerous activities. On Sundays we will find him out strolling, wife at his arm, walking cane in hand, greeting everybody with impeccable etiquette. And he measures himself against everyone he greets. By our standards, he is most certainly successful. He has a good job, a good wife, and a good station in life – by our standards. He finds criticism of society, his society, displeasing. Why? Because he lives by the customs and traditions of this society – and if you mock these, you mock him. But even more displeasing than criticism, is change. Change is treacherous, for it can lead to changes, even in the way one should view oneself. This is why he blindly defends the establishment against all criticism. He is a reliable, but not very well-reflected citizen that upholds the customs of society, and is primarily concerned with his own success – at work and as a breadwinner. Kierkegaard refers to this character as the objective cross-sum, representative of the average. Back in the 1920s, the German philosopher Martin Heidegger created another term for this figure: *das Man* (Heidegger, 1962). This figure, in the neutral, singular form, is more powerful than we imagine. It is to him we refer when we resort to reasoning such as: "that's not the way they do things" or "that's the way they've always done things". And quite often these are the arguments that bring a discussion to a close! Even though no-one has ever met "they". And this is precisely the point Heidegger wants to make – we cannot see him, because he is inside us.

It is very easy to transfer this to the world of leadership. There is Das Man in every organization. S/he is the perfect manager. The guardian of the system, high-priest of the time-honored tradition. It is easy for a leader to assume this role as part of the formal mandate, but there is a very real danger that this leadership style will deteriorate into the role of supervisor. The difference between a leader and a manager may be subtle, but it is crucial. While the leader should be concerned with making sure that the organization is doing the right things, the manager just wants to make sure that things are done correctly. Very different agendas. The leader emphasizes substance and change, while the manager focuses on control and stability. But, the manager, as supervisor, in the figure of Das Man, has excellent reasons: "This is the way we do things here. This is the way we have always done things. And that is the end of that." Which, of course, tends to stifle change and progress. Kierkegaard and Heidegger would argue that Das Man acts the way s/he does because going with the flow is much more comfortable, and involves much less tension, than actually questioning the appropriateness and significance of, and the responsibility for, doing things the way they have always been done. Management requires a pure and unwavering penchant for sticking to convention. On the other hand, leadership requires the determination to assume responsibility. It is easier to leave well enough alone, and simply refer to procedure, to the system, or to what has been done before. There is no risk, and no one stands out. Leadership it is not.

It is this nonentity that Kierkegaard wants to get at. The same one that scampers behind Dante's banner – always making sure that the guy next to him is keeping up with the rest. To Kierkegaard this is a dangerous existence, because this person never gets to find out who s/he really is. When confronted with such as question, the response is a menacing snarl. Thielst describes 'the Bourgeois' as: "A particularly conforming, almost robotic personality that blissfully slips into stereotypical behavior – a well-adapted citizen, who deftly plays the roles set out in today's script." (1989, p. 38). We are of course referring to the pillars of society. And even allowing for the powers of self-deception, Kierkegaard is wary of this lot. He argues that when the masses read: the herd, join together and shout "hurray" or "boo", this is about as far away from existence as we can get. We shed our identity in the masses, we are absolved from responsibility and the individual is diminished. Kierkegaard argues that the multitude represents untruth, because it absolves us from our responsibilities. And it undermines responsibility because each individual becomes a mere fraction of the whole when we are swallowed by the masses. According to Kierkegaard the herd mentality thwarts individuality. Cowardice is multitude. The crowd is untruth.

To Kierkegaard, the Bourgeois is only the beginning of falsehood. There are even more sophisticated ways of escaping from yourself. Just pick one – but herein lies the problem. It is risky to choose one, to have to stand for this choice. The only things you loose when you choose who you want to be are the things that slip away. All the things you will never get to try or be. Think about it! Think about all you could have done and everything you could have become! If you choose one thing, you exclude something else. And if you should choose to stand for something, there are a lot of things you cannot stand for. You forgo some options. You cannot remain stuck to one thing, because you could miss out on something else. You have to be true – but enough – to yourself. It goes without saying that this type of leader does not stay in the same place for very long. He has to move on.

But these methods of escape are more devious than was the case with the Bourgeois. He doesn't have a clue. But these people know that they have to make a choice. They recognize that, in the words of Carl Gustav Jung, life is a question that needs to be answered. They know full well that they should have chosen themselves and who they want to be, but they know how difficult this can be. So they have backed away from this choice. The thing is, you have to escape completely. Kierkegaard calls the character that represents escape *The Esthetic*, and within the esthetic there are a number of escape routes. As the term suggests, the esthetic view of life implies enjoying the pleasures life has to offer. The first that comes to mind here is the typical esthetic that enjoys speed, excitement, parachuting, or making new acquaintances – all wonderful opportunities for feedback. Nothing can top the sensation of hearing *others* say what a wonderful *person* you are! And herein lies the Esthetic's calling: to receive continuous reaffirmation from others about who you are. So you don't have to answer the question yourself. It is all about using others in the process and really enjoying the fact that it is all about you. New projects, acquaintances, or challenges are always welcome. And if things get too sticky, or too familiar, there are always new projects out there. This is the way things must be for the Esthetic.

A more subtle variation on this theme is the I-sickness. The Esthetic has got the point – getting everyone to notice himself as a turn toward inwardness. However, he accomplishes this by using a lot of inessential add-ons. New Rolex, new humidifier, new kitchen, new car, new suit, new membership at the gym, new body, new education. The possibilities are unlimited. You have to find the real you, and posing for yourself is taking up all your time, whether it is at the gym or during the self-development program. It is all about taking charge of yourself! As Kierkegaard sees it, this is all about escaping behind all the frills. The social images and sophisticated techniques are merely crutches for the self, useful for sidestepping the issue of actually relating to yourself. It is always easier to be the star pupil at a self-development class than to have to think for yourself.

Theories on leadership claim that leadership is a personal responsibility, involving choices, passion, and integrity. However, both consultant and leader would do well to take note of how easy it is to evade this responsibility. The escape routes are always available, in focusing on the project, in the pretending, on the business cards, job descriptions, bonus systems, and pension deals. Or in the organization's culture. The opportunities for avoiding questions about oneself are many. And as a leader the opportunities for avoiding issues like your position on leadership or even your own existence are numerous. The question: "Why are you a leader?" is therefore quite unpleasant for many. Many choose simply to avoid the question, or not answer it. Most respond that they don't have time. Or that one has just become a leader. But if the leader is to find his or her identity as a leader, the question requires an answer, even if this may involve some grueling soul-searching. And this is where many found the escape of last resort: they are always talking about how tired they are, how much they work, and how pointless it all seems. These gripes are not for every occasion. No, they are stored for when the big questions pop up and demand answers. Kierkegaard calls this a tendency to melancholy. Only bliss shall you seek! Gloomy observations are portioned out, to remind one, and the others, how tired you are and how pointless it all seems. At least you don't have to fight for anything …

The qualities common to all are the falsehood and complete lack of reality. They do not relate to their self, but rather to their exterior – as some essential condition that dictates their existence. And this was of great concern to Kierkegaard. He despaired of what would become of man under these conditions, where cowardice, acting and bravura, the masses, melancholy, or delight rule. And then he provides the answer himself: "For what do they achieve – those who make such haste? They will fare no better than the housekeeper who, in a complete frenzy because her house had caught fire, managed only to save the poker. For what more than this will they salvage from the great pyre of Life?" (Billeskov Jansen, 1993, p. 30).

There are a few things that suggest that Kierkegaard was frightened of the times he lived in. On March 1st, 1836 he read that a circus tent in St. Petersburg had caught fire and collapsed, killing many of the spectators, despite the fact that the clown tried to warn them, but received only laughter and cheering. Kierkegaard used this as a warning in his polemic: "And this is just how I imagine the end of the world; cheered on by a great crowd of simpletons – who thought it was all a joke!" (Billeskov Jansen, 1993, p. 31).

The indifferent that Dante encounters, the ones, he explains, that are so numerous. The ones that never choose for themselves, and never carried their own banner. Kierkegaard describes how this is possible – that the indifferent have not chosen life, but merely gone with the flow. That is why they have no names and no self. They have never chosen their own self.

Who were your ancestors?

Halfway to Hell, Dante encounters the antithesis to indifference, in the figure of someone who did stand for something, but did so with such fervor that he wound up causing harm. The upper layers of Hell are for those who have surrendered to passion. Further down, on the lower layers, we find those who deliberately wronged others. Dante encounters Farinata, a political opposite who died the year before Dante was born, in a burning coffin. Farinata was the leader of the Ghibellines, while Dante's family belonged to the rival Guelf burgers. The political struggles between these two factions escalated dramatically, debates turned into fights, fights into assassinations, and assassinations into war. Florence was torn apart – from within. The factions were so convinced of the legitimacy and absolute correctness of their own positions that they were willing to use all means to prevail over the opposing party. As they say, you cannot make an omelet without breaking a few eggs. The escalation of violence culminates in a terrific battle at Montaperti where Farinata, through treachery and by entering into an alliance with the enemies of Florence, crushes the Guelfs. A true patriot who, in the passion of seeking victory, betrays the city he so dearly loves. It actually got to the point where these enemies of Florence demanded, in return for the help they had given, that Florence be destroyed. But this threat stirred something in Farinata, and he defended his city.

Why this encounter with Farinata? Is this just Dante gloating over the horrible demise of an opponent? The conversation with Farinata has a less obvious interpretation. Virgil admonishes Dante: "Let thy words be fitting." We hear an echo from Dante's past, and begin to see why Dante is lost midway in life.

Shortly after Farinata's great triumph, the Guelf return – to defeat the Ghibellines for good. Farinata's palace is leveled with the ground, to make way for the new city hall that the Guelf intend to build. If you want to destroy someone, you have to do it thoroughly. Even with the Ghibellines out of the way, there is no peace to be had. The Guelf stand alone in victory, but they soon become engulfed in internal disputes. The factions are just as unyielding, and the bitterness as strong as it was between the Guelf and the Ghibellines. And Dante finds himself on one side of this conflict, holding political office. However, in 1301, he would fall victim to a political coup orchestrated by the opposing faction, who seize power and force Dante and his fellow party members from office. During his exile, Dante travels around Italy, making plans for a new coup. He wants to go back and settle the score. But nothing comes of his plans. The exiles never gain enough support to carry off their own coup. In the end, moderates wind up taking over Florence, and in the name of peace and forgiveness they invite the exiles to return to Florence. On one condition: they must repent their previous actions. But that is too much for Dante. He is supposed to apologize? Instead he answers that he can see the stars in the heavens just as clearly anywhere else in Italy as he can in Florence. And Florence responds in kind that Dante is exiled for life. And even worse: he is sentenced to death in absentia, his properties are confiscated, and the death sentence is passed on his sons. Bitterness begets bitterness. Retribution begets retribution. And that is when he commences his great work: "Midway in the journey of our life I found myself in a dark wood …"

From those who follow aimlessly behind the banner, to fanatics. Aristotle's admonitions about the middle of the road force their way upon us. Deficiency is no better than excess. Neither Dante nor Farinata have had any reservations about choosing what to stand for in life. They have chosen and made their choices painfully evident to all. Both of them burn with passion for what they believe in – a passion so intense that the indifferent in Canto III can envy them. However, it is dangerous to get too close to these torch-bearers when they burn with passion. The flames tend to consume all that surrounds them, and destroy as much as they illuminate. Farinata and Dante have let their burning passion consume themselves – and those who were close to them.

Self-destruction, unity, and fellowship are not unique to the 14th century. They are quite evident in our society (Bjartveit, 1998). Rather than working together for the greater good, people act out some *Lord of the Flies*-scenario and, in their quest to defeat imaginary demons and enemies, wind up stabbing each other in the back. This outcome is destructive, and any sense of community is destroyed while opposing parties try to finish each other off. Organizations can be torn apart – not from competition, market forces, or new technology. Internal strife will do the trick. Simplistic explanations for this type of event usually attribute everything to the power struggles or to resident evil. We are all comfortable with these explanations – they exonerate the rest of us. We will enjoy the sleep of the innocent. However, Dante's tales of his own life and of and his encounter with Farinata hint at a much darker explanation. Organizations don't self-destruct because some people are more power-hungry than others, or are a little bit more treacherous than others. Organizations self-destruct because people are fanatic and burn with passion for their causes. No, that would not be correct. In a constructivist perspective we don't burn with passion for a cause (Bjartveit & Kjærstad, 1996). We accept the most important issues as truths – on which we base our understanding of ourselves and our surroundings. And we don't mess around with our sense of reality. If we are utterly convinced that something is accurate and true, we will fight for it, and even go to war against a known enemy over it. Articles of faith, truisms, and opposing views of reality clash against each other – whether it is during the strategic power plays in the boardroom or in the sometime heated, but always Quixotic, exchanges between imaginary opponents in academia. And as we all are well aware of: you cannot make an omelet without breaking a few eggs.

There is every reason to sound the alarm when leaders start to, figuratively speaking, make omelets. When home-baked recipes call for something to be broken, we are usually a long way towards splitting things into dichotomies (Segal, 1974). These situations are not characterized by an abundance of middle ground or uncertainty. Everything is right or wrong, good or bad, black or white. And we inevitably see ourselves on the side of good. We are in the service of good, battling the forces of evil. This is when evil empires suddenly emerge on the horizon, or the US starts to assume all the traits of Satan. The scene is played out with Star Wars rhetoric and evil mythology. The major problem is that this scene looks identical from both sides – albeit with diametrically opposing interpretations. Right stands against right. Dogma against dogma. These situations tend to escalate, and unfortunately retributions and revenge become the means of destroying the falsehood that threatens our existence and all that we believe in. We cannot rest until the enemy is defeated. In this type of conflict, both Farinata and Dante will attack and destroy themselves and everyone around them.

It is easy to interpret the Contrapasso principle that applies in Hell as a punishment or retribution for everything you did during your life on earth. In that case Dante's God is just a cook in the omelet of Hell. But contrapasso can also be interpreted as the consequence of a life lived (Pertile, 2000). If this is the case, Farinata burns in Hell for two different reasons, proud and unmoved by destiny, and convinced he was right. Farinata's stubbornness and conviction frighten Dante when he realizes that he is gloating over the destiny that has befallen his family's enemy.

Trapassar del segno

Teodolinda Barolini (1992) argues that the most significant encounter in *La Divina Commedia* occurs when Dante meets Odysseus, Homer's great hero. Most readers are disappointed to learn that Dante has placed the greatest hero of Antiquity deep down in Hell. Surely such a figure should be in Heaven? But Dante creates his own, very ingenious, literary device –

he extends the legend of Odysseus. Banished for all eternity to the flames of Hell, Odysseus reveals the truth to Dante. He never returned to Ithaca. He did not end his life as king, peaceful and content in the arms of his beloved Penelope. No, a life of idleness was not worthy a man of adventure. He had to explore more, discover new lands, and new kingdoms. So, after meeting Kirke, his men are returned to him and they set sail on the Mediterranean. They finally reach Gibraltar, where Hercules had placed columns – to warn sailors against the dangers of sailing out into the open sea. And that is when the charismatic leader emerges, and with great eloquence and passion urges his men to follow the sun to a land without people. " … you were not made to live as brutes, but to pursue virtue and knowledge" (Dante, 1970, p. 279). His words touch the men so deeply that they immediately grip the oars and thrust the ship out into the open sea. But the journey is to come to a sudden and dramatic conclusion. The ship is sucked into a whirlpool, and the sea swallows one and all.

Odysseus had the sharpest tongue in Antiquity. Where other heroes relied on brute force, bludgeons, and swords, Odysseus used eloquence and wisdom. Even the Trojans of the Iliad admired his great power of speech and were of the opinion that no living soul could measure up to Odysseus. The Trojans gained first-hand experience of his immense wisdom, when the Greeks, following ten years of siege decide to follow Odysseus' advice and build the first Trojan horse. But Dante sends him – with barely disguised admiration – to Hell. As a mass-seducer and notorious offender.

Witness these serious attacks on our faith in these great leaders. Those leaders, who with a mere "I have a dream" or "our finest hour" can bring us all together to fight and obey. The ones we admire and write biographies about. The ones that have been summoned to the stars – as many a leader hopes he or she will be. Caesar broke down in tears when he learned that Alexander had conquered the world by the time he was as old as Caesar (Suetonius, 1957). There are but a few that are chosen who achieve honor and fame. As Dante so wonderfully illustrates, even these stars have a darker side.

The field of leadership worships its heroes just like others do. Because, there are heroes: the ones that burn with passion and inspire their colleagues and co-workers. They use their eloquence and passion to stir up the same passion in others. But where there is articulate expression and strong emotion, there is also Scylla and Charibdes. For there are even more pitfalls along this way for leaders and beguilers. Studies have shown that it is not just everyone else that is seduced by their eloquence – they can even persuade themselves (Conger & Kanungo, 1998). And not always for the better. It would seem that it is not just those around them that see these leaders as divine – they hold this view of themselves ... Great leaders are vulnerable to their own greatness. It can be contagious – from the project to the leader. The risk of narcissism is very real.

In a sense we are concerned with the leaders that are true to themselves and their goals, and who are willing to give all it takes. In this sense they are true to their ideals. Studies also show that by using their passionate drive and powers of communication to inspire others, these leaders can achieve great things (Conger & Kanungo, op. cit.). They have great visions and are full of ideas – they persuade the masses to follow, and they are willing to take risks. But this shining silver coin can be turned to uncover a shadow. The same studies reveal the adverse consequences of a burning passion and the ability to persuade. There is a phrase in political rhetoric that Aristotle once coined, and that Cicero later embraced: The speaker himself is the strongest piece of evidence. For if you wish to convince others, you must first convince yourself. And this is precisely what the great communicators are so good at. They convince their public – and themselves. Unfortunately, convincing yourself that you are right, and truly believing in this, may have some adverse consequences. The most prized qualities in rhetoric, pathos and emotional revival, also have an effect on the speaker. Emotions are stirred and the self-image is enhanced. Conger & Kanungo (1998) point out that this self-entrancement may have an adverse effect on leadership.

First, the leader's own perspective of reality may be affected, or, rather, warped. The great leaders often feel that they are the greatest, and delusions of grandeur will surface. As a result of this they tend to eschew the advice and support of others – because if you can master everything, you don't need help from those beneath yourself. Their focus tends to narrow, and this may in turn prevent them from noticing developments in their surroundings. And the ability to communicate deteriorates. Leaders that place too much faith in their own visions – and in the consequences of these visions, are often poor listeners. They tend to have inflated evaluations of their own abilities. As a result they don't respond well to criticism, and tend to get very defensive. They will often censure and deride any negative feedback. As if that weren't enough, they will maintain the illusion of control by attributing any negative developments to matters that lie beyond their control. They are in charge of everything that turns out well. And have had nothing to do with failures. Charismatic leaders that encounter these pitfalls, tend to focus almost entirely on themselves, and pay little attention to colleagues and subordinates. Rather than nourish networks, they tear them down, and in doing so, create rivalries. This makes them stronger, and they create dependencies by maintaining direct lines of communication with subordinates. This excessive control is interspersed with a unique ability for taking the credit for others' success, which also means that they fail to take the responsibility of grooming a successor very seriously. They are often absent from the day-to-day running of the organization – and thus fail to notice important details and developments. As Maccoby (2000) sums up, the research in this field shows that narcissistic leaders have many positive traits, but there are also some serious questions linked to their leadership ability. Some narcissistic leaders have entirely unrealistic self-schemas, they are hypersensitive to criticism, and they are poor listeners. Maccoby also notes that these leaders tend to display little empathy, but harbor a great deal of anger. They are always on the alert and ready to confront their surroundings, and display an overly competitive instinct – which is evident in the way they tend to see enemies and battles to be won at every corner.

It is almost a miracle to sail these waters unharmed when this doesn't lead to serious damage. There is often a shadow that lies over some of these great leaders – that tends to grow with their ambitions, until it is larger than their own leadership. These great persuaders don't just convince the audience, they convince themselves as well. Never has humility been more called for than here. Humility is an important part of the lesson Dante has to learn on his way through Hell and Purgatory. And this lesson is equally important for many of today's leaders.

There is a very thin line between Odysseus, the great communicator, and Odysseus, the trespasser (Barolini, 1992). His thirst for knowledge and new adventure drive him to great deeds, and beyond – he goes too far. Dante broaches the issue of whether an unending quest for new adventure and new things to conquer is always a good thing, or whether it is better to know and recognize one's own limits. Odysseus exceeds the limits of his being. Odysseus is driven by his yearning and passion to venture beyond

Hercules' columns — and to his downfall. Just like Adam, who could not resist the temptation to taste the forbidden fruit, Odysseus reminds us that *trapassar del segno*: man goes too far and beyond what is right. Odysseus ventures too far, for himself and for those who followed him. There are some places not meant to be traveled.

And this is where Dante encounters himself. In *Commedia*, the distinction between *erroneo camminatore* and *buono camminatore* — the wrong path and the right path, is fundamental. This is the point of departure for *Commedia* — in a dark wood … "for the straight way was lost". There is a connection between Dante and Odysseus. Two powerful communicators that lead themselves and others astray. Two travelers that wander the wrong path. Two souls so hungry for knowledge that they yearn for that which cannot be had. But Odysseus' journey is the antithesis of Dante's journey. Odysseus is driven by a twisted sense of reality and from a yearning for trivial pleasures. Whereas Dante wanders toward something that is of greater worth. In fact Dante's journey may be interpreted as the antithesis of Odysseus' voyage. Where Odysseus drowns, Dante is spared. Dante reaches humility and increased self-awareness, while Odysseus perishes along with his pride and self-glory. It is almost as though Dante needs Odysseus as a reference point to remain on the right path. And as Barolini suggests, this is why Odysseus dies for the sins of Dante.

If you follow your star …

There are several indications throughout Inferno that suggest Dante is assuming responsibility for himself, and for his existence. In Canto 15, Dante is given the following piece of advice from his old school teacher, Brunetto Latini: "If you follow your star you cannot fail a glorious port" (Dante, 1970, p. 157). But what is really interesting is Dante's answer: "… so conscience chide me not, I am prepared for Fortune as she wills" (Dante, 1970, p. 159). Dante reveals that he is no longer afraid for Fortuna, and he has started to find his own way. And he uses his aide's words as though they were his own — because it was Virgil who first spoke these words of wisdom! Virgil remains by Dante's side through most of his journey, but as Dante progresses he becomes less reliant on Virgil. This is a common narrative technique. When it is time for them to part, Virgil praises his pupil and companion: "Take henceforth your own pleasure for your guide. Forth you are from the steep was, forth from the narrow" (Dante, 1973, p. 299).Virgil lets Dante continue on his journey with these final words:"No longer expect word or sign from me. Free, upright, and whole is your will, and it would be wrong not to act according to its pleasure." (Dante, 1973, p. 301). The coach has completed his project, and must return to his place in Hell, while Dante has become his own guiding light. The person he so wants to be, poet, wanderer, and his own counsel. A wonderful illustration of existential force. Kierkegaard contends that when choosing, man is a synthesis of what is necessary and what is possible. Dante is a prime example of this.

Dante's journey is an excellent reminder to all leaders that it is never too late to choose or to change direction. The fact that leadership is, among other things, a personal issue, means that the leader has a responsibility to him- or herself. And this is the responsibility that Dante wishes to emphasize. To become a leader, you must be able to come to terms with who you are, and what you stand for as a leader. What of Virgil? What of the aide and companion? His exit is quite extraordinary. As Dante starts to make his way out of Purgatory and up to Paradise, he pauses to look back, but Virgil is gone. Virgil has vanished, before Dante really had a chance to thank him. Perhaps there is some truth to the old saying that the best aides never receive any credit and avoid the limelight. This was, after all, not Virgil's journey. Dante has once again taken control of his existence. After all his trials and tribulations, he made it out of Hell. It is easy to forget that he actually wrote his way out of Hell. But that was a choice Dante made.

Amazing what you can achieve on such a journey – with the help of one aide, and a sharp wit. Together.

References

Barolini, T. (1992). *The Undivine Comedy. Detheologizing Dante.* Princeton, New Jersey: Princeton University Press.

Bass, B.M. (1998). *Transformational leadership. Industrial, military, and educational impact.* Mahwah, New Jersey: Lawrence Erlbaum Associates.

Berglas, S. (2002). The Very real Dangers of Executive Coaching. *Harvard Business Review,* June: 86–92.

Billeskov Jansen, F.J. (1993). *Kierkegaard: Introduktion til Søren Kierkegaards liv og tanker.* Danmark, Forlaget Rhodos. 2. oplag.

Bjartveit, S. (1998). Organisasjoners iboende faenskap. In H. Doksrød (Ed.). *Kunnskap i arbeid – status og fremtidsbilder.* Oslo: Tano-Aschehoug.

Bjartveit, S. & Kjærstad, T. (1996). *Kaos og kosmos. Byggesteiner for individer og organisasjoner.* Oslo: Kolle forlag.

Collins, J. (2001). *Good to Great. Why Some Companies Make the Leap ... and Others Don't.* New York: Harper Business.

Conger, J.A. & R.N. Kanungo (1998). *Charismatic Leadership in Organizations.* Thousand Oaks, California: Sage Publications.

Dante Alighieri (1970). *The Divine Comedy. Inferno. 1: Text.* Translated by C.S. Singleton. Princeton: Bollingen Series LXXX/Princeton University Press.

Dante Alighieri (1973). *The Divine Comedy. Purgatorio. 1: Text.* Translated by C.S. Singleton. Princeton: Bollingen Series LXXX/Princeton University Press.

Fitzgerald, C. & Berger, J.G. (2002). *Executive Coaching. Practices & Perspectives.* Palo Alto: Davies-Black Publishing.

Flaherty, J. (1999). *Coaching. Evoking Excellence in Others.* Boston: Butterworth-Heinemann.

Freccero, J. (1986). *Dante. The Poetics of Conversion.* Cambridge, Mass.: Harvard University Press.

Goleman, D., Boyatzis, R., and McKee, A. (2002). *Primal Leadership. Realizing the Power of Emotional Intelligence.* Boston: Harvard Business School Press.

Heidegger, M. (1962). *Being and Time.* Oxford: Blackwell.

House, R.J. (1974). A Path-Goal Theory of Leader Effectiveness. *Administrative Science Quarterly*, 16.

Jacoff, R. (1986). Introduction. In J. Freccero, *Dante. The Poetics of Conversion.* Cambridge, Mass.: Harvard University Press.

Kierkegaard, S. (1989). *Sygdommen til Døden.* Borgen: Det danske Sprog- og Litteraturselskab.

Kierkegaard, S. (1991). *Enten – Eller II.* København: Gyldendal.

Kierkegaard, S. (1994). *Afsluttende Uvidenskabelig Efterskrift til De Philosophiske Smuler.* Oslo: Pax Forlag.

Kierkegaard, S. (2004). *The sickness unto Death is Despair. That Despair is the Sickness unto Death.* London: Penguin Books/Penguin Classics.

Kilburg, R.R. (2000). *Executive Coaching. Developing Managerial Wisdom in a World of Chaos.* Washington: American Psychological Association.

Maccoby, M. (2000). Narcissistic leaders: The incredible pros, the inevitable cons. *Harvard Business Review*, Jan-Feb.

Næss, A. (1994). Innledning. In S. Kierkegaard, *Afsluttende Uvidenskabelig Efterskrift til De Philosophiske Smuler*. Oslo: Pax Forlag.

Oreglia, G. (2001). *Dante: Liv, verk og samtid*. Lund: Hjalmarson & Högberg.

Pertile, L. (2000). Contrapasso. In R. Lansing (Ed.), *The Dante Encyclopedia*. New York: Garland Publishing.

Segal, H. (1974). *Introduction to the Work of Melanie Klein*. 2. ed. New York: Basic Books.

Suetonius, G. (1957). *The Twelve Caesars*. London: The Folio Society.

Thielst, P. (1999). *Kierkegaards Filosofi*. Frederiksberg: Det Lille Forlag.

Zaleznik, A. (1977). Managers and leaders. Are they different? *Harvard Business Review*, May-June.

Chapter 12 | Leadership as a possible mode of existence

OLE FOGH KIRKEBY

Summary

I will explore three issues that reflect new demands and possibilities, and these are related to leadership as a genuine mode of existence in this article, the concept of authenticity, the concept of force, and the concept of the event. My claim is that authenticity cannot be conceived of only through the framework of the reflective ego. Rather authenticity must be understood in relation to the event, as a way of being on behalf of Otherness, and on behalf of the other person. Authenticity is a process of becoming, not an acquired state, and certainly not a skill. Hence, the concept of authenticity must be exchanged for the neologism heteroenticity, "to be on behalf of Otherness".

When it comes to the issue of force, force must be seen as being very different from power. Force is a mutual, almost anonymous dynamism with an inertia that cannot, and must not, be transformed into the relic, symbolic structures of power. Force is beyond the dispositional framework of any established authority. Force is inherent in the coherency, robustness, and sensitivity of the organisation. The leader has to relate to it through identification, and through articulation.

Finally, the event, which should be seen as the core of our lives both outside and inside organisations, demands a certain ethos. This ethos can be embodied by the leader who "proves worthy of the event". This is the ultimate measure of a leader's capacity – to fully immerse him- or herself in the mode of existence as a real "Mensch", as a true human being. But the event also requires a guardian, one that anticipates and prevents the corruption of the event into an artificial construction or into an installation, and it requires a continuous effort to maintain its substance as a constellation, as a semantic, open entity in time, by guarding its secret. I conclude this article with five "eventuals": ways of being faithful to the event and that form the ethos of the new leadership.

Introduction

Within the field of management theory in general, and particularly within the traditions of value-based management, authors, and even leaders, speak of the challenge of "being true to yourself". It is thus presumed that it is indeed possible to establish a perfect union between individuality, or personality, on the one side, and the role as a leader, or even manager, on the other. By invoking the words of the Danish philosopher, Soeren Kierkegaard, "to step into one's own character", an illusion of *authenticity* in leadership is propagated without critical thought to the concepts that support this illusion: "Self", "character", "identity", "individuality", and "personality", and particularly, the meaning and essence of the "event" in which these take place. The extreme popularity of the presentation of the book *The Seven Habits of Highly Effective People* by Stephen Covey bears witness to this.

Today, every recruitment, at almost any level, will promise opportunities for "self-development". Similarly, we know that managers or leaders with an overt, reflective attitude towards their own ambitions, purposes, and pretensions, perform much better than the silent, obstinate, and authoritative ones. Character is at once the problem and the solution, and is perhaps the most important issue of genuine leadership.

However, when the Greeks invented the concept of "character", they called it *ethos*, and they were well aware of the importance of *etho-poiesis*, of "the creation of the self as a self", in relation to this concept: Individuality is a never-ending project, a pursuit of the Good to which there is no final solution. As long as leaders are human beings, no issue of leadership, no submission to any bottom line, can avoid this challenge. Hence, there is some wisdom to the approach of this article: applying a philosophical language, specifically Greek terminology, on issues of social interaction, particularly in relation to the practise of leadership. This should be fruitful for five reasons:

A   Philosophy forms a non-functionalist, non-strategic, perspective which an individual could apply to his or her own existence, or to that of others.
B   Greek philosophy constitutes an outstanding platform for thinking of an ethos for individuals and communities, and an ethos is a condition for leadership.

C Since the time of the Greeks, philosophy has served as the discursive fundament for social analysis by providing the basic metaphors and concepts used to explore the individual and society as reciprocal analogies.
D Philosophy forms the only existing meta-language of the social sciences that is neither shaped by dogmas, nor by common sense (*doxa*).
E Philosophy is the framework for thinking that only works when it transcends itself, and hence, it is the language of ethical and social imagination.

Authenticity

One of the fundamental propositions of the true character of leadership relies on us believing in the possibility of a fusion between the person and the role. This fusion is often termed *authenticity*, but the underlying notion goes back to a normative concept of general human existence. In leadership, however, authenticity is closely related to the expectations of the leader's ability to be "present", "to listen", "to be trustworthy", and "to recognize" new ways of creating legitimacy and devotion in the organisation. This concept of authenticity deserves to be examined critically.

The concept of authenticity is closely related to the existentialistic movement in philosophy, created by Søren Kierkegaard, and developed into a systematic framework for reflectivity by Martin Heidegger in his masterpiece *Sein und Zeit*. The frame of reference in which Kierkegaard writes is "Christology", while Heidegger's frame is definitely Stoic in character. Heidegger's core concept, *die Sorge*, is originally a Greek philosophical concept, developed by Plato (before Stoicism) in his late dialogue *The Statesman* as a virtue of the political leader, termed *epimeleia*, "care for others", and translated into *cura* during the Roman period. The meaning given to it by Plato, i.e., "the will and capacity to take care of other people", is, however, transformed by Heidegger into the ability of the individual to take care of its own life. Heidegger's maxim of, "to take one's life seriously by permanently facing the impending fact of death", thus transforms care for other people into a agenda of the reflective ego. "Authenticity", from the Greek concepts *auto,* "my self", "the self", and *einai*, "to be", is presented as a mode of being where the ego confronts itself in relation to a possible union between its "components", the "I" and the "me", the dialogue partners of the soul – to quote Plato. By using two Latin terms for the "ego", *ipse* and *idem*, "self", and "the same", we underline the fact that the existential claim to authenticity amounts to the possibility of uniting *ipse* and *idem* through a choice of mode of living.

I can choose to be the one, who I "really" am. Or, as the Stoic philosopher and emperor, Marcus Aurelius, put it: "Become the one you are!" The problem here, of course, relates to the ontological and epistemological content of the *ipse* and the *idem*. The question that arises, is whether the *ipse* presupposes the *idem* or vice versa, i.e., whether I am a "self", because I have a sameness bound to my body, to my peculiar or unique experiences, or to something "unnameable", a sort of substance, or an entity, placed "between" the body and the mind, and effecting their cooperation and controlling their development. Or, conversely, whether I am "a sameness", because I am able to say "I". In this case this sameness must be something which has to be permanently upheld as a kind of function, or even an illusion, of speech, that lies at the core of the possibility of social existence? The *ipse*, then, is regarded as a result of semantics, not as a substance.

This predicament cannot be ignored, especially after the post-modern era during which the autonomy and substantiality of the ego was severely challenged. It has become increasingly difficult to presuppose that authenticity can relate to a substantial entity that can be discovered through self-reflection on the one hand, and privileged, "ethico-pathetic" choice on the other.

The tradition of authenticity as a transformation, a process of turning away from illusion towards reality, has been vivid in Christianity since St. Augustin spoke of his own "conversion" in the *Confessions*, but it goes further back – to the image of the cave in Plato's *Republic*, and we also find this metaphor of turning around and seeing for real in the Holy Gospels. The women at the grave actually turn around (*epistrephein/conversio*) when called by His voice, and see Christ who has arisen. To turn around, to look into one-self, to be changed, transformed, to find one's real self by finding one's true vocation, to be wakened to a new life by the "word", to begin a "new creation" (a second creation of one self as St. Paul speaks about), these images are pertinent to the tradition of not just spirituality, but certainly also of philosophy, science, and the social theories of identity formation in our Western society.

In my opinion it would be futile to try to reduce these experiences and images to functional, explanatory structures. They must be taken seriously just the way they are, because they are the passionate core of our culture – or even better, they serve as testimony of "a thinking passion and a passionate thinking", as Aristotle spoke of in his *Nicomachean Etichs (VI, ii.5)*. However, it is also our duty to ask: How can these images be incorporated into our present social experience? And to ask: How does authenticity makes sense? The answer to these questions could actually originate in Classical Greek philosophy, as well as in Stoicism, because these "schools" tried to answer the question: How are you able to create yourself as a real human being? And their line of questioning did not originate in a concept of egocentric authenticity.

The Greeks were well aware of the fact that individualism is produced through the personal ability for making collective norms or "values" real, by thinking and acting. The ethics of Aristotle, and the theory of the affects (passions) as taught by the Stoic schools, emphasise this. The Greeks share a concept of – what one might call – *ethical perception*. To incorporate norms means that one is able to experience the world through these norms as though they were lenses. This presupposes an idea of a union of thought and passion, an idea of an "ethical imagination", of a situational sensitivity, and of a fundamental severity of consequence in applying self-reflection.

In Aristotle, the core concepts are the *ethos* and the *hexis* (habitus in Latin for *hexis*, hence, our, in this context misleading, concept of "habit"). These concepts presuppose that one is able to transform oneself into the image of the Good. Authenticity then, would not mean to "be one-self", but to act as if there was a "self", *autexusion*, as the Stoic said, to be a complete master of your own self. The self then, that is master of your own self, would be almost anonymous, would be the self of the *katorthoma*, of the ultimate wisdom, a position developed through hard mental labour, *askesis*, which transcends individuality, because it, in the capacity of a possible attitude, has left the realm of ordinary "psychological existence" behind. The Stoics spoke of the *prosoché*, "the refinement of attention". You must be aware of every tiny affect in order to transform your inner reality and its attitudes from the average "man" to the ethical human being.

The concept of *ethos* has two origins in Greek. One with "eta", the long "e", meaning "character", "place of origin", "set of acquired norms" ("values"), "moral disposition", "ethical talent"; and the other, with the short "e", "epsilon", meaning "the chosen behaviour", "the chosen principles for living". The concept of *hexis* unites these two meanings by referring to the reflective effort of realising the norms and values transferred to one from the community through the individual's innate as well as learned skills for doing the Good. The *hexis* is not a habit, it is non-automatic, beyond the "natural" ways of acting. Beyond the *consuetude* (the automatism of personality), the *hexis* demands permanent attention, and a "style" of imaginative interpretation of every situation in relation to the maxim of "doing the Good for the Good's own sake".

The paradox inherent in the concept of hexis concerns the fact that one cannot do Good properly without knowing it, and not know the Good properly without having done it, and is solved through a denial of the naturalism of authenticity. "To be the one you are" is a process which never finishes. There are no ultimate criteria for accomplishment, and no internal criterion for certainty. In other words: One is always working at it. It is easy to see that this paradox applies to leadership as well. To be a good leader, one has to know what good leadership is, but in order to know what good leadership is, one has to have practised it. The point is that doing the Good is a process where the Good itself is the agent, so to speak, not the ego. Aristotle describes the practise of the Good this way:

> "Whereas a thing done is an end in itself; since doing well is the End in itself, and it is at this that desires aims." (Aristotle 1994, VI, ii, 5)

and

> "on the other hand, it appears, there is a state of mind in which a man may do this various acts with the result that he really is a good man: I mean when he does them from choice (*dia proairesin*), and for the sake of the acts themselves (*kai autón heneka ton prattomenon*)." (Aristotle 1994, VI, xii, 7-8)

What Aristotle defines here, is *virtue*. *Virtue* is a way of acting in which one lets go of the reflective command of the ego, in order to let the norm perceive, speak, and act through oneself. This means that virtue can never create authenticity, because the virtuous person renounces his own authorship of the act – without, of course, denying his responsibility for it.

This concept of authenticity, then, could be re-named *heteroenticity*, and for three reasons:

A It does not have a definitive concept of a naturalistically given, or ontological, "self" that must be realised. It is nothing more than a movement in the direction of Otherness, i.e., it is a process in which one becomes by being oneself in the capacity of "another", the other that is able to realise the Good.
B The consciousness cannot exclusively posit its own values, because its choice is preset by the norms of the community. It seeks to accomplish something that at once belongs to all, and to no one.
C The criteria for accomplishment are linked to the assessment of others. To accomplish the Good is to be approved of by the community. There is no internal division between the individual and society. At least not in principal. The Greek elite formed a communion whose ideal was to be permanently climbing the steps of meta-learning, the *paideia* (the term was later translated into *humanitas* by Cicero & co.).

The task of achieving *heteroenticity*, the process of becoming the one who you might be if you are able to be the one who is permanently becoming, does not actually require exceptional situations or circumstances, although there may be situations and circumstances that facilitate and enforce the process of learning to live on behalf of the Good. The true leader might be spared any hardship, or s/he might be the one who has to overcome one disaster after the other.

It should be emphasised that this concept cannot rely on a firm definition of the Good. The Good is a "regulative idea", it is like a door in a wall – we know it is there, but it is covered in chalk. We have to find the door before we can even think about opening it. If we succeed in finding it, and do open it, we would however find another wall.

It is of immense importance to the concept of modern leadership that the leader does not attempt to determine the content of these absolute norms. To do this would not only reproduce a sort of organisational totalitarianism, but it would also frustrate the ethical imagination of employees. The leader must be a *hodeget*, the one who shows the way, not a *kateget*, the one who dogmatically interprets the text. The failure of ethical accountancy can be attributed to the process of deciding organisational norms by way of an feigned consensus. The power of diversity management, beyond the buzz word, lays in its ability to mobilize the different normative attitudes invested in different cultures. We must realise that norms are the fuel for acquiring and creating knowledge, and hence, of innovative behaviour.

Heteroenticity and leadership

We must ask ourselves whether there exists a *hexis of leadership*, i.e., whether the role as a leader can be seen as a mode of existence which is compatible with the life of the Good?

The insight that one cannot find oneself as a "self" actually precludes the question of whether there should be a true way of being a leader, i.e. whether one is able to find oneself as a true "self" through authentic leadership. Or, in other words, an authentic leadership cannot exist, because authenticity is an illusion. However, it still makes sense to speak of the possibility of creating a personal style of exercising leadership, through which standards of leadership are realised and posited in such a way that the role as "Mensch" (excuse me for this Yiddish concept), and as leader, begin to merge. It is possible to create oneself as a good human being *by* being a good leader, and it is certainly possible to create oneself as a good leader by being a good human being. This is due to the fact that one cannot be a person who tries to realise the Good, and at the same time be a person who does not care for other people, who does not care for the community, and who does not care for the future of society. The concept of "self-leadership" quite simply implies that one is aware of the fact that every tiny act is a contribution to the creation of a normative, social reality.

It would be much easier for the traditional type of *manager* – a concept which was originally used to describe those that train horses and display them at the circus – to be authentic, because his or her criteria for success are predetermined in much the same way as the physiognomy of his or her role. The leader – the word "to lead" is derived from an old, Nordic term, that means to go in front of, and to search for – can never be authentic, because the criteria for doing the Good, and the role which answers to it, are indeterminate, but s/he can try to be "ein Mensch" by creating a humanist leadership.

In the light of the fact that leadership involves making complicated and delicate decisions in events where it is not possible to act consistently by following any golden rule, leadership is certainly a very difficult, but very rewarding, "school" for creating oneself as a good human being.

The constant demands of having to communicate while maintaining a balance between empathy and control presents the leader with dilemmas involving genuine opportunities for personal development, provided the leader is able to resist the temptation to excuse his or her actions through strategic, functionalist and instrumentalist considerations, or through "pseudo-psychological" evaluations of his or her employees.

Heteroenticity is in fact a mind set where the ethical demand of taking care of Otherness, in the shape of the community and its future development, must be balanced with the care for the other, the individual, such that it precludes decisions being made along functionalist principles. The leader must create the event over and over by recreating the Good. If the need should arise, the leader can use his or her power, and certainly s/he will need to on occasion, but s/he should not seek to legitimatize this in relation to his or her own personal ethos, but only in relation to the care for the community. There is no authentic leadership, only a leadership, in which the demands of leadership challenge the leader as "ein Mensch", and hence, enforce him or her to deal with his or her own guilt. It is precisely the fact that the leader must make choices that makes him or her unable to realise him- or herself as a "self", because the choices s/he must make create victims, and an ethos of the Good does not allow for victims. However, if s/he is indeed a leader who searches for the Good, then the option of realising him- or herself as a person, e.g., through the narrow social role of being the "strong leader", would not bring him or her any satisfaction.

A leader that must choose between being two different CEOs in the same department can never be sure that s/he has made the right choice – if it is the interpersonal, communicative, and decisions-related qualities that are of essence. S/he has to use his imagination to envision them as real people acting out a play with a plot that s/he has to determine. S/he has to imagine them in future events, and in doing so, s/he is recreating them as characters. But s/he is never able to be truly impartial, because s/he is the one writing the script. S/he has to acknowledge that psychological judgement of any form is a fantasy, because it rests on a generalisation from a very delimited set of events. Ethical imagination combines with an "epico-pathetic" sensitivity, a sensitivity devoted to the "true story", to meet the demands of justice inherent in the Good. In this context, *heteroenticity* means the ability of the leader to act as if s/he were actually present at the premiere of this play, and present in the capacity of Another.

Above all, the impact of the concept of *heteroeniticity* in relation to leadership is that it directs the focus away from the "psychology", or "personality", of the leader towards something else. It directs the focus towards the leader as an anonymous function of virtues, and hence, as the one *through whom* norms and values come alive. Of course, the strategy demon might whisper: Then s/he is capable of exemplifying organisational integrity and corporate legitimacy … And we must answer:"That is exactly the point!"

When we speak of the canonical expressions of authenticity, the capacity for being present, for listening, trustworthiness, reliability, the ability to recognise, the ability to understand, the will to empathy, generosity, and distinctness and non-ambiguity in communication, in relation to meaning in general, and to information in particular, these expressions must not be seen as personal accomplishments. They are not results of the function of a "persona" – a word which actually means "mask" in Latin; and they are certainly not the effects of an ability to "be". They are an outcome of the will to become.

The leader *is* not trustworthy, *is* not present, *is* not caring; neither is s/he playing a role, and certainly not pretending. The leader is "just" trying to be part of an event in which the deep, delicate, and rich patterns of the attitudes of trustworthiness, reliability, and sincerity are acted out. The leader is striving to become another, which, of course, does not mean, that s/he should attempt to escape personal responsibility. In fact, s/he is trying to reach it a level of a new concept of the personal.[1]

The ambiguity, the Janus face of heteroenticity, which demonstrates that one can only be oneself as Another, presents the leader with an unsolvable dilemma between strategic and functional action on the one hand, and ethical passion on the other. This dilemma cannot be solved, but it can be softened if the leader combines force with the collective movement of the organisation, without giving up on personal responsibility.

Force and power

Within every human being, and in every community or organisation, there are forces at play. We know them personally as desires, as *conservatio*

---

[1] In this connection I shall recommend strongly the beautiful book by Paul Ricoeur (1990). *Soi-même comme an autre*. Paris: Editions du Seuil.

sui, "self-conservation" – as Thomas Hobbes named them when he founded modern, political theory in his *Leviathan*, or, spoken with the soft voice of Spinoza in his *Ethica* , the *conatus sese conservandi* , "the desire to take care of oneself". We know them as energy, as inclinations, as interests, as hope, as the will to live, as the reserve of strength and love, and as happiness. And in every human being, and in every organisation, there are structures of power, symbolic codes, ways of thinking, patterns of behaviour, and modes of experiencing and thinking, as well as institutional structures, rules, manuals and laws, that direct forces in a functionalist choreography.

The leader must be the champion of force, not power. Force, *dynamis,* or *kratos,* in Greek, is a force which never comes to a rest, and which can never be transformed into an instrument. It always appears in opposition to order, sometimes as a chaos, but also as a will to reinforce the essence of this order. In an organisation it can be sensed as problems with the flow of work, problems inside groups, and as straightforward malfunctioning; but it can also be evident as a demand for more freedom to move, cooperate, and to think; it could even manifest itself as the claim to more social responsibility from the firm.

The opposite of force, power, *fortitudo* in Latin, is a domestication of force, created through a sediment medium. Force is genuine doing, an act not hampered by reflection. It is mere expression, without being reduced to the production of an object. It harbours no aggressiveness, and is beyond destructive intentions. Force is genuine potentiality, *capacitas,* "capacity", (*capacitas*, is actually a translation from the Greek, *dechomai*, "to have received"). It is the inner core of practise. Its realm is creative action. It is not a will to power; it is a will to not wield power for the sake of power, but to transcend power in order to create the new. It galvanizes, rather than restrains, character.

Power, *potestas*, on the other hand, is always a consummated activity, and at the same time a perversion of force and its transformation into codes and control, into discursive dispositions, into role-and rule-bound personalities, into material and symbolic walls, and into the economic-technical apparatus. Due to its accumulative character, power creates its own motivation: in order to strengthen itself, it must increase. However, power destroys organisations, because it creates destructive cycles of action with itself as both a means and the end.

Every individual, and every organisation, is a potential arena for the clash between force and power. It is the struggle between becoming and being, between process and structure, between organising and organisation. We are well acquainted with these distinctions in economics, but they are not very well defined, because power also manifests itself as a process and tries to take over the ways of force. Power is a process both from the perspective of objectivism and of subjectivism. Objectively, power has the character of a process, because it has no fixed limits in relation to its concept. Power is never fully realised, it is never enough. Subjectively, power also has the character of a process, because it is impossible to know its actual goals, and thus, to know where it ends.

Force is explorative and creative, whereas power is demonstrative, symbolic or affirming, sometimes innovative, and often normative in relation to functionalist or ideological criteria. Both the medium for, and the processes of power need to be taken care of, whether it is through material and social mechanisms, through rules and laws, or through recognition and legitimacy. Power needs force. This means that the force that transcends power must be identified. This task is of great importance to the organisation. The leader must be able to identify and articulate force. S/he must also be able to recognize and diagnose both the visible and the concealed diseases caused by power.

From a sociological, anthropological, or ethnological perspective, force might appear to be an aspect of the phenomenon, which V. Turner baptised *liminality* under inspiration from Arnolds van Gennep's analyses of "rites de passages" (Turner, 1969, 1982). Liminality refers to states of great intensity for individuals or communities – states that manifest themselves through disturbances, chaos, or revolutionary forces, demanding a new order. Liminality forms the limit, or passage, between a structure, or an order, and its destruction or transformation into a new order. One might distinguish between three liminal phases in the life-cycle of organisations (Kirkeby, 2001). One in which liminality is smouldering, the pre-liminal phase. One in which liminality has erupted – infusing the organisation with new intensity and creativity, the ubiquo-liminal phase. And finally the post-liminal phase, where forces are being transformed into power.

Leaders must have a sense of intuition with regards to the force, a sense of liminality. If they try to stop the force prematurely, or to domesticate it at an early stage, they might destroy the possibility of change for the whole organisation. But how do we describe a leader who must have this liminal touch in order to come close to it, and to be strong enough to set it free?

First, I think s/he must have the sense of – what the Greeks called – the "ta ef' hemin", that which is within our power (*in nostra potestate*), and hence, that which is not. This is also the meaning of the event – as we shall see shortly.

The stereotype of the poor leader is the manager, who is prone to imagine that much more is within his or her power, than is actually the case. S/he might be inclined to use "managerial tools", or to secure these from a consultancy firm, but fundamentally, s/he assumes s/he is capable of transforming the attitudes of any employee, the atmosphere in the firm, as well as its corporate image. Such a person has no sense of the delicate and charming sensitivity of force.

If I may quote Dylan Thomas:

"The force that through the green fuse drives the flower
Drives my green age; that blasts the roots of trees
Is my destroyer.
And I am dumb to tell the crooked rose
My youth is bent by the same wintry fever."

The leader must be capable and open-minded. S/he must not fear force. S/he must dare to open the curtains and let the light in.

It is important to realise that the new type of leadership must be extremely aware of these conflicts, and that the genuine leader must be the champion and advocate of force. Naiveté, on the other hand, leads to nothing but disaster. And it is naive to hope for the existence and persistence of a force which is choked by the channels of power, and interpreted through the convoluted symbolisms of modern institutions. Nevertheless, we can not escape the question of what kind of institution is leadership.

There are indications that a concept of leadership that goes beyond the traditional borders of economic, technical, and social, control that used to characterise the role of the private and public leader is emerging. This is not only due to the fact that leaders are increasingly becoming pares inter pares, nor is it entirely due to the fact that structural and procedural creativity is on the agenda or to the roles played by knowledge, innovation, and communication in the corporate world. Perhaps the most important factor is that leadership is beginning to grow into a new institution, the institution of taking care of life – the life of the leader, of stakeholders, of any individual in society, and of life in general. I do *not* wish to emphasise the negative sense of a "biopolitics" – a set of strategies for exploring our biological and mental life, which recently has become a topic of focus in academia – among the followers of Foucault, Deleuze, Agamben, and Negri. I wish to emphasise the non-strategic, positive aspects, that grow out of an urgent need for creating a sound foundation and new modes of operating, for social responsibility and sustainability. To take care of life however, is to prove oneself worthy of the event.

The eventum tantum

The concept of strategy arose from the needs to control the event. The necessities of war prescribed it; the ability to use nature as the source of survival; the realisation of desire; the demands of raising children; the founding of cities and states; and the ceremonies of religion – all require that the event can be defined and handled as an object.

Most metaphoric language of the event emphasises the relation of being inside and outside, something in time, and something in space or place. However, the event is also seen as a substantial entity intruding on our reality, or as a process decomposing it from inside. Virtually anything could be the agent or the victim of an event, from nations to shoes. Even abstract concepts such as love, insight, possessions, and attitudes, could "event" or "be evented". Even the event itself could "event" or "be evented".

However, there is a strong line of demarcation between that which actually happens at the material level, and the meaning which we ascribe to it by giving it a name. The Stoics called the material level of the stream of events *tunchanon,* and the act of giving it a name, *pragma*. They didn't operate with a causal relation between the levels, nor with total ontological autonomy, even though they claimed that *tunchanon* was corporeal, and *pragma* incorporeal in the capacity of meaning.

If we do not want to advocate a naturalist, voluntarist, or constructionist conception of the event, we must follow the Stoics. The event of meaning and the meaning of the event must be conceived as two separate functions (Kirkeby 1994, 2005). Or, the event is something transcendent: We can never realise what "really" happened.

This state of equivocation in the event suggests, of course, strategic manipulations, canonical interpretations enforced by institutions, and direct negotiations, in relation to "that which happened" – all parts of the game of constructing History as our "Lebenswelt" – as well as attempts at discovering levels of description that lie beyond any ontological doubt (the temptation of physics). In this context we are able to distinguish between *constellations* and *installations* in relation to the event.

A *constellation* is a state in time and place, constituting different phases in the fluxuations of life, of which we can say, they form a "natural" entity. However, we can never completely grasp the meaning of such entities, even if we, with utter conviction, could say that "the firm was closed to day", or "he betrayed us".

An *installation* is an attempt to construct and control such an entity completely in time and space. Installations pretend to be able to create meaning, and to be able to control all the important components of the event.

However, we create installations, but constellations create us. Even the best prepared, and most convincingly performed installation is circumscribed by a constellation. Economists know that event-management is vulnerable to this, and theatre directors would agree: the most well-rehearsed performances may convey aspects of a meaning that were never intended. I think it is very important that leadership should be *constellative* in character. By saying this, I do not advocate passivity, but a certain modesty of interests, an interpretative moderation, and a certain degree of respect when it comes to action.

A genuine historical consciousness, so essential to leadership, must prove itself worthy in its ability to create a balance of knowledge between the event and its contextual framework. Sobriety in judgement and generosity in thinking might not be that easily coerced into inflexible descriptions and interpretations. Understanding must free itself from the *doxa*, the rule of obstructive, common sense – it must reflect the event of thinking the event. This must not be interpreted as resentment founded on the predicaments of "bounded rationality". It is in fact quite the opposite – these considerations signify a confession to a limitless rationality. It is a proclamation for the realm of the possible, the realm which deserves the name "the real". The real meaning of the real is a sense of the possible. This is the leadership-virtue per excellence, because it reflects an *epic* attitude to reality.

An epic attitude has very little to do with so-called "story-telling", because the epic attitude is sharp, merciless, sober, and fantastic, all at the same time. Its goal is neither strategic, nor tactic. It is neither directed towards any group, nor even towards a public. The epic attitude creates the never-ending story. The epic attitude is a way of proving oneself worthy of the event, because it is faithful against that which happened, but did not take place. It guards the secret of every event. It guards the *eventum tantum*, the "great event", because this event might be taking place right now behind our backs in an entirely un-spectacular, humble, and quiet world, of which we are playing an important part, without even knowing it.

When we guard the secret of the event, we take care of everybody involved in it, including ourselves. This is exactly the opposite of a strategic and instrumental attitude. It defies functionalism, as well as "symptomatology", in every shape and form.

One way to guard the secret of the event is to facilitate the recognition of its inherent self-referential structure. Every event is an event in an event, because the perception of an occurrence as an event is itself an event, and this infinite self-referential movement can only be stopped by creating a *haecceitas*, an image of facticity, a "*this* happened". It is up to the leader to balance between cutting through the mess and loosing equivocation. This balancing act is actually a hermeneutic one, and the leader must perform as a genuine "Hermes", a messenger between the visible and the invisible, while at the same time being a dealer in, and a thief of, thoughts and intentions.

The leader's obligation to be visible – obliged to make decisions that carry a distinct content of meaning, as well as his or her duty to be visible in the event, and as the interpreter of the event, must not tempt him or her to submit to the perils of rhetoric, nor to those of the authoritative exegetic. The leader must guard the secret of the event by performing through *heteroenticity*. S/he must be able to set the event free as Otherness, an Otherness by which the multitude of the Others slowly can be transformed from a *plethora*, "a manifold", into a *pleroma*, "an ethical abundance" of a community in a process of creation that allows for dissidence.

The ethos of the event

The character of *heteroenticity* as an attitude, the opportunities given to us by force, and the ability to guard the secret of the event, can be presented analytically through a framework that I have called the *catalogue of eventuals*. They form the cornerstones of the ethos of the new leadership.

The *eventuals* are not the result of a quasi-transcendent ego, like Heidegger's "existentials". In fact they are quite the opposite, as they evolve from the secret of the event, conducted by our participation in it, because we are always lost to the others. They reflect the dependence of the I on the Other. I have chosen five *eventuals,* all of which constitute the probable domain of *heteroenticity*:

The first eventual is the positive powerlessness. It is the ability to distinguish between that which is in our power, and that which is not, and still be able to act properly. This is the domain of practise.

The second eventual is the ability to ascend to the meaning of the event through free acceptance. This is the domain of autonomy, and of the critical attitude, the *"krinein"*. It is the anti-naturalist, post-ontological, attitude towards the event, the way of guarding its identity. It is the ability to enforce a distinction between word and concept, the will not to accept meaning-making at any price.

The third eventual is the void in space given to us by force, a force manifested through the freedom inherent in the bodies of the others. It is the will to want the essence of space and of place as the freedom of others, and to experience one's own body as a place: The pampas of the skin.

The fourth eventual is the ability to receive time from others. It is the invocation of an emotional, or organic, logistic. It is the ability to receive the layers of time grown into the foreigners through their cultures. It is the belief in a fertile abundance, in the beautiful untimeliness of the event.

The fifth eventual is the force of being able to be "evented" by the Good, to be a part of a process of eventing which is dedicated to normative perfection. It is the will to conquer oneself without defeating sameness.

The consequences of these thoughts for leadership and for consultancy

The first eventual alerts the leader to his or her own limitations. To acquire the ability of true leadership means to be able to push these limits, but only to a small extent, and only very carefully, while observing the ever-changing conditions predetermined by the coming of the event.

The second eventual advises the leader to be very careful when interpreting the event. As Nietzsche once said, it is the prerogative of the victorious to interpret the event, and the leader must take care not to position him- or herself as a victor in advance. S/he must earn his victory. However, s/he must never negotiate the meaning of the event, because such behaviour would mark him or her as a manipulator. S/he must keep the scene of meaning open. S/he must be able to wait for the *kairos*, for "the right moment", when meaning chooses to arrive, and then grasp it.

The third eventual commands the leader to place him- or herself in the middle of the organisation, as a synoptic centre. Thus, s/he must become the body of the organisation, the image in which the other bodies reflect themselves. The point is that whatever happens to the organisation, happens to him or her first, and with no mercy. The worst thing a leader could do is to make him- or herself a favoured exception.

The fourth eventual dares the leader to postpone. If you are able to postpone fruitfully, you are also able to fulfil. The leader must be a fulfiller of the different thoughts, memories, and values that are gathered throughout the organisation. S/he must try not to miss the point where the lines of times and flights intersect. S/he must be able to let diversity manage itself.

The fifth eventual summons the leader to be the servant of the organisation, at any time, and at any place. S/he must make his or her mind up ahead of time to lead this organisation the same way s/he would lead him- or herself. S/he must be the *homo creator, factor et fabulator*, the (wo)man that creates the organisation inside the event, and the event inside the organisation; the one who throws the ball, and the one who catches it; and the one who is allowed to testify. The consultant's role then is to:

- advise the leader to develop *prosoché*, the hexis of ethical attention, and help him or her master this sensitivity to the tacit levels of the event, to the level where something is preparing itself.
- counsel the leader to develop the ability that Epictetus called the *parascheué*, to the power of *anticipation*. We can try to control and install the event, but our only real power over it is through anticipation.
- advise the leader to be gentle, because in gentleness lies the capacity for receptiveness.
- warn the leader against the temptation to install. You can prepare for the event, and even partially control it, but it must be allowed to take place in accordance with its own conditions.

- teach the leader to listen even as s/he speaks.
- advise the leader to transcend the role of being timekeeper, and instead try to be the one that provides time for others; the guarantor of an emotional logistics, the patron saint of breathing space, a master of the syncope.
- advise the leader to be the one that bears the pain for anything that happens to anyone within the organisation.
- advise the leader to compose the organisation, not as a letter, not as a play, but as a poem.
- advise the leader to improvise, and to prepare carefully for improvisation, because an improvisation is just the emergence on the surface of the social of the play that we did not know were the one, which actually betook us.
- advise the leader to narrate, but to do so in such a way that demonstrates that s/he is already informed by his or her own story. S/he must emerge him- or herself in it, and always in the capacity of him- or herself as another.
- advise the leader to be true to that which happens to him or her. This means that s/he should admit to ignorance, to his or her lack of omnipotence, to his or her vulnerability to fate, and to his or her impotence towards ambiguity, but at the same time affirm his or her keenness, his or her zealousness, and his or her will.

References

Aristotle (1994). *The Nicomachean Ethics*. Cambridge, Mass. and London: Harvard University Press (The Loeb Classical Library).

Diogenes Laertius (1995). *Lives of Eminent Philosophers*. Cambridge, Mass. and London: Harvard University Press (The Loeb Classical Library).

Epictetus (1996). *Arrian's Discourses of Epictetus*. Cambridge, Mass. and London: Harvard University Press (The Loeb Classical Library).

Heidegger, M. (1967). *Sein und Zeit*. Tübingen: Max Niemeyer Verlag.

Kirkeby, O.F. (1994). *Begivenhed og krops-tanke. En fænomenologisk-hermeneutisk analyse*. Århus: Modtryk. (Reprinted: København: Handelshøjskolens Forlag 1998).

Kirkeby, O.F. (2000). *Management Philosophy. A Radical-Normative Perspective*. Heidelberg and New York: Springer Verlag.

Kirkeby, O.F. (2001). *Organisationsfilosofi. En studie i liminalitet*. København: Samfundslitteratur.
Kirkeby, O.F. (2005). *Eventum tantum*. København: Samfundslitteratur.
Plato (2000). *Republic*. Cambridge, Mass. and London: Harvard University Press (The Loeb Classical Library).
Plato (2001). *The Statesman*. Cambridge, Mass. and London: Harvard University Press (The Loeb Classical Library).
Turner, V. (1967). *The Ritual Process*. London: Aldine.
Turner, V. (1982). *From Ritual to Theatre. The Human Seriousness of Play*. New York: PAJ Publications.

About the contributors

Mats Alvesson is professor of business administration at the University of Lund, Sweden. He has published extensively on subjects such as leadership, identity, gender, organizational culture, methodology, and knowledge-intensive organizations. His latest book is *Knowledge work and knowledge-intensive firms* (2004). Oxford: Oxford University Press.

Carl Reinhold Bråkenhielm is professor of systematic theology with studies in worldviews, at Uppsala University, Sweden. He has studied classical theological problems as well as contemporary worldviews and ideas of nature. He is the author of *Forgiveness* (1993), has edited *Världsbild och mening* (2001) and *The Relevance of Theology* (2002), and – working with Torbjörn Fagerström – recently published *Gud & Darwin. Känner de varandra?* (2005).

Kjetil Eikeset is a philosopher and economist with degrees from the University of Oslo and the Norwegian School of Management. He is a well-known lecturer in the field of organisational psychology, through both his teaching at the Norwegian School of Management and his partnership in the Management Consultancy Firm Bjartveit & Eikeset AS. His areas of interest include political philosophy, applied ethics and leadership, and he has also worked as Organisational Manager in Coca-Cola and Orkla Borregaard in Norway. Most of his assignments involve organisational change, team development, group processes, leadership development, and executive coaching.

Carl Erik Grenness is professor of psychology at the University of Oslo, Norway, where his main focus on Business Administration. He has published the book *Kommunikasjon i organisasjoner* (1999). He is now a senior researcher at the Norwegian Defence Leadership Institute.

Bengt Hansson started out as a teacher in the social sciences, doing research on education in the 1970s. Since then he has had different managerial positions in the educational sector and in various public organisations. At present he is head of the department for contract research at the University of Uppsala, Sweden. His experience in coaching, mentoring and management consulting in reorganisation- and development-processes, extends back to the 1980s.

Heidi von Weltzien Høivik is professor of business ethics and leadership at the Norwegian School of Management and a much sought after consultant for both Norwegian and international companies. She is a Fellow of the Harvard Executive Program of the Institute of Education Management, and a Fellow of the Harvard Program on International Negotiations.

In 2002 she published the book *Moral leadership in action, building and sustaining moral competence in European organizations*, E. Elgar. She is on the editorial board of the *Journal of Business Ethics* and *Business Ethics – European Review*, the *Journal for Business Ethics Education* and a reviewer for *Journal of Business Ethics*.

Ole Fogh Kirkeby is professor of management philosophy, and director of the centre of Art & Leadership at Copenhagen Business School in Denmark. As a philosopher of phenomenology he has published many works on the significance of the event in our lives. He has also written the recent best seller *The new leadership*, which encourages managers to transform themselves into leaders by exemplifying genuine moral virtues, and by yielding to their immanent capacities of art. His central theme is that organisations must be the new protagonists of a radical humanist attitude.

Flemming Poulfelt is professor of management and strategy and vice dean of research communication at Copenhagen Business School in Denmark. His research and consulting interests focus on strategic management, managing professional service firms, knowledge management, change management, and management consulting, and he has published widely within these areas.

Andreas Werr is an associate professor at the Stockholm School of Economics. His current research interests focus on the rhetoric of management consulting, the procurement, use, and consequences of using management consultants for client organizations, and the management of consulting companies. Andreas' work has been published in journals such as the *Journal of Organizational Change Management, Organization, Organization Studies and International Studies of Management and Organization*. Andreas has taught courses on management consulting for both graduate students and practicing consultants.

Hugh Willmott is a professor at the Judge Institute of Management at the University of Cambridge. He has published widely on critical theory, labour process, power and subjectivity. He has edited a large number of books, including *Studying management critically* (Sage 2003, with Mats Alvesson) and co-authored several books, including *Management lives* (Sage 1999, with David Knights).